SOLUTIONS

A Wiseacre's Guide For Cleaning Up

The New World Odor

© Philip Kosdan

The Wiseacre Press
Carrboro, North Carolina

Library of Congress Cataloging-In-Publication Data
Kosdan, Philip.
SOLUTIONS, A Wiseacre's Guide For Cleaning Up The New World
Odor/Philip Kosdan
    p. cm
Includes Bibliographic References
ISBN 978-0-9910687-0-8
1. Politics 2. Economics 3. Sociology 4. Ecology 5. Education 6. Interna-
tional Relations I. Title

Library of Congress Control Number: 2013952446

Cover Design by Martin Nibali & Watercolor by Linda Griffin

To My Wife, Pat,
For Friendship, For Love, For Humor, For Family,
For Most Everything
and
To Everyone and Anyone Who Has Ever
Talked With Me, For Better or Worse

Table of (Dis)contents

Forward
With My Best Two Left Feet Forward

This book, citizen, is no less than of how we get from our present New World Odor to a less noxious order literally and socially. I make no apologies for what is to follow. Still, I know it is too big a task; yet, even so, I believe this book is up to the task. Of course, what I believe may be fine for me, but irrelevant in any picture bigger than the territory of my ego. I need to convince you and many others of you to expand the space of these ideas beyond my little wise acre.

This book is an outline. Each chapter in this book could itself be the introduction to a whole other book. Were there words enough and time, I would forthwith give you a much longer and complete university-approved and referenced work with a review of the appropriate literature, including precedents from Nietzsche, Marx, Freud and The Frankfurt School, Habermas and Foucault, America's Orestes Brownson and Fitzhugh, Plato and Milton Friedman, J.J. Rousseau, Tom Paine and Thomas Jefferson, et al., a ghostly host of venerable dead political and economist poets — and, then, many a quantitative study from top of the line peer reviewed journals.

Much of this is actually purposely left out so as not to bore you, but it is readily available where you can get depressed and bored all on your own. There are umpteen studies complete with all manner of stats and graphs documenting where we are headed and at what speed, not that we do not know already. We have pretty well scanned the route and the distance on the road to hell. Heck, we have surveyed each cobblestone and each of its chinks on this proverbial down-the-tubes highway and we have quantitatively measured it all ad nauseum.

Not that facts are absent here, nor is this a work entirely of fantasy, although there is a good deal of hyperbole here and there. I believe this to be a work of practical imagination and, I hope, beneficial imagination at that. In fact, I believe this book is a work with an actual and fairly accurate factual description about how our socio-politico-ecological-economic world works in general if not in all its grueling and gruesome detail and then most importantly what we should do about it.

This book is also a political literary work. I have never been very good at either the writing nor even of the reading of poetry. Yet, my writing style appears to be a bit poetic, full of metaphor and long-winded and winding sentences with alliterations sprinkled liberally about that would fit better if it were perhaps a poem. Although clearly this is not a poem. I feel I am in good company in this regard as James Joyce said that he took to writing novels because he just could not write poetry. His novels are brilliant examples of what one can do in prose with a poet sensibility. I am hardly a James Joyce — could any one be, actually? — and I am two removes from poetry besides, writing non-fiction and prose, not just fiction prose.

This book is intended both to be amusing as well as to make points. Policy wonk writing just does not appeal to me and I am afraid if I tried to write that way I would find myself, I am quite certain, slinking down the halls of Tedium Hospital in an intellectual wheelchair, slip sliding away to a premature and unhappy mental and emotional death and never finish this book. There are many others who do wonk far better than I, even making it all amusing and informative. This is not my gift or intent.

That said, I hope beyond measure that I shall light many fires — metaphorically speaking, of course — under our collective conscious and unconscious about how we arrange our political and social and economic relationships. The ideas are not meant to burn us up but to put us on a different trajectory and away from the hot claustrophobic greenhouse hellish Earth we are making, indeed, have made!

My friends have complained that upon reading parts or the whole of this book that I have the horse and the cart backwards — actually I think it still works that way, too, at least if the horse faces the direction you want to go — that a change in the collective consciousness needs to change before my proposals will make any sense to anyone. Well, that may well be true, futile effort not being absent from several if not most parts of my life. Still and all, not only do I believe our consciousnesses are high enough to understand what is written herein — it just is not that tough to read and understand it — but that human beings, especially younger Facebookers across the planet are ready for the next and greatest democratic revolution and reasonable and rational government and society. It is about time.

Anyhow, how do you become more conscious if nobody around comes up with new, elevated ideas? The intent of this book, indeed, is itself to raise our collective consciousness. Thinking, intuiting, channeling these ideas from brain to consciousness and from memory to paper has, I believe, raised my consciousness.

So which comes first, the chicken or the egg, the consciousness or the new idea? Too tough a set of questions for me. I will just write the book and someone else can figure out all that. I am not sure I really know what an elevated consciousness is anyway and whether this book represents one or not.

The World As It Is

I am a bit put out, put off and otherwise not in a very good mood about this whole shebang. "New World Order," my foot. What an odiferous mess. And, there is most likely more and worse to come. Much worse perhaps. Read any report and summary on climate change, environmental depletion, species deprivation, bird flu possibilities, population growth in the areas that can least handle it, the health of small children on poor continents, the shortage of food on many a continent, you name it. It does not bode well; it bodes ill. Monumentally, tragically, ill.

I suspect you know what I am talking about. I know, I know, you do not want to get involved in politics or even hear all this negativity. We all just want to save one person, usually a family member or, if not a family member, some wayward non-familial soul who really does need your help, and feel we have done our part. It would be in other times and places, but maybe not now.

I also know that it is better for your vibe and mine if we do not watch the news. Better if you do not read any books on global warming. I understand. Because if you do watch the news or read a book on global warming then you get depressed and feel hopeless. "What is a poor little me to do?" we all sigh "I am so small and the problems are so large." And, "besides, how would I, how could I? I have so little influence or power. Better to go about my business and do my part, recycle my garbage and love those around me and pray for the rest. Others have the power, the know-how, not I."

I understand, really I do. I have said it. I have meant it. Nonetheless, to me, that perspective is now really a great problem. Why have you and I been shut out? I think you and I need to be a part of the solution, to have more power, to participate in the very decisions that matter to you and everyone you know and everyone else. The power elite — governmental and corporate alike — have been derelict and without very good ideas and running the show in some version of their own interests more or less. And that, my fellow planet riders, leaves us with a terribly, horribly, mucked up world.

Frankly, and as one who has been there and done and said that, avoided doing anything about cleaning this mess up, we are being not a tad bit irresponsible, you and me both. Not only have we been shut out, we have shut ourselves off.

This is our world, our planet, our country, our society. It is ours, at least for a little while, on loan from God Him or God Her or The Great Spirit or whomever or whatever, The Tao, or some mischievous Bodhisattva world creator or long lost Thor or Odin or just plain old scientific evolutionary survivors' advantage. Letting it go to pot with a futile and breathy sigh without so much as a proverbial quixotic charge at a windmill or two, well, come on, let us, me and you and everyone all the way to Timbuktu, roll up our psychological and practical sleeves and get to work.

Hey, the chains are off, workers of the world: take back the world! The merde has already hit the fan and it is far past time to put the big mop to our living space and clean it all up. Some are trying and it is time for all of us to try harder; and not only try harder, but get it done.

Are we going to just let Assad kill women and children? Are we going to let glaciers fall into the sea without a fight? Are we going to let our politicians of the corporatocracy run the show, tell us what the issues are in their corporate media and then gridlock themselves in Congress endlessly so nothing gets done? Or even when it does get done, nothing really gets done. Shall we let money speak as we agree to be kept silent?

Of course, there are a few among us who work voluntarily for organizations trying to make a difference. They do but not enough. The way The System is rigged — "rigged" says Elizabeth Warren running for The Senate in Massachusetts — it is so awfully hard to make a difference when the powers that be want to keep The System in place come hell or high waters. And, it is, indeed, high waters that are coming, literally, not just metaphorically. Ask the residents of Far Rockaway and The Jersey Shore. What happens when that shelf of ice the size of Rhode Island and parts of Texas falls off the edge in Antarctica? Ask Mr. Gore. Ask the residents of New Orleans, now, even before the ice shelf goes splash in the night.

I admire The Tea Party, not because they project intelligence or good imagination to come up with solutions (hardly!) but at least they are speaking up that they do not want to take it anymore. Guess what? They are actually being heard, at least for their 15 political minutes or months. Could you imagine the effect if they had good proposals instead of being a front for aggrandizing conglomerates, stupid politicians and oil companies? And, The Occupy Movement, even if they refused to have proposals, at least they proposed that we think about proposals for the 99% of us. We need to occupy the whole planet! Even so, it is not nearly enough whether dumping tea in the polluted Boston harbor or harboring vague and general revolutionary intent. It is not enough, being now too little too late.

What we most desperately need, I sincerely believe, is a plan. A really good comprehensive plan. It is really not enough to do as the Nike advertisers screech to "Just Do It!" Do what? Why? Will it make a difference? "Just Do It!" Ker-plunk right off the fiscal and environmental cliff.

The plans and scams that pass for plans, the proposals of The Parties, Democrats and Republicans, Barack and Boehner, the schemes and themes, are not getting us going anywhere that is worth going to. If they worked, if their past plans worked, we would not be where we are. We need a better plan, a Newer New Deal. Then, and only then can we "Just Do It." We sorely need to think about a world that we and our children and grandchildren and great grandchil-dren, out to 1500 years at least, could live in, in peace and harmony with nature and each other.

It is not hopeless. We are not hapless. Yet, as far as I am concerned, it is far past the time to think outside all these constraining psychological, political and economic boxes. Iron clad boxes they are not, but chimeras, foggy illusory residues of our shortage of belief in ourselves and what we are capable of. The old way of seeing and doing is no longer adequate, if it ever was. Neither Orator Obama of golden tongue nor Mighty Mitt of Fifty-Five Point Plans, nor Cheru-bic Billy Clinton nor, our next president, Hillary Clinton, are going to save you and everyone from the entropies to come.

End Times In No Time

According to the ancient Mayans the plane of the ellip-tic of our solar system hits a point perfectly in line with the center of our Milky Way galaxy during late 2012. For the Mayans, this does not signify the end of the world as some have conjectured. For the Mayans, actually, this is only a cosmic move from the Fifth to the Sixth World Era. Something is ending; something is beginning, who knows exactly what, except maybe a laid back and secluded modern Mayan shaman or two far from the ruckus of our demises.

I do not know Mayan astrology and whether the meaning of this alignment means what this or that paranoid interpreter says it means, end or beginning, Armageddon or the utopian millennia. Yet, this I do know, either we move pretty quickly to put things right on this planet or the end of the world as we know it will entail a set of sufferings too gruesome to contemplate.

Really and truly, actually and factually, there is precious little time left before... So for the sake of our grandkids — I say that now that I am a grandfather — let's ... Otherwise, future generations surely, if there be much future for future generations, will see us not as baby boomers but as a big baby bust.

Introduction
To Our Little Dystopia

It is generally said that as you get older you complain more. You contract grumpy old man syndrome, with scowling flabby jowls, whiney strident voice, flipping off here and there on one or another irrelevant mad tangent, mad at the government, mad at the Tea Party, or mad at Barack while being a member of the Tea Party, mad at the majority of your clueless fellow citizens or mad at the numbskull rascals of the minority. Us old grumps harrumph to nobody in particular, "Why can't they, a world populated by a whole host of 'them,' be as rational and clear thinking and know it all and know what to do about this disagreeable world, just like us? Can't these dummies even increase the debt ceiling without bringing down the whole bloody system? Good grief!"

You know how the world is. There is always some new angst and life threatening dilemma going on for days, maybe weeks, not much longer — or it gets too old to be good news for the prime time news hour TV ratings. The news cycle flips us through Libyan protests and Gaddafi exhorting his African mercenaries to quickly martyr protestors and they desirous of martyring him or the devilish mass murderer Assad ordering his troops and thugs to shoot down women and children first or our Afgani and Iraqi wars on radical extremist Muslim pseudo-clerics prone to fire their guns in the air, issue fatwas and send boys strapped with bombs designed with a fatal button to ignite in a crowded outdoor market. Then, we are whooshed back to the political gossip world of U.S.A. politics and with whom and when Newt went nude and left a wife and then another in the lurch or Sarah Palin blathering on in run on sentences about what he said and "isn't he a liberal ninny for saying it and don't you liberal women defend me I don't need the likes of you," or Donald the Frump trumpeting all over the place trying to fire the President, still and all a much better man than he, or a general or two screwing up by, well, having unauthorized sex. Then we are zipped back out across the Pacific to a tsunami challenged nuclear plant burning its rods and sucking in and then spewing out seawater, nuclear-izing a beach and its ocean in Japan and a good deal of the outskirts of Tokyo, and will it or will it not it happen in L.A? What has Mighty Mitt paid or not paid in taxes; and, what was it that he said to his millionaire minions about approximately half of us?

Here it is, the news farcical circus, all this and more, ladies and gentlemen and children of advanced ages, hour after monotonous hair-pulling hour, all with requisite talking head experts going over and over again and over and over again and then again the dimensions and constituents of that road to Hell, and the world just seems to be getting worse and more hopeless by each CNN 24 hour news day. Do you turn the tube on or off when the news comes on? Years of that, days of that, would make anyone grumpy, so better to turn it off and hide one's head in a barrel, at least until they repossess the barrel.

As for me, I was older when I was younger, not that I am literally ageing backwards — only psychologically — because I griped a whole lot more all the way through my youth and my middling age about all kinds of personal, interpersonal, work related, societal, environmental, national, political, economic, and international distresses — you name it — always giving me any reason to complain and, perhaps, forget about my part in making this grandiosity of a mess, just like any curmudgeonly coot. I was a socio-political grouch.

Yet, from cranky crank all these years, now, perhaps I am losing my bitter and vinegar edge. I seem less apoplectic at the state of the world and more cool, calm and imaginative, even sanely wiser or so, I think. I do not believe that the human beings of this woeful and wonderful planet have suddenly made amends and then gone off and made it all alright. Far from that! To what then do I against all odds owe my latter day sanguinity?

I seem to be experiencing, popping up out of the clear North Carolina Piedmont blue sky of an aged mellowing brain, actual factual solutions to just about everything. Just like that: here a pop, there a pop and each and everywhere a monumental world class dilemma is solved. It is comforting to know the answers to just about everything — sociologically, politically, economically speaking, of course. These immodest proposals seem, to me at least, fairly and sanely reasonable. Although, how would I really know if I qualified for being diagnosed by a representative of the latest edition of DSM — Diagnostic and Statistical Manual of Psychiatry — and its bureaucratic rendition of who is contemporaneously certifiably walking down the street nuts or just out and out politically insane like the rest of the politic world?

Yet, nuts or not, I think I can show us a way of doing things on a great big societal wide scale, how we might want to arrange our world in a fashion far more orderly than what we have now. I have ideas for how to reasonably reorganize and reverse the trend to global warming, the endless wars and small genocides here and there — Rwanda, the former Yugoslavia, almost in Libya, in Syria for sure at last count, still in the Congo — and then unemployment and underemployment and giving up on employment and crimes and punishments and errant despicable multi-multi millionaire TV stars screwing who knows whose wife and others while ingesting who knows what illegal pharmaceutical concoction and alcohol and, and, and, and the list goes on and my wife turns off the TV late into the evening so I won't become too crotchety as we grow old together. Enough of all that.

Who knows? Maybe in the better future as we all grow older with whomever we grow older with, we might not become more and more ornery at all because we have so well arranged our personal, social, national, international, economic, and political lives in such a reasonable and effective manner that the only real complaint left could be, "darn, do I have to leave so soon?" What would poor rich Ted Turner say when his cable TV child and its reporting commentators had nothing more to prattle on about and things were just fine and dandy? I am sure Ted would be alright simply roaming a Dakota trail with his buffaloes, out to pasture and happy as a lark on a buffalo. Ted's buffalo burgers are not half bad, by the way.

Socio-Personal Suffering

There is a quotient of suffering in the world that is innate to the rules of the game, life and death, pleasure and pain, joy and suffering, the golden yellow sunset with hints of reds and oranges on the darkening shore lapping lake, the fragrance of late afternoon honeysuckle, the hustle bustle and singing of the birds who did not get the early worm but who did get the worm that did not get up early either, the sigh that vacation is passing and that life is passing and then it passes maybe or maybe not in agony, maybe peacefully, just a sigh and you are gone, or, less cataclysmically, the big toe stubbed and bruised black and blue on a root sticking out surreptitiously on the trail, or the fear in the dark or the cosmic flush of birth and then, all the voluminous multitudes of experiences of life there for the being and doing, feeling and thinking, the movement and the stillness, the pleasure and the pain, as it is, as it was, as it will be, for ever and a day, for a day and forever, underlying it being the miracle of being alive and then the miracle of all that is there for the living. There is much to worship; there is much to grieve. It is life. It has its exquisite pleasures with great variety; it has its awful pains of great intensity. And the world has boring ordinariness as well.

Then, there is the suffering that is not necessary, that we create, that we create with others, that we create in society, that causes all of us — rich, poor, young, old, happy, unhappy — to suffer more than is necessary beyond the rules of life on this planet. This unnecessary pain and suffering, is the pain and suffering I wish to deal with here, to talk about with you, to think over with you, to come up with a way to get us beyond this suffering that is unnecessary.

There is already in the nature of things, enough suffering to doubt God's goodness — being so hard on Job and the rest of us — to not give over to faithlessness. Yet, given how we pile on the pain over and above natural pain, is it any wonder that there is relentless and overwhelming doubt about the goodness of the good Earth, about life itself? God and The Devil are not entirely to blame for evil in the world. We are, too.

Why do we do it? Is there an "Original Sin?" What could it be? What does The Good Book say?

In judging the world, our incisor minds pierce and chew on the cinnabar apple of The Tree of Knowledge of Good and Evil, and therein lies the problem. This "Original Sin," that we somehow associate with sex — how so? — has far more to do with our self aggrandizing arrogance of judging, critiquing, quantifying, controlling and conquering The Creation, The Garden of Eden, the here and now. Therein is the rub, that grating, chafing, blistering rub, the endless thorn in our sides and in our hearts. God stated clearly and unequivocally "it is good"; yet, we are not so sure. We want to be the judge; we bite of the fruit of deciding what is good and bad. "Original Sin" being then our judging instead of our accepting of: The It All: Life, for all its good and bad.

It is not God who throws us out of Eden. It is we who stride out in a snit declaring that we are going to do something about all this, this imperfect creation with its evil and ugly as well as its good and beautiful. We are arrogant, full of hubris, full of ourselves in cosmic revolt, dissatisfied with it all. We do not want the pain of the world that goes with the pleasure of the world. We judge.

Within our denying souls, we deeply desire that this world, the natural world, the world that God, and Gods and Goddesses, and angels and demons, or just cosmic quantum-ized chance and fortune created should not, must not house the foul rot of our corpses. We know it will but we try to deny it. We try to deny it so awfully hard.

While we recognize the pure innocent playful silly joy of childhood there is Buddha's old age and death scourge lurking. We feel we must quickly and diligently educate our kids so they can get a good job and live a financially solvent life with enough left over for a golfing and mall-shopping retirement, not to mention a good health insurance policy that somehow never really saves us from the deterioration we most fear.

And that, ladies and gentlemen, is how we become such a pain in the ass to ourselves and to each other. More ironic still, we decide what is "sin" and then what is "good" and what is "virtuous." That, too, in assigning "sin" to our acts and the acts of others is an arrogance as well. If God said the world is good, God meant us, too. We lay the guilt upon ourselves. We even say we are "sinful," that we are involved in the "Original Sin." It is all so doubly twisted and ironic, a closed loop of psychological angst.

We reach and strive with our hidden palpable sense of cosmic biblical deprivation for a better world, at least we pray that our children may live in such a world, knowing that for now, for ourselves, for this life, it is impossible to get to the sinless there, the vision of what we want the world to be, the sweet without the bitter. We become workaholics to a fault, workaholic architects, exterior painters and interior designers and builders of fantastic and phantasmagorical cities. We create Singapore and Capetown, Baltimore and Rio, and towns of all shapes, sizes and character, and towers of Eiffel and walls and The Great Wall, all the time refashioning our world, working for a better, an improved what? A pro-growth paradise of artifice is what we get for all that. Yet, we long for Eden. We forget that Eden has a set of down-to-Earth rules we do not care for.

We willfully cannot fully and whole-heartedly even accept as our due the pleasures of the world because it implies insistently the pain and a final end that is its part and parcel. In our trying, effort-ing and then ultimately forcing, and wanting and desiring oh so badly for life to be only the quintessential-perfect-essence of youthful sun drenched life and forever more, we shun and deny the neglected and awful night of our ageing and the dying of our light and the pleasures of the nights as well as the real and natural ones of the day. We artificially light up neon bulbs arrayed in commercial advertising sequence at Times Square sometime around midnight, and in that light, our artifice of light, our wanting only a virtual self created perfection, we swoon.

We go out for dinner and a movie or croon with Dancing With The Stars. "Ah, life is good, isn't it?" We take a pilates workshop at a Mexican resort by the sea. "Ah, life is good, isn't it? Isn't it?" And the wage slaves stroke our quadratus lumborum and bring us tea with vodka. Is it, this other-worldly man-made world that we create within the good and natural world, is it good?

Is this it? Really?

Presumptively, crazily, tragically, in powering up our motor car for the climb up to The Shining City on a Hill, teetering Ronald Reagan's senile vision, we burn it out, city, hill, countryside and all. Then, we make excuse after excuse. On and on we perpetuate one denial after another, over and over; and, like Sisyphus, like the gerbil on the treadmill, like the wage worker working in the hand cuff factory nine to five each and every day over and over again, we manically manufacture our very own personalized and professional-ized machine made manacles. We blame, not ourselves, not our ancestors, but God and Mother Nature, not remember-ing what we have done, what we are doing, what we should stop doing.

The marathon of civilization huffs, puffs and wheezes its hyperactive industrious way to our foul and fetid dystopia that we call home, the civilized world of our miscalculated making. And if for old Marx, religion was the opiate of the masses, today, the numbness of the masses comes from the dumbness of the television.

The world as it is today: dystopia and Facebook. You and me both, are we not crazed crazy creatures who do not appear to know what is up; do we know what we have lost; do we know how to get back to Eden? Where is the trail, where is the way, who is the politician, the Indian guru, the evangelical Baptist preacher, the late night TV host, who will show us The Way back or forward? What is up with all this?

Grumpy, I want to escape, put my head in a barrel.

Paradise Found & Lost

Hiking the trails around Mt. Rainier in Washington State, not unlike other dirt paths in other national parks, my wife and I were practically alone, a few hikers here and there while the masses of our friends and neighbors were toiling away elsewhere, back out of Eden. Around the Rainier volcano is what we call an "old growth forest," seeming, I am sure, as it was a few hundred years ago. In point of natural fact, the whole of the hemisphere north and south was similarly beautiful a few hundred years ago — B.C., before Columbus — the humungous ferns, the thousand year old patriarchal trees, the misty foggy wisps of clouds blowing through the impressively grand pines, the rocks pummeled by a zillion gallons of crystal clear cold stream water, the thorns warning that you better be careful picking these berries cause I'm going to give you pain for your eating sweet pleasure if you are not careful, and everywhere life abundant with predator and prey and trees, oh so many trees. Oceans of wavy land called now "The Plains" and snow pocked rocky mountains and alligator-ed and mosquito-ed swamps of gargantuan water logged cypress and hot dry sandy deserts of eucalyptus shrubs and ephedra stick plants, and everywhere was a national park — although not called a "national park" — but was just what it was and glorious to behold and lucky you were if you lived in it at those times as did the Narragansetts and the Cherokees, the Iroquois and the Sioux, the Cheyenne and 500 nations.

If a tree fell in the woods and nobody heard it, it was all the better for the tree, because a bit later on our grandfathers would be sawing down that tree and then that woods and building a nouveau riche Roman style American Empire out of it. And then, there was simply much less woods to be heard from again. Now, all that anyone and everyone hears everywhere even where there is a bit of forested woods is the racket of internal combustion engines or sees and smells time and again the sludge in the water from the fuel oil gunk gushing out of the floor of the Gulf of Mexico. Everywhere is obscured the magnificent soft rustling of the simple green leaves of what is left of common deciduous trees. What would Thoreau say? Would he have somewhere to hide? In a barrel, I am certain, and not The Walden Pond.

If God thought it was all good and said so, I do not think He quite had this in mind, that we would take away the good Earth to fight The Bad and make it all so ugly. The Creation has been turned into a toxic trash heap, as the poor glaciers in the Himalayas all melt away — how will the Chinese and Indians feed themselves without the run-off water? What will happen to our thyroids when the walls of all our nuclear reactors melt away?

The world as it is today: dystopia, eco-dystopia, the Garden of Eden ravished, polluted, going, gone.

My Life As It Was, Is

I grew up for the first five years of my life in the raging middle of the Bronx, New York, on University Ave. on the first floor of a rounded eight story solid stolid brick apartment building whose contours fit the large avenues and sidewalks at its front and whose back doors and yards led out to streets of single family homes. In back of the single family homes was a stubby elongated hill. Here and there and in the backyards of the single family homes were some scrubby neglected trees, afterthoughts, a bit of an embarrassment really, I am sure, in 1952. In the front of all the buildings were sidewalks and then, of course, city streets and on one side of my building, a very wide boulevard or so it seemed to me as a child, a very wide and dangerous place for me, so my mom and dad said. There was an interior courtyard to our round apartment building, but even here, no grass or trees, only flat concrete without contour, except for the lines you could not step on or "break your mother's back," or so the other kids said. I remember them saying that.

To me, a child, it was all good, whatever it was. Concrete with its lines that I would be sure to vault: fine. Lead laden toxicities from the tail pipes of early 50's autos: fine. The stores on the street, especially the luncheonette candy ice cream store: very fine. I did not hear the word of God saying it was all "good" — I was not so attuned or well read at 3 — all of it, no matter what: fine and dandy. Life was simply good, urban and all. And I liked the trees, too; and the dirt making up the hill in the back. I did not pooh-pooh a little back yard dirt and a few shaggy elms. That was good, too.

By 21, now in Brooklyn's Park Slope, the up and coming gentrifying neighborhood of renovated brownstones from a prior century, I felt overwhelmed and I felt the elms' strife. Inside and out I could not escape the distance from I did not even know what exactly. The dust itself seemed covered in grime, the dirt in and of the air all feeling unnaturally dirty; and the feeling I had I really have no words for, a pain so new to my young adult life, so anguished, a hopeless anguished pervasive angst of skin and body and soul.   There is probably a category of distress or pathology in some new Eco-Psychiatry DSM complete with numerical code numbers for this feeling: Depression of the Eco-Soul? 942.5? Existential Dread at the Heart of the Organic Soul? 942.6? Not creepy in a horror story imaginative way, this was horribly creepy in a soot-based reality way.

Here we New Yorkers were, living in our own machine smoked and soaked debris from horizon to endless polluted horizon — or what we could see of it — and me and everyone else wheezing on the pervasive putrid manufactured flatulence. I looked out from the tar roof of the renovated brownstone I lived in, having nervously climbed the rusty black paint peeled metal fire escape, to a view of the roofs of the other brownstones and on down Atlantic Ave. to the minor metropolis of downtown Brooklyn and further, looking at the narrow gargantuan Andes-like colossus, Manhattan. I felt fatefully, if temporarily, imprisoned to my bones, eco-claustrophobic. The best intentions go straight down

Broadway past 42nd St., straight to Hell and its kitchen. I did not love New York.

Walk along the Salmon River outside of Portland, cruise the Black Hills, listen silently and intently to the stubbornly clinging wind swept grasses of the Sand Hills of Nebraska, imagine the lands before the white man, imagine Manhattan before New Amsterdam, the wave and wind swept Outer Banks before Blackbeard. See Texas before it was Texas, Colorado without resorts, the soft trees of the Shenandoah. Then hear those crying in these wildernesses, what wilderness is left, "O' America," they whine. Hear the prophets crying and weeping and chastising and despairing. Al Gore is one of them, Thoreau and Whitman, too. Do you know Crevecoeur? Many of us know in our hearts what is lost and gone forever. Read our contemporary poet-philosopher Wendell Berry, crying out from what is left of natural Kentucky.

America is beautiful in isolated enclaves, here and there, out of town and out of the way, places to drive to for hours, for days. It takes a day or two to get from Milwaukee to the South Dakota Badlands, longer to the volcano's caldera that is Yellowstone. It takes that long to get back to what was everywhere and everything a couple of hundred years or so ago. It takes the very same gasoline that tarnishes the very purity we drive to in order to get there. It takes a bit — maybe too much — of imagination.

Decades later, a much older gent, I sit on a bench in a park in St. Louis by the Mississippi and strollers from the stainless steel grand gateway arch look at a foolish tall balding man but do not see him hallucinating the native Eden past. He is crying, big, big, primordial tears and they cannot fathom in the least why. Why am I so very sad, head tearing at heart? I look straight ahead and then to the sides and see the industrial boats and the beams of machinery for unloading and the fetid drek that the river has become. I am the man crying, crying to my bones, tears dripping on my spirit. Not crying in the wilderness, but crying for wilderness.

As It Is

Sorry. America is not The Beautiful. America is a mockery of the good life in too many ways, an ecological and social wasteland, a modern day dystopia. Still, at least we can shoot our mouths off and dis our President and all the members of Congress of both parties when there are nations on Earth where such blathering will get you shot. At least we have that and it is no small thing at all.   There is worse ecologically, too, around the world; outside of our dystopia, worse dystopias. There is a worldwide collection. Haiti is worse; and was worse, far worse, even before The Earthquake. Most cities in China are far worse. Brazil is following in our footsteps. There are strip diamond mines in the Congo and a slow leaking genocide. There are the slums of Rio, Manila, Capetown, New Delhi. Former Communist East Europe and the Soviet Union are still cleaning up or may never be able to. Think of Chernobyl for 10,000 years.

Consider it this way: hundreds of years ago, the natives, before it was America, before they were "Native American," lived in "The Garden of Eden." For better and for worse, in sickness and in health, with one social form or another, they lived and died in "The Garden of Eden." Where do we live now, where is the progress? If it may not have been a perfectly golden past, it is not a glowing present by any means.

In our patriotic genuflection, do we even begin to recognize the ugliness that our fore fathers have left us? Virtual reality has such wonderful appeal because the un-virtual world has become so appalling ugly. We retreat into little shells of illusions, delusions, denials and other forms of personal and social retreat, TV virtual life, computer virtual amusement, a Disney fantasy life at best. Plato might think that we live in the corner of dank dark caves peering and panting at screens that contain pictures of what is left of the spirit of the world. We live, perhaps, in the latter days of the Dark Ages. Why is Edvard Munch screaming?

As we pillage The Garden of Eden and misshape God's

good Earth into eco-Hell, the least we could do is to throw a good party for everyone and let's all have a good time. Hardly. Even the Devil has to be disappointed. If we have turned Lake Erie into a dead cesspool, the least we could do would be to give the good citizens of Ohio and Cleveland a bang up Roman orgy of sumptuous gourmet bacchanalia and round the clock love making. All those open pit mines in West Virginia and Kentucky and you would think that all the gracious hill peoples who opened their mountains and forests to the monstrous paraphernalia of coal production, trucks the size of Tyrannosaurus Rex, coal trains the length of small nations and run-off that pollutes so far down stream that it makes it to the dying ocean of mercury poisoned silver fish would be filthy rich and gorging themselves on one and another goody. No, just a middle class salary at best if that and there is soot in their blood and the occasional mining disaster. An early 600 foot-down underground grave.

And the diamond miners in the Congo? And the factory workers, women and children, slaving away in sweatshops in China and the Philippines making all the stuff and junk for everyone on the planet. The Brazilian timber tree cutters decimating the rain forests, do they live The Great Society life? Do they tell you on CNN or NBC or Fox or CBS about the very high suicide rate at the Apple factory in China? Ah, what a hero-genius is Mr. Jobs, rich on the backs and minds of overworked, underpaid, horribly suppressed Chinese workers.

You would think, given that we are eating our very own planet's surface and a bit below it whole that we would all be rolling in do-re-mi to beat the band. Hardly.

Of the 6 billion + of us on the Earth, there are probably one billion of us who live on less than $1 per day. There are probably about one billion of us who do not even have that dollar. We, and the United Nations, do not know how they stay alive, scrounging on garbage dumps, if they are lucky. And then, I would guess, another billion live as poor as church mice in a church hovel in a dilapidated neighborhood. Another billion are just pretty drastically poor. More than half the world's population lives now in cities and corrugated sheet metal hovels overflow with the grossly poor. Slum Planet. Even as some of the wealth spreads around to newly minted high growth capitalistic China and India, still the suffering goes on for the vast majority even there.

The suffering this represents is not being heard by our Western ears. Are any of these voices ever heard from? Do we know of the conditions under which 2/3 of our fellow human being live and how they get by? For the one Slum Dog Millionaire, billions never get to dance across the bright silver screen and tell a triumphal story of youthful glory and go on to fame and fortune.

Yet, in the fallen shanties of Haiti, the hill slums of Rio, the back streets of Manila, Mogadishu, Capetown, Detroit, there is laughter, drama, spirit, fulfilled and unfulfilled lives, desperation, personal triumphs, disputes, miracles, violence, love, sadness, and all the rest. As the natural world has its nature, so do we have human natures as we are a part of the world.

Regardless of the degradation of the natural world and the human world, still, the sun rises on a field of corn in Kansas and the wheat steppes in Ukraine and children play in a playground in L.A. as children play next to open sewers in Jakarta. They run and they laugh and they make up the games that they play. Perhaps a teen-child in South L.A. takes a bullet for another gang member from another member of another gang who will himself later be shot by another gang member of another and different gang and the malnourished child in Jakarta dies of dysentery at 6. Or perhaps not. Or they start out in sweat shop factories making sneakers for other children in other countries.

Two-thirds of our species live most likely under intolerable conditions of desperate poverty and the other third are progressively better off, most not by much, but at least better off. Hundreds of millions in China, India, Europe, the United States, Canada, Brazil, Chile, South Africa, and here and there get to be middle class even as the middle class life is threatened by the predatory 1%.

A very, very small minority, a portion of not even 1%, a small percentage of 1%, are the winners in the global economy. They are the wealthy and super wealthy, the object of supermarket magazine attention and mass adulation and envy. Or they hide away with their old money lives behind gated country clubs and off-shore tax havens. They control, count up, occasionally charitably dispense in some small, but well publicized, proportion as they spend, horde and invest the wealth of the world to geometrically gain even more.

I have personally known a few of the winners. Are they any happier than the rest of us? Does money, great fortune, bring happiness and a great life? What's the point of the whole bloody system if these people cannot be joyous beyond anything the rest of us experience? All this and it sucks for them, too?! That would just be too much for a mind and social conscience to bear. Is Lindsay Lohan happy? Trump's wives? Grumpy Trump? Was Jobs?

It is true that the super wealthy may be able to attend the NBA finals, flying to the game in their private jet and then sitting on superbly cushioned seats while servants set a buffet of lean filet mignon, Norwegian salmon and hollandaise soaked asparagus. They may be able when life seems a little too staid around the museum mansion and the country club crowd doesn't seem to compensate to take a trip to a ritzy St. Thomas holistic health spa and soak up mineral baths for a month or two as they work their pilates core muscles around a diamond studded navel in private tutorials. They may be able to buy really indulgent adult toys like biggest screen TVs or whatever car tickles the latest manifestation of their ego or a great antique Mauser or a Van Gogh at which to aim the Mauser's discharge. Wealth has some advantages, of course.

Yet the issues of life, of relationships, of fulfillment and purpose, of the joy of the taste of a really good tart hard Macintosh apple or the spray of waves on Montauk or the

Oregon coast, or the early death of a child or spouse, or good conversation with good friends or arguments with enemies, or the feeling inside the ribcage when you have helped another mammal, human or feline or canine, these have little to do with your position in the lopsided global hierarchy. Life and Nature and Spirit have other demands.

I have seen the wealthy winners screaming paranoid and naked down the streets of their town, drunk to nervous oblivion and sick and tired of life and moneyed fate. And I have seen others of them ecstatic as all get out nursing twin babies at her two breasts both at the same time.

You can be just as miserable and crazy or happy and fulfilled covered in lucre as you can without it. It is not winner take all, at all. The issues of right life are not settled by money. The point of a competitive system, a world political economy that produces a very few winners and a mass of relative losers and a greater mass of lumpen-losers, is absurd beyond measure. No one gets The Life Trophy the way we kick each other about. Absurd dystopia beyond reason and we seem so stuck with it, this unnecessary suffering on a mass scale. Not even the little coterie of super wealthy winners knows but a glimpse of Eden. It really is no fun being destitute, even if it is remarkably futile being filthy rich.

So, in the end, the organization of our species that creates the material suffering for the many and does not wholly compensate any of us properly, is out of harmony with a natural rational order — what we and the Catholic Church used to call "Natural Law" — if there is some such way of doing the human social world. It is all too bad to be true.

At the immediate moment in America there is a whole set of other social, economic and political problems a result seemingly of The Great Recession but really endemic to an irrational system: high unemployment when there is plenty of work to do, the wealthy get wealthier especially those dreadful scheming bankers and financiers who game the economy while making no product and perform their socio-economic functions for their benefit alone and could care less about what they have wrought as they brought the whole economy down around everyone else's ears — as opposed to the vastly overpaid and overrated CEOs of manufacturing companies, e.g. General Motors, who actually seem to produce something, cars, if pretty poor cars — as the rest of us get poorer and poorer when there is plenty to go around.

Wealth does not trickle down; it gushes up in the direction of a very few. The education of our American young is second rate when there is plenty of intelligence to go around. American medicine is exceedingly expensive almost in direct proportion to how inefficient and ineffective it is.

And so on and so on into greater and greater debt socially and governmentally until bankruptcy will bring the whole edifice and the Social Security Administration crashing down. And then, maybe then, Tea Party goers might actually have something real to complain about.

America, too, lives with one of the highest crime rates in the world, with one of the highest obesity rates in the world, with one of the unhappiest populations in the world, and with a politics that is second to only Italy and soap opera Berlosconi in its Rush Windbag stupidity and radio talk show roughhouse inanity.

It really is so pitifully easy to go ranting and raving on and on; there being all too much, all so very much, all too too much, to rant and rave about. Where is the old man's barrel about now?

The Big Cleanse & How

So. What to do?

I will be getting to that. "Yes, we can" indeed! We just need a really good plan, not just the idea that we can somehow do something, but we need to know exactly what to do. "Yes, we can do," but what?

In order to get my head out of the barrel and back to the world, I will be outlining ways to get not "the greatest good for the greatest number" — sorry, Jeremy Bentham and John Stuart Mill. I have, I think, a better set of proposals than that and a better goal for us all. A better formula would be: THE GREATEST GOOD FOR US ALL.

God said it was all good. Should be easy. It is already here, "the good news," that line that the Sunday evangelical preachers squawk from their preposterously prosperous pulpits, while degrading the message.

Still, there is "good news." Life is good, after all. Eden is here without even asking.

How do we clean up our mess? What do we do? How do we get back to the Garden? How do we live in Tokyo with 12 million? What do we do about Palestinian teenage suicide bombers blowing themselves and dancing teenage kids to smithereens in discos or Gaza with Israeli warplanes up your mother's behind? New Orleans and its Ninth Ward if not under water then under the incompetence of bureaucracies federal and state? Chicago's South Side of gangs mutilating and killing each other in juvenile stupid warfare of guns without roses? Outer or Inner Mongolia? the slums of Bombay? Yemen? And, of course, The Spill in the Gulf? Libya? The tyrant in Syria killing his citizens for demonstrating a bit of displeasure with this rule, and where and what next? Federal bankruptcy? What to do?

Somehow I do not believe that the way out of our misery involved electing Mitt Romney or Barack Obama President, that either one offers the magic trick we need, unless either politician magician has a whole lot more bunnies in their empty hats. Did either of their plans really add up to much of anything?

That is the topic of this book: how to arrange things, how to put together our society so it comes out right. A book of creative reorganization. Yet one more book, why?

There are literally libraries full of books that delineate the problems of the world and America. I could spend your time and mine in just a book that listed all the problems, let alone describe each one, which would take, well … a library of books of time. Yet, most books, articles and essays on this or that problem usually come up with moderate recommendations about how to fix an individual problem or, at best, two. Some good proposals are even adopted here and there especially if they preserve the existing rotten chaotic New World Disorder and Odor and do not rock the leaky ship of fools too much.

Of course, I know better than to imagine that the proposals and ideas of The Wiseacre's book are the last word on ideas. You, too, can come up with some that might be better. We need a bigger and bigger parade, a parade of ideas, marching down every street and boulevard around the world.

Actually it is going to be easier than you think.

Starting From Back Then to
The Here and Now

I am a kind of pre-Mesopotamian conservative. Give me the good old days, the really, really old, very old days. "Well," you say, "how backwards, how unprogressive and your life will be short and brutish and there will be no dishwasher to do your dishes, although you won't even have dishes and you will scald your fingers on scraps of charred mealy moldy meat because you don't have bone China and stainless steel forks and you will live in a clammy cold cave and your children will die in infancy and you will toil and travail from before sun up to after sun down and never have enough and you will be chased around the open savannah by ravenous lions or North American Ice Age mammoths with huge tusks; so, you want to be a Neanderthal? Good luck, buddy. Life expectancy was 18 years old then; you would be dead by now, instead of being a grumpy old man, you lucky guy."

Well, that is all not exactly how it really was. In fact, the work week for "primitive" tribal members is about 16 hours, depending on location, the outback of Australia, way back away from modern Brazilians in the Amazon rain forest or wherever or whenever "civilization" is not around to manufacture and sell its labor saving devices.

Ask your local anthropologist, if you have one, if you know one. You might not be able to find one because once they learn what a cushy life Neanderthal cultural-ists live, they leave the university department, its publish or perish mandates, disputatious faculty meetings and boring teaching and head for the hills that are way back and out of sight.

Of course, I am taking slight academic liberties with working hours and anthropologists and employing rhetorical hyperbole besides as working hours for prehistoric tribal members might be 18 to 20 hours and many an anthropologist might like life back in the states. Still, the factual truth of the matter is life just was not as bad as it was made out to be and, for many a "primitive" soul not so primitive after all.

So they asked my hypothetical anthropologist when he came back before he lit out again for the territory obscure and never returned what these poor primitive souls did with their free time, having so much of it on hand. Were they not bored out of their skulls without iPods and Facebooks? Well, he said, actually, these poor "primitives" do their hobbies and raise their children and dance until dawn to ecstatic drum beats. There is no juvenile delinquency in most old tribal societies because parents spend enough time with their kids to take care that they are raised properly. They have lives and adventures instead of voyeuristically not having lives and watching someone on a screen who seems to have an actual life but are actually acting out an adventurous life.

As for those lions and tigers and bears oh my!, munching on your carotid artery and liver well, now we have cars called Mustang and Cougar and other wild beasts. And I am quite certain that the rate of being mutilated and killed by or within one of those is far greater, percentage wise, than that for a tribal society facing down hungry hyenas, woeful wolves and portly polar bears on a Sunday outing visit with the relatives.

As for the food? I once went to a workshop in Northern Virginia titled "Wild Edibles." It was not a workshop on growing your own organic vegetables or herding domesticated goats. It was: go out in the woods and pick up your unpackaged, un-priced, un-supermarketed, un-shelved, un-shipped, all natural, all organic, all pure and untouched free lunch. We came back to camp with armful loads. No plowing, no seeding, no weeding, no work except harvesting. Oh, by the way, there was another workshop given by the same group in hunting for free and unspoiled and un-hormone-ed and un-antibiotic-ed meat, what we call "wild game."

If I ever had any notion of the poor and starving primitive that weekend dispelled it. North American Indians, at least on the East Coast, ate well indeed. The cod off the Cape, by the way, was so abundant and dense in the ocean you could not help but spear it. Oh, yes, and salmon in the Northwest.

All this is in addition to all the corn they grew.

When the white man came to Virginia and Massachusetts in the first colonies, the Cherokee and the Massachusetts Indians among others could not believe how short, scrawny and ill looking the first Europeans looked. Of course, they did not know the half of it. The illnesses of the intruders became the source of the decimation (90% of the population by some reasonable estimates) of an Indian population genetically unprepared for smallpox, hepatitis and all the new diseases coming their way. Spanish pigs brought illnesses ten-fold. The reports of the "pale faces" writing back to Europe was how magnificent and healthy the native population appeared — until the epidemics.

The native Americans even had time for fun and tattoos and hair styling that the puritanical Pilgrims, the puritanical Puritans and the drab English in general, thought was ungodly. The Indians thought the settlers dull prudes.

Longevity and sophisticated medicine was also the fortunate lot of the "primitive," as well, depending on the tribe. The worst life expectancy in the history of the human race is the 19th century Europe and America. It is not the case that the further you go back in time the worse health and life expectancy get. Well, yes, they did not do well in Athens when the Spartans attacked and they had to wall themselves in and pestilence and starvation became their lot, the end of Pericles included. But that was rather exceptional. Oh, yes and the Chinese and European bubonic plagues cut into life expectancy in a big way back several hundred years ago, too.

The big marker actually in the decrease in longevity and health winds up being the establishment of civilization and agriculture and cities to begin with. The last three to five thousand years. Recorded history.

On the other hand, hunter-gatherers most likely lived nearly as long as we do now and had a life style, living in the real world of nature — not the nature that you must drive to — in many ways, to my mind, far superior to ours.

(I know this is difficult to believe given how we have all been taught and propoganized ever so many times. As an antidote, please read the scholarly Mark Nathan Cohen's Health And The Rise of Civilization. Or research the Kung group in the Kalahari.)

While taking an anthropology course at Hunter College in New York City on "Native Americans," I did a final paper on Iroquois medicine. The herbal medicine of the Iroquois was at the time of their meeting Europeans certainly as sophisticated and efficacious as the medicine of the Europeans of that age.

The idea of social "progress" that we have learned from school and media, is, frankly, poppycock. It does not accord with the facts of life. Are things getting better? In some ways they have gotten worse and all the modern and post-modern machinery may not be making life and love and death and taxes substantially better.

But can we have our cake and eat it, too? Is it all hopeless and forlorn and must we live a machine dystopia nightmare all the days of our lives and our children's lives? In fact, can we keep some of the machines and have natural genuine fun, too, without being in ruin? Can we keep dishwashers — my personal vote going to the dishwasher for the greatest invention of all times, just barely ahead of the clothes washer and dryer and refrigerator and central heating — and can we keep all this and the Eden of forests, too, the life of the tribe and a clarinetist toning Mozart's Clarinet Concerto in B flat on my iPod, and my computer, and cell phones and all that? Oh, and can we have a government that works well, and no more gross poverty or the greedy rich, no taxes sucking away at ½ our incomes and still get all the services we require?

"Dream away, deluded dreamer," you say. "Take a winter vacation in Jamaica, drink a little rum, drink a lot of rum, listen to some revolutionary reggae and come back to reality. It is not really all that bad," you tell me.

Worse, I reply.

A Really & Truly Free Free Market

Actually, it could all be free, all the modern goods, if we looked at it perfectly objectively and followed the logic of the facts. We could have it all without much effort at all, the pre-civilized and the best of the civilized. If we did it right. And all free. And all free! Eden with free dishwashers. Could it be so?

How many of us in America who are working actually do productive or essential labor? That is, what is the percentage of all those who work who produce all the products we consume and possess; and then, what is the percentage of us who perform essential services — doctors and nurses and fire fighters and the transporters of goods — and only that which is essential and necessary?

Less than 1% of our American population feeds us all. They are the farmers and farm laborers. About another 5-6% do all the productive labor. Now, of course, much of the labor of producing all this stuff for us is now done in China, but even so, if we had to do all our production ourselves, a few more percentage points and we would be self sufficient, production wise. So let's just estimate that what we need is about 15% of the current labor to produce everything we have and do what is necessary.

I need to say this a couple of times to make sure we are clear about this. All goods. All our present abundance of goods of all kinds. All goods and essential services. Not a minimum of essential goods and services. All essential services and ALL GOODS!

What are the rest of us doing for work currently? Basically, fundamentally, living off the labor, mostly machine labor, of others. Easily more than 50% of all labor is paperwork. Whole industries and workers are simply paperwork done by paperworkers: advertising, banking, insurance, government and its bureaucrats, lawyers, financial advisors, the check out person who rings up your purchases at the supermarket, all accounting and bookkeeping and so on and on and on. Unnecessary.

(Again, if you want table and charts that show facts that are difficult to accept at first glance given our training, see the classic Small is Beautiful, Economics As If People Mattered by E. F. Schumacher)

In an America and world in which everything were free and you did not need to be induced to consume ever more and more, we could get by with about 1/7 of the current amount of work.

Every sales person in the country would be out of work. Talk about unemployment: 85%. Yikes! And still everything would be produced and taken care of. Put the goods up on the shelf and let everyone take what they want. From each according to a minimum and to everyone, anything. Karl is flipping over in his grave as I write.

If we then divided that work evenly so that, in fact, there was no unemployment, then what would be our work week? 15% which is essential work = about 1/7 of the week would then = one day of work per week for everyone. About ½ of what the typical aborigine had to work. Ah, the marvel of civilization and its inventive productive machines; it has cut the work week in half. That is, if we did it rationally. We would actually have improved on Eden.

All the automobiles — non-polluting, of course — all the computers and iPads and iPhones and iThis and iThats, all the food, all the dishwashers and everything else and all you would have to work would be 8 hours per week. And say, you wanted to put in your allotment of work when you were young, at say 40 hours per week, then by the time you reached your early thirties and counting your potential longevity at say 85 to 100 years, you could retire very early indeed. Retirement at what, 32?

But this would be a completely rational society. Too rational. The consciousness we now wear on our sleeves and fuss and fume to keep at any and all emotional price is both detrimental and limiting and the source of our earthly suffering, but still it is surprisingly difficult to raise precipitously — whatever that means, of course, "raising consciousness." We just appear not ready for a reasonable world. Are we simply so awash in garbage and attached to our ways of living and thinking that a world where everything was free, everyone had access to every free thing and where everyone need only contribute one day's worth of work labor is absolutely totally inconceivable, except as the fantasy presented here? Perhaps.

Yes, maybe it is a fantasy. How naïve can I be? Good luck getting this through our locked uptight Congress.

It will, I would estimate grandly and loosely, take a thousand five hundred years of consciousness-raising to get us to a world looked over by "machines of loving grace."

In the meantime I would like to propose a set of interim steps and goals to head us in the right direction. I am going to cover in this book everything from high unemployment in which some are denied work and the ability to obtain money and, therefore, to obtain goods, even life sustaining goods. I will also cover the drift of a productive industrial base out of the USA, obesity and the nutritive value of tomatoes, urban sprawl, trains-planes-and-automobiles, schools, social classes, democracy and a dysfunctional politics in America — and Italy and Iran and Russia and China —human rights, poverty and food and water and sewers and child labor, amongst others. Well, maybe not the tomatoes and Italy, but a good deal else, in any event.

The task is rather overwhelmingly prodigious, I know. There is, after all, no fool like an old wiseacre. Still and all, I am an old wiseacre that is not grouchy anymore.

Summing Up & Out Of Dystopia

Right now, it is an Old World Odor instead of New World Order and then, what to do? Even protestors, left liberal and right conservative, hardly know what to propose. There are not some good proposals out there, sure, but there is far too much nonsense. Comprehensive and workable solutions and a fix for the whole thing? Hardly!

I am quite sure we can do much better than this. I am quite sure that you are not so sure and maybe you believe that I am a bit nuts. You shall see. While I will not pretend to know the answer to every social problem, I am going to try solving at least most of them. Who knows, maybe if I throw enough bull manure around some of it will stick to the social ground and sprout some manifest futurist institutions better than the ones that today pretend to function for our benefit.

This book is nothing but and nothing less than a little book with very big ideas. I hope you will be writing another one, too and, then we can compare notes, add them up and change the world. It needs us, as we need it. And we need each other.

40

Chapter 1
U.S.A. Politics

Caveat Politico

I do know that there are many of us who find the American political scene so disagreeable — and for good and sound reasons — that they cannot bear to hear about it, let alone think about it any more. So, for all of you who feel this way, you might want to consider just skipping this chapter and go on to the next. I will understand. It is not necessary to torture yourself with things as they are and going nowhere at breakneck standing still speed.

However, it might help to read about the current political stalemate to see how we can take the best from the worst. That is, I believe that we can take the best that the current batch of politicians has to offer and use it to make a better future. So, if you have the proverbial stomach for it, I do suggest reading this chapter as well. It could be helpful. Otherwise, see you at the next chapter.

Such As It Is

For a brief and luminous moment, even though the event — the victory celebration after Barack Obama's first election — was late in the evening, it looked like it would all change: politics, economy, society, the world. There has been change, no doubt, but then again, so much has not. The unemployment lines stay long, if not as long. The stock market has doubled in value and more after having been down by half. Yet, the multiple branches of government cannot agree on much of anything especially money and budgets. The climate is changing and Long and Staten Islands and the Jersey shore are recovering from their underwater misadventure as the President talks about climate change and showcases that emissions levels for cars will be changing, if not nearly fast enough, or well enough. Libya has changed. Tunisia and Egypt have changed for the better, maybe the worse. Syria is changing, if murderously and tragically. Still, North Korea has an hereditary authoritarian dictatorship and threatens Seattle with nukes; so no change there.

Then again, what was about to change, actually? What did we expect, actually? It is something, the change that has taken place. Is it marginal, evolutionary, revolutionary? Is it enough? What would we really want to see?

On that late November night after our national day of voting, news commentators crooned with studied proud aghast, having once fervently believed they would never ever in their liberal, conservative or centrist lifetimes experience the election of an Africa-American President, yet in fact, right in front of their panning cameras, right up Jesse Jackson's nose and in his face as he profusely shed not a little bit of eye water, it was so. That was one change at least and a significant one at that.

I had not really considered the issue in that racial way at the time even though I grew up in part not far from where the Chicago crowds filled that Lake Michigan waterfront meadow. It was another time, another psychological space, in a 1950's racist world, the north side of that very same Chicago, where except for the occasional black maid trudging to or from one or another house or apartment to clean and whiten the interiors, the ethnic composition was mixed, a melting pot of sorts that was nonetheless wholly, totally, absolutely and intentionally low melanin toned. That is, whites only.

On a school bus traveling to museums on the South Side of Chicago where the future Michelle Obama would grow up and the future Barack Obama would organize, I could unmistakably hear my shouting and gesticulating classmates, seven year old children of tender age but malevolent mind, blurt out loudly and derisively the "n" word from school bus windows at African-American passersby. No teacher scolded them.

We, in a generation or so, have seen a rather quick and deft change about town and nation, racially speaking, much to our general moral and human credit — much to our collective conscience's relief. Yet, that Mr. Obama was of darker hue than all preceding presidents was, to me, a big bonus, but not altogether monumental that inauguration day. I had other changes in mind.

All racial and ethnic stereotypes aside, the electoral seismic shock for me was not that Barack, a black non-WASP man won or that Hillary Clinton, a break-the-glass-ceiling woman, would have won, but that we really and truly elected a politician of intelligence, emotional maturity and several obvious degrees of personal and professional dynamism. I was simply not at all sure that I would live to see the day that a calm and measured intelligent rationality would bless the nation's highest office again. It had been awhile, especially as the last president, George B. II, appeared in public and probably was in private, too, such a macho strutting airhead, almost but not quite the air-head equal of the ultimate non-reader — Couric was most likely on to something — Sarah Palin, whose caricature of a politician is still taken seriously by about the same quantity and quality of the American electorate that is a caricature of free citizenry.

Nonetheless, even with Barack in the Presidency and Hillary at his foreign policy side, the off chance that we would then create a good country, let alone, the late great "Great Society," was long odds. Long odds and fat chance. Check it out now. There is a sighing disappointment on a grand scale, even as we have elected Barack for a second term. Don't we want more change? Whither goes change?

So, while Obama stands head and shoulders, often Lincoln literally, but also rhetorically, above an elite group of politicians conspicuous for an absence of good sense and any palpable vision of the future, the terms of un-endearing debate that passes for Congressional civil civic discussion makes clear and unfortunate that we will be going nowhere fast for a long time and treading water at best even as the rising of the waters inevitably presages mass drowning. Whether that drowning is literal in the climatically challenged oceans rising or, in Armageddon actual, as in a new strain of AIDS going airborne or as in al Qaeda or some other group of violent nut cases gaining access to a couple of Pakistani silos and its contents and wasting Philadelphia and Denver or that we and the country or the whole continent of Europe go stark raving bankrupt or that there may be any number of pandemic disease mass extinctions likely coming down the devil's viral pipeline or that a pipeline of one kind or another, gas or nuclear, will rupture and we will pollute the whole of the oceans and much of the shoreline as well or, similarly, the aquifers of Nebraska and Kansas. We are treading water out at sea and hoping — we like the idea of HOPE — that the next swelling wave reveals a floating boat of rescue, not just more water to swamp us all.

Though the electorate voted for change that could be believed not only is the reality that change is not really and truly happening, but under present political conditions, it will not for a long time and we instinctively know it. Sorry. Hope is believable; its results not inevitable. In a second Barack term, what exactly do you expect? And in a first Mitt term, what exactly would we have gotten? Heaven have mercy upon us. Are the rich not rich enough?

On the other hand, it seems to my overly optimistic old mellowed mind that both American political parties, Republicans and Democrats, for all their boneheaded inability to get anything done and even when they get something done it turns into another debacle — "sequester"! — at their core might actually have some good arguments. But only at their core and even then we must think our best about them. It is at times a torturous mental rack stretch but maybe we can make something of it all, if not exactly on their present terms.

As any pollster will tell you, we, the public, in great majority sentiment, understands clearly and with irritation bordering on attitudinal insurrection, that there is nary a thin slice of brain pie in Congressional politicians' presentations and pronouncements. We, the citizen public, appear to think that their current dumb ideas are dumb — dumb-ed down, by media accounting and their politically cynical calculations for the supposedly dumb electorate, "nothing above the 6th grade level, please." I do not appreciate and I am quite sure you do not take pleasure in being talked down to like we are a bunch of know nothings and that coming from a bunch of knows-even-less. This in a society that values democracy? We actually had Republican candidates for the Senate of The United States from Indiana and Missouri who said exactly what about rape? Too stupid even to repeat. At least they did not get elected and get to spread their appalling ignorance to D.C., where there is enough hurtful lunacy already.

Getting to the parties core positive side and values means therefore, working one's way through a whole lot of blithering, blabbering, bothersome nonsense and political gesticulating. It just all seems so impossible to get anywhere, do anything, help anyone, fix the economy, punish the unjust, make love not war, save Social Security, as neither Grand Old Tooting Elephants nor Asinine Donkeys can transcend their pitiable rhetoric long enough to find creative ways to accommodate the important and positive core of each point of view.

I know this will sound a bit odd, but perhaps neither end of the political spectrum of politicians and their moneyed makers need compromise, with all due deference to The Compromiser-in-Chief, President Obama, but instead integrate socio-political-economic policies that on their surface appear in opposition and mutually exclusive, but properly fused produce a sum greater than their two disputatious parts. The Tea Party drinks a blend of Back Bay soaked tea leaves with the L.A. to Seattle latte house Occupy Movement. Possible?

I know that in point of political fact in many cases and issues this will not be possible, say, in the case of funding Planned Parenthood and the general abortion issue or for that matter the government's own voluminous debt. But on the other hand, there is plenty of room for both parties to live in the same house, the same country, the same political universe and actually in law and in practice, solve problems and help to make laws that promote a society where it all comes out right. We can — God and the ghost of Maynard Keynes and Mr. Hayek help us — even pay off that bothersome federal debt. I will attempt to show just how possible this all is.

So what I will be proposing: much smaller government, no income or sales taxes. Shall I repeat that not less income tax but NO INCOME TAX — and yet everyone and their Aunt Rose is taken care of as she should be, having brought up all the brothers and sisters with mom when dad died prematurely. That should satisfy everybody — maybe. We would not even be required to endlessly debate whether the top 1 or 2% should have to pay 1 or 2% more or less in taxes or whether everyone else should pay less. None for everyone! Therein could be the end of the devastation of our politics and society — again, maybe. It may take awhile; although, as we all know, we must start somewhere, somehow, sometime with some real solutions and not an airy fairy empty hope for the best or, as present proposals are generally, only slightly less than nothing.

"No taxes," I say and I say, "it is all OK." Can you believe it? I am proposing not only George Bush senior's "no new taxes," but simply: no taxes, period. And yet, Democrats and Progressives alike might even enjoy this more than Republicans. Tune in.

Intellectual History of
Democrats and Republicans

First though, it might help perhaps to know where exactly in what boggy political and philosophical ditch we are located and spinning our proverbial wheels in order to have some idea where to apply the proper leverage to get us moving out of perpetual divisive governmental gridlock. It really is a very bad intersection, in Washington, D.C. and more than a few state capitals besides.

In advance, please excuse the following simplifications. If in essence and overall, if not in specifics and all the time, and certainly not every last politician, and with lots of un-specified caveats as well, what follows is what has gone on politically in the USA since the early 20th century and a bit before that as well. What this summary will hopefully reveal beyond the specifics of the philosophies and policies of each party over time, is the underlying good core and good faith of either side, putting aside by holding our mental and polit-ical noses, those parts of specifics that are neither good nor faithful.

Dems

The wonk-ish Democrats, for their part, have been repris-ing versions of FDR's New Deal— and Teddy Roosevelt's Square Deal and Woodrow Wilson's ideals — ever since 1932 or so and gotten away with it right under the elephan-tine Republicans' nosey trunks all the way through Kenne-dy's The New Frontier, and Johnson's The Great Society. They managed to pass The Voting Rights Act, Medicare, Medicaid, and poverty programs galore; although, until recently they could not push through comprehensive health insurance for all.

The unquestioned popularity of Square Deal-New Deal-New Frontier-Great Society ended more or less philosophi-cally and practically when Ronald Reagan pulled the words out from under them Dems, angrily and apocalyptically pronouncing that "government is the problem, not the solu-tion." Conservative Republicans and not a small part of the general electorate as well have been in love with Reagan-ism ever since.

Thus, very quickly indeed ended decades of Democrats promoting and passing "progressive" government programs to solve social problems that, by the way, were inadvertently, indirectly, advertently, or directly created by corporate America, et al. Progress may be corporate product, but problems are its by-product and Democrats love to solve them — but are not similarly skilled at correcting them so they do not happen in the first place. Republicans see those social shortcomings as just part of doing business; and they believe it would be better to ignore them than burden business and the tax paying public with a government bureaucracy designed to absorb the expense of the cost to everyone else of doing their corporate business. Business loves to externalize costs. Why should mine operators pay for miners' black lung disease or childhood asthma downwind from the coal plant? Yet: why should we pay in the form of our tax dollars for a problem they created?

Reaganesque progress would have us progress in a different direction than the Teddy and Franklin Rooseveltian Woodrow Wilsonian Leftist progressivist direction, out with Big Brother and in with Big Business. To the conservative Republican mind set, Reagan put America Right and right and rightly so. With Reagan in The White House, the business of America became business once again. It was "morning in America," even though Ronnie slept through a good deal of the afternoon. All the Dem's progressive horses and all the Dem's progressive men cannot quite put Humpty Dumpty, Hubert Humphrey or The Great Society back together again.

Do we even remember poor Hubie? Hubert proposed a "guaranteed national income." Even Richard Nixon flirted with the idea. Change I could believe in. Fatter chance.

It did not help the Democrats that when Reagan was President the economy did, in fact, perform much better — not exactly right away, but eventually and even right on through the rest of the century, until George II Bush mucked it all up by continuing Reaganomics, as if it would work forever.

Of course, too, what much better means is defined by Republicans: the rich getting richer and the poor living in the tunnels between stops of New York City's underground subway. That, for them, is irrelevant to the fact that the rich are getting richer and the middle class picks up the dribble down of economics.

Yet, note that when tall Boston Brahmin Big Brother, the politically tone deaf John Kerry, paternalistically promised in his acceptance speech at the Democratic Convention of '03 that "help is on the way," you could almost hear a shameful shudder sift its way through the assembled lauding applauders and guess the sentiment of the skeptical millions watching on the tube. Americans — including myself — do not like to be told by the upper crust that they "need help." It was the beginning of the end for a campaign that never got started. Besides which, Kerry, while hinting that he was The Peace Candidate, started his convention speech militaristically intoning, "John Kerry, reporting for duty," implying that he could conduct the unnecessary Iraqi war better than the incompetent Bush.

When FDR promised help, everyone knew that he meant it, since everyone did need help, and everyone cheered all the way to the polls and happy days were here again. When Kerry, sweating above his upper lip through an overly serious oration, offered good times, no one could relate and there was no happy days ditty humming through our lips. He just did not look very happy those days or any other. At best, for the assembled convention politicians, there was only a half-hearted happy daze.

John, "we would rather do it ourselves, thank you!" And that was that. Mr. Reagan's mindset had squashed Mr. Kerry — even though it were two decades later.

Yet, the progressivist progress made a mild comeback with Obama and the Democratic controlled Congress at least for a short, compromise-filled two year congressional term. Still, even then it seemed that a Presidential Gipper-ish ghost haunted those proceedings, spurring on Tea Partiers and Republicans-all right into the next congressional election and the end of Obama-Dem progressivism.

Still, there is a bit, and not a bad bit, at that, of progress in the kinds of social reform promoted by the Democratic Party and carried by slim Congressional majorities, even if legislation based on its philosophical preferences is not what it used to be. Hey, they got health reform through if by the skin of their congressional grinning gritted teeth, and maybe it is a good thing they did. Although politically "Obamacare" is still not entirely popular with the majority of Americans, nor will it fix a boondoggle medical system with problems of its own. Still and all everyone will be getting healthcare and some of the grosser abuses of the medical insurance system may be done away with. Maybe, if not likely. I think, though, that we can do much better than that.

Republicans and Reagan-clones are still at it — when majority, when minority or both, majority in The House, minority in The Senate, always depending on the last election. Republicans like to think that they are the second coming of the Enlightenment's Adam Smith and his 18th century vision of bright beauty ever so perfect self regulating markets, born again laissez-faire capitalism at its most virulently fecund. Yet, what they offered not too long ago and got elected as a Republican President was George W. Bush, a true believing Reaganomics Republican if there ever was one, who looked more like Warren Harding each day he strutted and stammered and slap dashed his way through two terms — George's first term as ill-gotten as it was.

At least the Republican Warren Harding had the minimal intelligence required to know that he was out of his league and voluntarily refused a second term, mercifully dying after an awful and awfully corrupt first term. Harding's father, not one to mince words, said of Warren that — and I paraphrase — it was good that Warren was not born a woman because he simply did not know how to say "no." Warren's friends and colleagues had used and abused the federal government as their personal money gathering and laundering machine. I have always wondered what father George H.W. said behind closed doors about son George W.

Personalities aside, from Ronald Reagan and Margaret Thatcher to Newt Gingrich, and even our past ex-Fed Chairman, Alan Greenspan, among others of power and influence, lurking behind their political and economic thrones was the writer-capitalist-cheerleader Ayn Rand, an egotistical money grubbing Adam Smith on steroids. She was part and party to a philosophical tradition called Social Darwinism, the 19th Century justification for the ill gotten gains of the corporate wealthy Gilded Age, and the Rockefellers, the Carnegies and other fitter than fit individuals — at least to their own greedy and enormously oversized egos.

Much of our very prominent current Republican leaders read her, worshiped her and more or less adopted and adapted her latter day Social Darwinist philosophy to the real world of multi-national corporations and public and private finance. They probably would have come up with all this regardless, but it nice to have it all neatly wrapped up in intellectual charismatic and articulate packaging, in novels and essays.

Ayn Rand notably wore each and every day wore a diamond studded dollar sign pendant that kept together her bat black omnipresent cape. Philosophically, she was the archetypal female Gordon Gecko mouthpiece, yet she has been and continues to be enormously influential. To bring us up to date, Paul Ryan is a later latter day follower.

It is not too difficult to sum up the randy A. Rand philosophy of "Objectivism": money first and damn everyone else; business first and damn everything else; free markets will make me rich and damn the poor everyone else; me first and foremost and damn everyone else. And, she concludes: nothing gets done because the politicians muck it up trying to help the poor, "the 47%" or more who live off the hard work of the ever deserving 1%.

It should not be nearly such scary stuff, yet given the influence and power her followers have, given that they have sat at her mind's feet, bowed their moneyed heads and kissed the diamond broach, it is telling. It tells us what these corporate elitists, these 1%ers and their apologetic politicians have in mind.

In all fairness to the Midas touch Ayn, there was a socially redeeming rationale in back of all her self-aggrandizing chutzpah. Ayn Rand believed that the only genuine productive members of society were the creative entrepreneurs who brought product to market and were responsible for the great capitalist cornucopia that we see around us. She may at least have a very little bit of something there, certainly not everything — maybe only a bit, as no man or woman ever does it alone. In other words, she is not right. However, Steve Jobs and iPads may be a fine example of the better side of her argument. Yet, I am not as sure that the CEOs of Enron or GM or Goldman-Sachs or BP should deserve her $ Broach Award.

By the way and not coincidentally, the high rate of suicide among exploited workers at Apple factories in China is more than a bit of a black mark on the deceased Mr. Jobs, telling us much about The Dark Side of Rand and her predecessors, the Social Darwinists, William Spencer and William Graham Sumner. They make a good afternoon's revelatory read, by the way, when you realize how very 21st Century Republican they truly are.

Following her leadership, the neo-Social Darwinist leaders, Reagan, Thatcher, Greenspan, Gingrich — and now the youngster Ryan and Mitt himself — and most present day Republicans are all for: freedom for business, free and unfettered and unregulated and unencumbered business out and over-producing more than enough and then some. Oh yes! And then they would also like to build up the military so the military-industrial complex businesses can make money, lots and lots of money. For everyone else, however, there is at best a modest trickle down effect to placate all of us — the unproductive, uncreative and undeserving poor and middling types — even as we do all the work. "Let their children eat ketchup!"

Credit card consumerism satisfies and mollifies the masses when the trickle is not really quite sufficient. You can always borrow your way to the resemblance of upper class life and read about and voyeuristically participate in the shameful excesses of the rich in supermarket tabloids. Right after the Evening News, there is the Entertainment News.

Personal restrictions like those on abortion or gay rights or marijuana smoking and so forth, consistent with supposed traditional religions and sensibilities are reintroduced as well to swell the Republican voting ranks with reactionaries, but even more importantly, as a means of keeping the lower orders — especially women — in their traditional place with more dos and don'ts circumscribing all behavior that is not involved in buying the products manufactured by large manufacturing and retail corporations. There are things they simply do not want you to freely do in your freedom, like take drugs that are not sold by pharmaceutical companies or make your own moral choice whether or not to get an abortion or take birth control pills or join a labor union or protest the next war or get off the grid and so on. "And do not occupy Wall St. or Main St. or any other place you unwashed huddled together unhappy jobless."

There are limits to freedom after all for the undeserving masses, as there are less and less restrictions on companies and corporations to damage the environment and trash the banking system in their very, very own personal folly-get-rich-quick way. While business is taken care of, nobody else is. Everyone else is on their own in the free market society even as nothing but nothing is actually free; it costs, one way or another.

Republicans, at times, if only sometimes, sound a bit like good old boy libertarians with their persuasive talk of less government, more freedom. George Bush II sprayed out of his inarticulate mouth the word "freedom" more times than any previous government official in history, especially as his U.S. military freed the poor put upon Iraqis, bestowing on them "freedom" not only from Sadaam but in the hundreds of thousands, "freedom," too, from earthly existence.

Yet, when it comes right down to your personal freedom they are well known to coddle up to preposterously prosperous mega-Church maniacs who plunder their male secretaries and want you to live by the Golden Rule, that is: the golden green bucks rule. The Evangelical Right is not infrequently an impious version of Christianity that allows the rich to squeak through the needle's eye and promises everyone else a GM Camel put together by cheap Chinese labor, on GM credit, of course.

In the final analysis, it is really all business freedom. Forget about mine safety and human growth hormones in the beef, and give more power to mine operators and Monsanto and BP. Let the good times roll right over you. They, of course, hide it a bit, paper it over, keep it quiet and secreted away, depend on Limbaugh and Beck and their well paid front men and women to blame the Liberals and liberal media for all the ills such policies create. Yet, underneath the surface and not too far underneath at that it is simply a rationale for unfettered, unabashed, unethical Big Corporate Entrepreneurial Capitalism. Government is the problem, not free enterprise.

Yet, still, again, as much as I hate to admit it, there is something at its core that is good and worth keeping. Although I do think it needs a little more work to get to its better nature since at its core is also simply: greed! All in all, Free Market Capitalism does have a nasty habit of out producing and out creating any other economic system so far, especially its leftist defunct nemesis, Communism. The Chinese Communists seeing the writing on the economic wall, finally — after Mao's death — adopted, Free Market Capitalism. Telling.

Freedom for entrepreneurs may not be a bad thing at all. Yet, here in America freedom to the max has turned into unbridled license and harm. That is another question and one I shall deal with shortly. And where unrestricted corporate Republicanism leads to mass repression, especially repression of women, that is something else I shall need to deal with, too. Change they believe in looks more like a Roman orgy for the 1% and industrial serfdom for the rest of us.

Dems Again

Democrats have their own solutions for all this problematic excess and socially intolerant free market bonanza. Democrats, at core, want everyone taken care of. Whereas in Republicanism, winner takes all and the losers — just about everyone except CEOs being losers in this philosophy — are just such losers and that's just too bad. Dems and European Democratic Socialists, bless their patronizing compassionate hearts, do not think that there should be losers or, at the very least, if you are a loser you should not be stepped on too briskly. "Help is on the way, loser, you need help." And you should have some opportunity, if you are skilled and aggressive and lucky enough to be able to join the ranks of the very super wealthy. "Facebook's founder did it and so can you." Barack appears to believe with a little more and better education, we all can get ahead.

Dems and European Socialists try to ameliorate the inevitable downside of a social Adam-Smithian-Social-Darwinism-Ayn-Randish run away Capitalism. As they are ever so wonk to say, Democrats "solve problems with common sense solutions" — or they use some such equivalent phrase. At least they acknowledge problems. For Democrats and Socialists, the Capitalist system creates problems that they are more than willing to correct with government programs that they, the politicians, create and then oversee.

Of course, you must love and appreciate them for that and elect them again and again and pay their progressive taxes, lots and lots of taxes. You may not have made the problems in the first place, but you are sure to be the ones to pay for their solution. The corporations, after all, have their loopholes big and small and while they may have created these problems to begin with, do not want to pay in just proportion for what they have wrought. "We want to be free!"

they inveigle. And dem Dems "want to take away our freedom by taxing us all."

Dems are also, and to their credit, reformers of a system that has a speculating tendency to step on its own feet and go Depression or Deep Recession suddenly bust in the night. Not only do they want everyone taken care of, but they also know that the Capitalist system itself needs regulating so that greedy bankers and/or greedy entrepreneurs and/or greedy corporations do not get so god awful greedy that the whole shebang goes boom and then bust and things are even worse than the usual bad.

At core, I find it easy to like Democrats, even though they come off as not a little bit snobbish, dour, and ultimately, self-serving as well, Big Brother-ish or Bureaucratic Earth Mother-ish. Even Barack seems a tad overly serious to me, even as I like his caring and clear intelligence against the non-caring and power mongering of Republicans. Still and all, Democrats are far more interested in personal freedom and democracy than the corporations-first freedom Republicans.

Republicans, at the positive side of their core, like freedom and economic expansion. If they could give up their desire to control the masses with a retro-repressive religiosity, I would like them, too. Which is why Ron Paul gets more liberal votes than one would think possible for such an extreme Free Market kind of guy. If they would make freedom available across the board, more like their Libertarian cousins, they might even rule for a generation or more. Still, I think Ron misses an essential political point and gets so few votes because of it. Republicans are not libertarians for everyone, only for business and they are certainly not going to dismantle the military-industrial complex to suit some marginal Congressman peacenik from Texas.

There is a positive and optimistic bent about Republicans at times too, a Ronald Reagan glint in the eye that says that everything will be alright if we would not be so gosh almighty politically and progressively correct. This is the endearing thing about Republicans even if, underlying the wry smile is a sinister smirk that says, "who cares about anyone else but rich me."

Of course, the only problem with letting every business-man to run wild and free is that there is a tendency, more than a tendency, in fact it is a definite trend, a veritable certainty, for things to run amok in any number of ways. Even maximum freedom needs limits. Let oil companies and mining companies dig anywhere and everywhere and, yes, there will be lots of energy to burn and jobs and money to be made, but downstream, or on the Louisiana-Alabama-Georgia-Florida coast, rich and middle class and poor alike may pass their days swimming and fishing in an oil slickened and sickened watery oily dump.

To my mind, maximum freedom has its necessary limits. This is where, Democrats come in, of course, usually after the proverbial turds, oily globs washing up on pristine Gulf Coast beaches and all the way to the southern coast of England, have hit the proverbial fan. The Great Depression. The Great Recession. The Great Climate Change. (Not that Democrats, except Mr. Gore, have said or done much about global warming.) The Great Oil Spill.

Not that we should not maximize freedom, creativity, new products, new ways of producing products and every other good deed of unbridled entrepreneurship, but maybe, just maybe, we might want to add a touch, even perhaps more than a light fingering, maybe a whole hand of responsibility to this potential and actualized messy mess.

Democrats like to regulate a bit more than Republicans. Still as the corporate donations come in to assure their next election, they are often with the Republicans in watering down the rules governing the cleaning of the water supply. It is, as Jeffrey Sachs has pointed out, a virtual "corporatocracy."

Summary

Yes, it is time for a evolutionary-revolutionary change, but we could do worse than save the baby with the bathwater and take the best that the progressive left liberal Democrats have to offer and the very best that the conservative right Republicans have to offer. The trick is knowing which is baby and which bathwater and how to fuse Right and Left in such a way that baby gets a new pair of shoes to boot! Which freedom and which responsibility and what is the limit to both? What is the correct balance? Where is the best Middle, the reasonable and sensible Middle, a Middle we can believe in? We need a Middle that changes the political-economic-social equation by solving it.

If we just let Dems and Repubs go about their business as usual ad infinitum-nauseum, then we shall all go down the proverbial drain with them, baby, bathwater and all of us. I think this is not the proper or efficacious way, the way of the current political, social, economic ongoing chronic debacle. As bright as Barack is, as professorial as Newt is, as Witless as Mitt is, as out to lunch as Michele Bachman seems to be, still we require an entirely new Middle to head us away from one Armageddon or another and toward, if not The Great Society or The Shining City on a Hill, at least a reasonable world where we can all pursue some degree of happiness.

In sum, at their core, I think we can give the Republicans a good deal of their business freedom; yet, we should not allow them to give all businesses complete license to do exactly what they please. Certainly, we will not give them laws to repress anyone or everyone else but the 1% either.

I think we can give Democrats their core values of having everyone taken care of adequately on the one hand and on the other regulating business. Yet we do not want to stymie business unnecessarily in such a manner that more social problems are created.

On the one hand, freedom. On the other hand, responsibility and caring. Might just work out. The question is, of course: how? Rationality is knowing ratios, that is, the just correct proportion. Freedom and responsibility and caring in just and rational ratio. Saying it is so simple; it is the planning it that is so tricky. Keep tuning in; do not drop out.

Chapter 2
Premises On The Premises

Having archeologically summarily unearthed the half
buried foundations of Right and Left, I guess I should try
to dig out of my back mind my very own better nature and
philosophy as well. Time to pull out my premised beliefs
from deep down in my brain hippocampus to shower on my
pre-frontal lobe and out to you. It is only fair.

Philosophical underpinnings, to my mind, are a combination of personal preference and preferential reason, seeming
all the more reasonable if we present a good argument with
certain kinds of evidence. We require the required statistics,
of course, and impeccable logic — complete with the forms
of syllogisms from Aristotle or a course in Symbolic Logic,
perhaps — and then the argument.

Yet, there is nothing inherently cosmic or necessarily
true about any of them. They are approximations, attempts
to order a world that is ultimately unfathomable if oddly
regular, it being difficult if not impossible to understand
all the world's regularities, even as we realize that maybe it
is not so regular after all. Quarks and leptons, quasars and
spinning galaxies, dark matter and super strings — all these
might be mysterious but they do seem to do the same things
in motion over and over again, more or less. And, of course,
when one tries to deal with values, let alone politics, things
get stickier still.

It may all be clear to God or whatever gods may be,
but you can tell that someone is trying to pull a fast one on
you when they preach down in hysterical rhetoric that last
Thursday they spoke with God's son or holy ghost, or Allah
or his messenger on Earth, or Yahweh on the highway or
whatever Spirit of the times knows all and only reveals The
Truth to the one and only representative of their particular
Almighty in question, the preacher up there at the rostrum
generally either a sneering murderous and nasty Ayatollah
demanding blood revenge on his citizens protesting a rigged
election, a belligerent Baptist inciting — oh yes, again —
blood revenge on abortion doctors or any other very sure of
themselves nut cases, be they religious cashew, psychiatrist

peanut or run of the mill mixed up nut firing on an unarmed congresswoman and her friends. They are confident of their own point of view, absolutely, to a fault. The delusory omniscient truest of true believer knows how it all hangs and what we should do about it, even if it means sacrificing your life and roasting all dissenters forthwith tied to the nearest burning bush. Maybe they ever so sincerely think they can place the whole wide worldly one and only Universe in a sea captain's bottle, but they are giving God or whoever or whatever a bad name — all things considered. As it is in religion; it is so in politics. And politics has a worse name.

As much as I am in love with my own solutions to modern problems, as much I cuddle up to my philosophical premises, or blabber on about the faults of politicians, no celestial Bodhisattva, nor, for that matter, devilish bona fide creepy crawly demonic monster out of Dante's Inferno, nor anyone else but my adored wife whispers in my ear late into the evening. As wise — or wiseacre — as I think I am, my philosophical underpinnings, my solutions to all our economic, social and political dilemmas, my ranting and ravings, nostrums and nonsense, have much more to do with simple personal preference, a simple personal sense of what is fair, right and rational. Simple, not cosmic.

I neither prayerfully beseech God, nor does God write on a tablet — now a computer tablet — to me, laying down The Ten Things I Want You To Tell Everyone To Do or Else. Not that secularists, by the way, are any less prone to absolutist murderous nonsense. You do not need belief in God to be an absolutist. You can be a born again Skeptic, too.

It might behoove those who are now in power and control in many parts of the world and in our own polity to get off their colossal cosmic high horses — yes, you, Mr. Sanctimonious Santorum — and get down here with the rest of us unsure stumbling bumbling human beings and try to fashion a social world that works without the hyperbole of "we are the real Americans" or "we are the backbone of Syria" or "après moi le deluge." It would not have been such a head rolling flood if Louis XVI's grandfather had not asserted the divine right of kings and "l'etat c'est moi" a couple of generations earlier. There are not a few tyrants around who might want to meditate on the shadow of ye olden Parisian guillotine before they order up another round of troops, bullets and missiles on peaceful demonstrators who are compatriot citizens, their own women, children and fellow countrymen who disagree with them.

My philosophical underpinnings, first and foremost, require creative synthesis — as I have suggested already. That is, taking the best from what is there already, even when what is being put together comes from what might seem like irreconcilable points of view. Whether it is Newt the Grinchy Gingrich or Eliot the Spritzing Spitzer, Mighty Mitt-wit, Rick Sanitarium, whether The Tea Party or Acorn disorganizers, Pelosi or Boehner, Barack or Hillary or Sarah The Growly Bear Paleolithic, as much as I might disagree with how their arguments are framed or what the implications of their policies would be if they were to take effect in governmental law and budget, they have made sincere if sometimes misguided efforts to use their intelligence to solve social problems. As critical as we all should be of what is said and proposed, I believe that using the best of what they have to say and propose will work well instead of starting from the proverbial square one and reinventing the wheel.

Political office holders even have wholly good ideas sometimes. Although, from CBS, NBC, CNN, New York Times and everyone's polls, you would think that hardly any percentage of the population accepts that as so. And you might even very well think that I think they propose very little. Well, actually that is so, but it is only partly thus. I believe that underneath all the woeful rhetoric, there is something genuine that we can use. This may be a case not so much that I tweak their point of view, as much as that I stretch the truth. Forgive me my accommodations.

The history of the 20th century is bloodily strewn with total solutions that mightily waged total war to reset history.

Hitler tried to sweep aside in genocide The Communist Left, all Jews the Nazis could get their hands on, any one deemed weak and non-German or anyone in dissent in any way from the regime. In Stalin and Mao's egalitarian genocides, the self-righteous Commies looked to annihilate The Fascist Right, many of their own Leftist friends and anyone that had a little more of anything, whether expertise or a mule or in any way dissented from their regime. Neither side of these Right-Left arguments should win. Both sides have something to contribute to a non-lethal debate. Winner take all means that there a whole bunch of us who are left empty handed or without Right or Left hands or heads.

I believe then wholeheartedly in creative synthesis: the best from each for the good of us all. Ignoring or trying to do away with the other side, wanting some ultimate political-social victory will not do and is ultimately and tragically destructive. Nor really, for that matter, will injudicious compromise do either. Although compromise is certainly better than nothing, being a kind of synthesis.

A creative synthesis is more than compromise, not a meeting half way but skipping joyfully arm in arm together, laughing and howling in glee, our differences worked out, a new world of a new reconciled synthesized order created out of the partial good judgments and proposals of all former seemingly incompatible points of view. I will try to demonstrate what I mean by it in most of what follows.

My other prejudices are: democracy, the more participatory the better, human rights, non-violence and freedom (libertarianism, if you will). I think not really that bad for prejudices. Then, add an effective medicinal dose of responsibility to freedom and we might all be better off. Even Cicero, the quintessential Roman Republican Senator, himself, would have approved the idea of responsibility and duty within a democratic republican framework.

Democracy

I am an admirer of Thomas Jefferson and the ancient Athenian Greeks, among many others — Tom Paine, Frederick Douglas, Elizabeth Stanton, Emma Goldman and on and on. Neither the slave holding Jefferson nor the slave holding misogynistic Athenians who ordered up a hemlock cocktail for Socrates — and offered another to Aristotle — are without hypocrisy and come up hopelessly short when it comes to human rights for anyone not of their social class or gender. Some of the original intent of the U.S. Constitution writers, by the way, was to preserve slavery and preserve privilege, both political and economic. I blanche political pale when I hear contemporary Supreme Court justices, but especially Clarence Thomas, an American African-American, declare that they want to preserve "original intent." Did Clarence think about what The Founding southern Fathers intended that he should be doing?

All that said, in contrast to the authoritarian regimes of their times, and even in contrast to the nightmarish authoritarian authoritarians of our times, the ancient Athenians and the revolutionary era American Founding Fathers have much to recommend them, even if we need to take their inspirational hints and go far beyond their initial lead.

I believe, if we took a look at contemporary societies from the perspective of a far more democratically and freer structured future, we — even in the more enlightened and politically democratic parts of the present Western world — do not yet demonstrate a society that is democratic enough. Across many other sectors of power in the society that are not government it is demonstrably not so. Very few are the corporations where workers vote for their CEOs and Board of Directors. Very few are the banks where depositors vote for their bank managers. Very few are the public utilities like electric companies, oil companies, telephone or cable TV companies under the control of the public. Very few are those in most kinds of positions of public power that get voted in.

Democracy. I will be suggesting ways to extend democracy to social enterprises of all kinds that we could and should make more democratic. If you do not believe that people have a right — and a duty — to control the very institutions within which they live, then you might consider reading no further — although you might want to read further if for no better reason than to know how to squash my arguments in some future debate, if, by wild chance, we ever have one.

Participatory Democracy Week At N.Y.U.

I was a freshman at New York University, Washington Square College of Arts and Sciences in 1966. As a naïve eighteen year old from the outer reaches of culturally and linguistically deprived far southeast Brooklyn, land of Jamaica Bay and the gigantic caldera shaped mound of waste disposal, the City Dump, on its shore, I was just learning the meaning of such phrases on posters taped on the glass doors of campus buildings as "Uptight with the Draft? Contact … " Honestly, I did not know what "uptight" meant. I was not yet in synch with 60's rebellious lingo. N.Y.U. was situated around Washington Square Park in Greenwich Village and the center ground of latter day beatniks and early hippies (two years before 1968 and The Summer of Love) and, to its west, in the West Village, one of the quintessential meeting places of gay America. I could not converse in the appropriate hip tongue yet.

I went to and then participated in my first demonstration, first year. It was a tuition strike supposedly. The strikers were by far in the vast minority and any resemblance to a real all-students-out strike was far fetched at best. The administration was going to raise our tuition for the next year maybe $100 or $200. Being on full scholarship from a variety of sources, state, federal and the college itself, this would mean that I would be actually forced to pay upfront money for my college education, $100 or $200. Since I had worked summers and I commuted to school from way out in Brooklyn and my parents' apartment at a city housing project where I was housed for free and my mom fed me meal after meal, the money was not a big deal.

Yet, here I was sitting in the main lobby of the college of Washington Square listening to speech after speech of the demonstration's organizers on into the night, and overnight and then into the next day. It was a completely new experience for a new freshman, a new world, a new exhilarating sleepless world. Not sleeping all night was a new experience too; and, I felt rather dizzy and tired in a funny way — I thought at the time.

The organizers said it was serious and there was a melodramatic tone to the speeches and there was talk about the administration calling in the police to bust up our squatting in the lobby of the college overnight and bash in our young and innocent intellectual skulls. Still, it did not seem all that serious to me. It felt more like play than anything of real consequence and violent moment. I thought it odd that one of the speakers wore a sport coat and tie and blue jeans. The brother of a friend from high school sported a long beard and he was one of the main instigators. Wow, was this cool or what?! I was just learning to use the word "cool" and realized you could grow a beard and wear blue jeans with a sport coat at the same time. I mean, naïve!

Yet, there was a lesson from this my first demonstration — even if the events of those early days were a pseudo-quasi rebellion — that sticks with me to this day. This lesson colored my next few years at a college that saw demonstration after demonstration, each becoming larger and larger and more hysterical and historical by the year, ending with the shootings at Kent State when every student, professor and administrator not only at N.Y.U., but in the whole country, was out of the classroom and demonstrating.

This first demonstration was different. Not only was it open mike and any of the relatively small number of us could and did speak in turn until a good portion of the 50-100 tuition rebels actually said something. Moreover, and most dramatically for me, all resolutions about issues and decisions about tactics were made democratically. It was participatory democracy during a fine, if inconsequential hour, even at times late into the evening and the next woozy morning and a long commute on a New York City subway back to the far reaches of Outer Brooklyn and the last stop of the number 7 train, New Lots Avenue.

Later, reading the Port Huron Statement and other literature of the fledgling Students for a Democratic Society, I was impressed with the overarching commitment — not to Left Socialist ideas, rejected consciously and deliberately — but to democracy. But not the limited democracy of pulling a lever every two and four years, but to what they called "participatory democracy," desiring consciously and deliberately something like the participatory democracy of the ancient Athenian Greeks at their height of their relatively inclusive system, with the caveat that the S.D.S. brand of participatory democracy for America would not be at all limited to all well propertied males who had the time to participate. I instinctively loved the idea and my first demonstration was a good introduction to how that might work.

Demonstrations and protests after that moved into more the serious territory of the Vietnam War, the continuous struggle for racial equality and civil rights and then women's rights, and gay rights and abortion rights and environmental issues of all kinds, all the needed and necessary rebellions against oppressive restrictions and problematic degradations of a civilization in distress. Yet, in the process of all the justly self righteous shouting and anger, the idealism and the angst, the changes of life and consciousness of so many citizens young and some older, what seemed to get lost was that wonderful participatory democracy, that camaraderie and respect that still to this day is, for me, a prime motive force.

Participatory democracy and S.D.S. were not at that intense historical moment of the 60's and 70's allowed to develop and grow at a slower and more deliberate pace. I think that this was unfortunate, if inevitable, given the times and all its shortcomings and the Vietnam war.

You shall see that many of the proposals contained in these essays have much to do not only with democratizing vast stretches of our society and culture, but really, capturing the spirit of participation, of excitement and involvement that only democracy, participatory democracy brings — not to belittle at all once every so often pulling a lever or making an ink mark or punching a cad.

That old cry of the ever so repressed Black Panthers "power to the people, right on," still begs for expression and implementation. What does that "power to the people" mean to me? It means, as I will show, democracy and participatory democracy far across the spectrum of the institutions of society. Power to the people really is POWER TO THE PEOPLE, and then not only politically, but economically as well.

It is my prejudice and I am rather fond of it. I think it is an American prejudice as well. It is more traditionally American than even the proverbial apple pie we think so quintessentially gastronomically historically American.

FREEDOM. DEMOCRACY. FULL CITIZENSHIP. Writ large on the souls of Americans! Written, of course, into the texts of history we read as children and young adults. I read. I listened. I liked very much what I heard.

And yes, democracy is hardly perfect. The Athenians, during the time of Pericles, in the participatory democratic era of the great cultural achievements of those times, yes, they too screwed up, tried to maintain a small empire and then fell to Sparta. Yes, Plato, if you check out modern day America, screwing up the environment, trying to maintain an informal empire — keeping the world safe for Capitalism and oil imports — and falling and failing under its own weight, democracy can lead to tyranny and climate change.

Still, where are the pluperfect philosophers who would rule us, where is the modern ideal of an Aristotle or Confucius? Well, nowhere to be found. Therefore, I will go with the next best thing: democracy.

Human Rights

Thomas Jefferson and John Madison and Ben Franklin and George Washington, et al, did us enormous favor by creating a human rights space in government. Within our American Constitution is that section called "The Bill of Rights." Except for the part about guns, I am an unabashed lover of these particular statements of law. Even the part about guns and the right of self protection makes sense to me until all violence across the board and across the world is done away with. Self defense, including armed protection from the encroachments of a fully armed and ready government, is not to be sneered at. Of course, AK machine guns in the hands of mass murdering nut cases is not a very good idea either.

The right of everyone to free speech and free press. The right of everyone to assemble and demonstrate. The right of everyone to their beliefs and religion. If any beliefs come close to an absolute good for me, it begins, even if it does not end, with these. The Fourteenth Amendment after the Civil War, even if it has taken more than 100 years to implement and is still in process: equal protection of the law. Oh my! How very beautiful and essential!

Yet, again, even within liberal democratic societies, while these freedoms extend to a not insubstantial public area, supposed liberal democratic government have sometimes tried to curtail these rights, even within our lifetimes: Nixon condoning the killing of unarmed student civilians by the National Guard at Kent State, J. Edgar Hoover and his G-men FBI guys spying to get the private dirt on Martin Luther King, the Chicago police assassinating Black Panthers asleep in their beds and night clothes. In a previous generation, there is Woodrow Wilson incarcerating Americans and the American socialist Eugene Debs for opposing Wilson's World War I. Further back, President Andrew Jackson ordering even against the wishes and votes of Congress the ethnic cleansing of the Cherokee from Georgia and North Carolina (among the most ignominious genocidal acts of American history, although certainly not unique in our history either). There was John Adams, in The Alien and Sedition Acts, attempting to squelch the speech of those, including Jefferson himself, who opposed President Adam's foreign policies favoring the English over the French. It took more than 100 years for white women to get the vote and several hundreds of years for black Americans to be treated as equal citizens. Our American authorities threw Emma Goldman in jail for speaking, yes, just speaking out in favor of contraception in the early 20th Century. The list is long, all too very long.

So, as a nation, we have not been perfect or even very close to perfect in the human rights regard. Yet, as with Jefferson and the Athenian Greeks, we have done better than the former apartheid regime of South Africa or Mugabe in present day Zimbabwe or Ahmajinejad in Iran or the Assads of Syria or Mao's Cultural Revolution or Stalin's purges or Hitler's genocide or Turkey's slaughter of Armenians or the British as the greatest drug dealers in history before and after the Opium War, or the genocide of older women, too easily designated as witches, in late medieval Europe, all too many more examples of the terrors of histories, human rights abuses galore.

HUMAN RIGHTS. I will be suggesting ways to extend the reach of human rights as well. On our planet in our supposedly enlightened times men, women and children can be shot to death for peacefully protesting an insensitive government or a rigged election. On our planet in our times fundamental and essential human rights are not accepted as fundamental and essential and are routinely and outrageously violated. This should be, to my mind, a source of world wide human shame. I feel personally a great gaping emotional bleeding wound every time I hear of what is going on in Syria in the present moment: abuse of rights, murderous bloody abuse of fundamental rights. North Korea, stories told and untold. Chinese factories. A young woman is shot in the head by the Taliban for advocating for education for girls. We should all be horribly ashamed and horrified that this should take place on our watch, in our times. I think we are. I think it long past time to stop these abuses across the world and around the planet. There is no excuse that this continues.

All Together Now

The side of me that identifies with everyone and believes that everyone should have a fair shake and that we should make sure, as much as we can, that everyone is cared for and that everyone is deserving of equal rights and an equal chance in life, that side of me, besides being instinctive, was nurtured by my parents and especially my mother, by example and explicit philosophy.

I lived as a teenager in a New York City public housing project in the far reaches of Brooklyn in a six story apartment house. We were, to classify us, working class or lower middle class. Today, we might say we were working poor. I was impressed that my mother was consistent in believing that everyone was deserving of respect, all our neighbors — and there were quite a few around.   My mom would sit outside our apartment house on the green painted park bench in front of the house and talk to, with equal respect, any neighbor who would sit and talk to her. There was no snobbery about my mom whatsoever. In conversation it was clear, I believe, to each person she talked to that she cared about them. She paid strict attention to what each person had to say and she showed appropriate sympathy or, for that matter, humor when called for.

She believed it, too. She believed that all people, rich, poor, black, white, women, men, all were equal and deserving of respect and kindness. She would say so if you asked. She would adamantly tell you so. And when she heard of abuses of persons and rights, she was appalled. Appalled. She cried watching the televised news, too.

I was impressed. I have tried to keep my mother's attitude — and my mother's memory — in my heart. It was a great lesson to be taught that and to be taught it consistently. She really cared and she cared worldwide; she truly did.

Another set of experiences taught me a similar lesson. As a young man, in my twenties, not like other young men in that age group, I felt socially awkward. I would not say I was shy, just awkward. I certainly, like everyone else I suppose, had my likes and dislikes of people. If there were a crowd of people walking by, just by looking at their faces I could probably, at the time, tell you whom I would like and whom I would most likely have disliked. Some people just looked mean spirited to me, the look on their face sending me the message that I probably would not want to have any dealings with them because the encounter would be difficult. And, as I already felt socially awkward, an awkward interchange was not what I wanted at all.

Years later, out of New York City and now a medical practitioner in the granite mining town of Barre, Vermont, an acupuncturist when acupuncture was a beginning novelty, I treated one person at a time, face to face. I literally placed thin needles judiciously in the richest person in town, the poorest, the very elderly, the young infant, the woman who ran the dry cleaners and the founder of one of the granite mine companies, the miner, the sculptor of granite, the jewelry store owner. Now, I was not thinking about it when I began, but frankly, if I had seen some of my clients on the streets walking around before I met them in my office, I might have looked at them and thought I would not like them. Possible.

Yet, to my surprise, one at a personal time, in talking and needling and talking and needling some more, I found, one by one, that I really and truly liked everyone without exception. And, to be honest I came to have a new respect and liking, by extrapolation, for everyone, everyone in the world. And to boot, I lost any social awkwardness I had ever felt.

Feeling this way is not a superficial feeling. I feel an

empathy for everyone now and an ability to relate one way or another to everyone, something that I did not feel before I started my practice. I had previously held an intellectual feel for equality and respect and empathy, but just sitting with patients, now for 30 years, I feel in my heart, in my bones, at my core, that I can like everyone, that I can love everyone, that I respect everyone, that I believe everyone has a right to life, liberty and happiness. I may not agree with anything anyone says, still, I feel at one with everyone, instinctively, culturally, whichever way you want to see and say it. Deep in my marrow, in my consciousness.

Human rights for all; fairness for all. It is a prejudice of which I am rather fond, too.

Non-Violence

I am also an unequivocal admirer of Jesus, Mohandas Gandhi and Martin Luther King, among others.

It seemed to me that just after 9/11 George Bush, who made not a few claims to being an evangelical Christian and a regular reader of the good and Holy Bible, did not take a Christian view of the scurrilous and murderous dastardly surprise attacks. I am not at all unsympathetic to self-protection or going after the criminal scoundrels who sneakily executed the execution of ordinary citizens and our skyscrapers. Yet, it seemed inconsistent to me to no small extent that Mr. Bush, having heard the words of Jesus to "turn the other cheek" and "resist ye not evil," did neither. Instead, in his best John Wayne Hollywood cowboy pose, he nailed "Wanted Dead or Alive, Osama bin Laden" to the White House pillars and shipped the Air Force and Navy posse across the seas to hunt down and shoot on sight the bad guys, Osama and company.

I understand. I understand that al Qaeda's kinds of acts cannot be allowed to just happen and no response. Criminal acts of murder, especially on that scale, should be punished. I may be an admirer of Jesus' pacifism, but I am just not there yet. Justice should be served to those who disregard the sanctity of life, al Qaeda, the Assads, Mugabe, et al.

Still and all, Bush's response was not Christian. When the Roman soldiers came to pick up Jesus at prayer for sedition and being a general nuisance to their occupation of Jerusalem, when his followers resisted and one of them even cut off the poor ear of a Roman soldier, Jesus scolded the follower, not the Roman soldier. Jesus did not fight back, he did not act in self-defense, he wanted to be led away to avoid more violence. I am even quite positive that he knew what was in store for him in Roman custody, it being no secret what Romans did to loving and kind rebels predicting the end of Roman rule and the beginning of God's Heavenly Kingdom on Earth.

Jesus was non-violent, period. I am an admirer. I am an admirer of M. Gandhi, who in the most genocidal murderous awful century in history, the 20th, tried to show, he said, "the world a way out of the madness." He was, to my mind, the greatest political thinker of the 20th century and will not be forgotten for many more centuries, as Jesus has not been forgotten now for two millennia. Martin Luther King, too, used the same strategies of non-violence as Gandhi, as Jesus, appealing to reason and right, to love and humanity, speaking up about injustice loudly and forcibly.

I believe that violence between human beings must end, completely, absolutely, forever. It is no longer tenable; it never was. It is my prejudice, a preference I admire. That does not mean that I think personally that I could do what Jesus, Gandhi or King did in the face of violence. I simply believe it would be a good idea if we took very seriously Moses' rendering of God's commandment that: "Thou shalt not kill." You do not have a right to violence. You have a right not to be violated.

God has that right, in the end, killing us all. We all die. Yet, we do not have that right, to kill or violate another human being. It is a usurpation to do so, whether the usurper is bin Laden, George Bush or, for that matter, Barack Obama and drones. It is not that I do not understand or sympathize with the Presidents. I do not, however, admire their actions like I do Jesus, Gandhi and Martin Luther King.

Still, a system needs to be in place to stop all this for good and all time. I will be proposing how we go about really getting "peace in our time," and for all time. Certainly there are too few in positions of influence and power who argue for the total cessation of violence, as much as I believe it is the fond wish of everyone. "Peace on Earth, goodwill towards men," and women and children and everyone, I would add — and, not just at Christmas.

Freedom

I do have a prejudice in common with Ayn Rand, Ron and Rand Paul, even — heaven forgive me — the loopy Michele Bachmann, Noam Chomsky, the Libertarian Party, 50's Beats, Jack Kerouac and Allen Ginsburg, 60's hippies, Abbie Hoffman, and Tim Leary and, poet singers of all stripes, Bob Dylan and The Jefferson Airplane, and even the most mediocre president in US history, Mr. Bush. And of course, John Locke and Adam Smith. Again, it is: FREEDOM, individual freedom.

Yet, whereas the freedom that Ms. Rand and Messrs. Paul, Bush, Reagan, and many others in the Libertarian Party would reserve as liberty for business and upper class rich individuals, I have a much broader prejudice in favor of individual freedom. That is: for everyone. Freedom is not just for rich Rupert Murdoch, rich Rush Windbag Limbaugh or rich BP executives on yacht racing sail boats.

I also believe in freedom for Chinese factory workers to unionize, freedom for Russian journalists to write about the connection between the Russian mafia and the Russian government, freedom for a Nebraskan teenage pregnant girl to make her own moral choices, freedom to their lands for the Lakota Sioux, freedom for Detroit auto workers whether to make the decision to move their factory they are working in and making a living working in to move to Mexico or China or where ever else there is cheapest labor, their freedom to make the decision to keep their factory right where it is, those are freedoms, too. There are so many others: the freedom to marry whomever of whatever sex the freedom to smoke whatever kind of cigarette, be it cancerous tobacco or mind altering marijuana, and so on and so on and on and on …

Here is my prejudicial rule for freedom, where it starts, where it stops. It is the Doctrine of No Harm, a doctrine that starts with The French Revolution's Declaration of the Rights of Man that we would do well to adopt, in principle. John Stuart Mill, English political philosopher, said it well:

> ...the only purpose for which power can be rightfully exercised over any member of a civilized community, against his will, is to prevent harm to other. His own good, either physical or mental, is not sufficient. He cannot rightfully be compelled to do or forbear because it will be better for him to do so, because it will make him happier, because, in the opinion of others, to do so would be wise, or even right. (J.S. Mill, On Liberty)

Many others notable and not have said the same.

As long as you are not hurting anyone else, you can do what you damn well please and more power to you. Freedom ends, is irresponsible, is detrimental, where your freedom of thought, writing, speaking, action, what you say or do, harms another. You are not free to libel; only to tell the truth. You are free to manufacture; you are not free to pollute. You are free to believe what you want, but you are not free to start an unnecessary riot. You are free to commit suicide, not to murder. That is for starters. There are, of course, many more examples.

Much of what will follow in the next chapters are my account of where the line runs separating freedom and irresponsibility. It is a boundary that is very distinct and clear in some cases and ways; and far more problematic in others. Sometimes, I do favor the lines we have drawn in law and practice, many times I do not. When George Bush yelled "freedom," I was ready to head for the exit. When Martin Luther King raised his voice and heart and proclaimed "free at last," I marched with him.

As I have said already, I am in partial agreement with and have some sympathy for the philosophical political posturings of all those dastardly Republican Conservative Tea Partiers and Glenn Beck, Sarah Palin, Michelle Bachman, Rick Santorum, Ron Paul, Grover Norquist, Paul Ryan and not a few other congressional Republicans who are more or less and usually more than less hinting THAT: the government of the U.S.A. should be cut back to very little.

I am, after all, a Baby Boomer child-adult of the 1960's and have not trusted the government since the ridiculous-tragic Vietnam War and the presidencies of that ultimate patronizing Brezhnev clone, Lyndon Baneful Johnson, and the spasmodic bodied and paranoid-minded Richard Nixon. Thus instinctively since early college adulthood, the FBI photographing us as we demonstrated time after time on campus at N.Y.U. for less tuition and then civil rights and then against the Vietnam War, I have a long ago and hard fought wariness of government.

It is more than just a gut feeling, my Boomer generation's early experience with the downside of an out of control government putting many of us in partial sympathy with these latter day Tea Partiers. They have something important to point out to us and before long I will say exactly what and how to accommodate this point of view without doing away with the functions that welfare, "Obamacare," education or the national parks perform.

I believe that media drenched conservatives would on their more honest days when they do not have to hedge their political bets to get elected trash just about everything that our government does. Certainly they would do away with just about each and every government regulation and government oversight of banking, the environment, beef inspection and just about everything else that appears to require peeking in on companies and corporations who, these folks believe, would do much better without the snoopy government mucking up their ever so smooth productive works. I very clearly would not go so far as them on that. Not at all. Not even close.

What would they really do with Social Security and Medicare, too, if they had their druthers? "Entitlement reform," is their mantra; implying that "entitlements" are bad. It is not too difficult to surmise ulterior motive. I think with druthers, they would simply eliminate "entitlements." As we shall see, I would take "entitlements" out of the hands of government. Yet, I would certainly not eliminate them, not at all.

I have sympathies, too, if not much more so, with the Occupy Wall Street group as well. In fact, I believe that Occupy just needs some good ideas and proposals and they should go much further. I think that what follows, the proposals of this book will inspire those from Occupy. Of course, I hope it might inspire The Tea Party too, but I would not hold my breath — so to speak.

Now let us see how to make proposals consistent with what I believe are very nice all-American prejudices: democracy, human rights and non-violence — (although, the last, not very American actually at all, given our history.) On to the actual proposals!

Chapter 3
No Taxes,
Anywhere Anyhow Any Kind At All

So here we are, and the rest of the way is proposals, proposals and more proposals. By the time you wind your way through the thicket of these ideas in the chapters that follow, they all should add up to a thorough democratic and human rights reorientation of society, economics and politics. Still, as I said, we will give Leftists and Rightists, Socialisms and Capitalisms their due and not throw out the best — and their best is considerable — each has to offer. Rather, we will put it all together in such a way that it comes out far better and better balanced. As bonus, there are ideas here that even go further than the policy positions and the current limitations of political and economic philosophies, actual novel ideas, not just the best of the old.

So here we go. I am sure some of you will classify each of these ideas as pleasing to The Right or The Left or The Center or The Independents. I will do some of that with you.

First set of ideas.

Taxes

• None. Not only no income tax, but no sales taxes, no property taxes, no excise taxes, no social security taxes, no this tax or that tax. Gone. All taxes gone forthwith.

You heard it here, folks. Not only senior Bush's "no new taxes," nor junior Bush's "tax cuts," but no taxes whatsoever anywhere, federal, state, local. Can you guess who is going to like this? The Right and anyone in their right mind. Do I have your attention yet? The question then is, as you might question me, how do we pay for government and all that it does whether we like what it does or not?

Coming up.

Federal Government

• Not a social service agency in any way shape or form. One and only one function for the federal government: makes laws and regulations and enforces them.

What? Is this guy nuts or what? But I think those Righties are getting into it. We shall see.

The Price Tag

• All citizens are billed equally for the price of government. This is not a tax, but a fee for services.

Here come the groans: you are just renaming it and it is a flat tax on everyone. No, not really.

And oh yes, this means:
• No government debt ever again. Everyone is billed at the end of the year for what the government spent to be the government with its one function of making laws and enforcing them. That is it. That is that. No debt. Again, I hear seats squirming on The Left and hosannas on The Right. Fret not, I will be sure to alienate everyone before I am done — except, I hope, you, dear reader, a rational citizen human being. Still, everyone needs to hear out the whole shebang to see how this all works out. These proposals are interlocked, one depending on the other. This is holistic and democratic social reorganization, so do not stop now and think that this is it, not at all.

Explanation

To my Occam's Razor political mind, the one and only one function of government and the only necessary and legitimate and essential function of government is: to make laws, rules, regulations. That is that and only that: the government creates the terms by which the society operates. That is: no murder, no theft or fraud; and you can keep your patent secrets for a certain number of years and make a bundle.

Why the government of the United States has become everyone's best friend for all kinds of handouts and good works has much to do with information you can solicit from your history teacher or professor, it being a tall tale complete with historical histrionics and bull moose Teddy Roosevelt. As the Tea Party well knows — with its excitable members referencing The Boston Tea Party and rebel yells of "no taxation without representation" although they are represented all too well in the Congress and not that Tea Party favorites, Bachman and Palin appear to have much of any real idea what is true and what is fiction in American history — it is long past the time to write a different kind of American future history.

For one thing, just eliminating all the other functions that the U.S. government has taken upon itself and limiting it to making law would be a whole heck of a lot cheaper than the trillions and trillions in debt the U.S. government is squirming under, trying to subsidize everyone for everything: citizens who are too poor to feed their children, farm corporations who will or won't plant crops depending on whether the government will pay them for more or less planting, billion dollar profiting oil companies who have enough spare change to bribe Congress to give them all kinds of incentives to make more billions, and so on and on, right up to a government that it is so in debt that it does not know quite what to do — as we all and Barack Obama, Rand Paul and Eric Cantor know all too well.

The poor beg the government for more; the wealthy are privileged and rich enough to "lobby" the government for more. Who do you think gets more of your hard earned tax dollars? Mitt thinks Barack won the last election by offering handouts; while, if you check out Mitt's potential giveaways, he would have handed out even more to his stock bloated buddy billionaires.

Does the government, as wealth distributor-in-chief really have a right to your income? By what divine right, other than the right of saying it is right? It is the right of: I will take away your freedom or your property, if you do not pay up. I think they do not have right on their side, only power. If it is written down, as in The Constitution, is it then any different that just saying it is so and enforcing that?

Then, without the U.S. government's dubious business of being all things financial to all people in need or greed, the only cost of government would be the cost of making the laws and incarcerating the law breakers and running a military to protect the country against criminals from beyond our borders bent on murder and terror. Compared to what we have now, it would be blessedly cheap. Although, given the size and number of our prisons that incarcerate at a rate greater than almost any of the rest of the nations on the planet, plus the boondoggle that is the military-industrial complex in which we spend about as much as all the other nations on the planet combined for fighting wars that we are actually fighting and also fighting wars in our imagination (we are still fighting the old defunct Soviet Union and speculating on going to battle with the Chinese in about 50 years) plus the cost of congressional perks and privileges, maybe not as cheap as it should be.

Yet, reduced to just those functions, maybe, just maybe, I would then go along with those Tea Partiers who want to shrink the government to a fraction of what it is now. I would be very much for shrinking the military precipitously and congressional perks precipitously, although the prison system a bit more slowly — drug users out of jail right away, violent criminals, not at all.

How to pay for this far smaller government bill?

Again, let me repeat, the only function and the only cost of government is now in the making of laws and their enforcement. Nothing else.

Then, with this in mind, bill us. As above: bill us all equally, each and every adult citizen equally.

We are all equal citizens under the law. We should pay equally for the writing and enforcing of the law. Simple. Direct. Everyone and their relatives can understand it and understand why they are doing it. If you want a government, if you want the rule of law, if you want the rule of law in a democratic society, then you pay for it. Equally. You are an equal citizen. You pay equally. Therefore, everyone, in all ways, is equal before the law and should expect no more or no less than everyone else, including and especially financially.

I shall insist on payment equality in funding the government because if some were to pay more, they might assume, as in some sense some of them do already, that they deserve more under the law: more justice, more subsidy, more bailouts. Which, in oh so many ways, they get. The one grand big insurance company called the federal government is all too ready to jump in just in case laissez faire capitalism fails them and, they, the super wealthy, fall into the pit with the rest of us. One day you are fitter than fit in a social economic evolutionary way, the next, you are going the way of the extinct unfit. Think: bank executives. And then they are back up, way up, perks perked back up care of Uncle Sam.

In fact, government has become not only an insurance company when things fall apart and the corporate center cannot hold, but an economic and social preventive mechanism as well. The U.S. government has been stimulating the U.S. economy since F.D.R. If what really took us out of The Great Depression was World War II, not just the W.P.A., Social Security and the rest of the alphabet soup of stimulus package of The New Deal, doesn't it make sense that the government, in its function as preventive medicine economics physician, keep priming and pumping the economy's heart muscle by putting as much money into the military as if we were at war forever and a century? The Cold War.

The War on Terror. How convenient for the economy and Lockheed Martin and all its employees and all those generals who go to work for Lockheed and Grumman after the government retires them from overseeing the requisitioning from Lockheed and Grumman.

The wealthy and corporate America are as dependent on the federal government as any poor welfare single parent mother. We can afford the poor; but can we afford the wealthy and its money made for perpetual war? Does Grover Norquist really want to shrink that part of the government? Romney said he did not; the military is worth a lot of jobs and cutting the military would cut jobs; and then he sobbed "poor, poor weapons manufacturers."

Yet, ultimately in the last 70 years, it has been all far too costly. The payments for this boondoogle are your tax dollars; and the payout is continuous and far above what the government economic insurance company is taking in. Not only are all the chickens coming home to roost, but whole flocks of a variety of species of foul fowl, a huge foul deficit threatening government default and bankruptcy.

Forget the whole blood sucking contentious tax thing — as The Tea Party regulars might describe it — the income tax, the excise taxes, Social Security tax, Medicare-Medicaid tax, this tax, that tax, everywhere a tax, tax. Sarah Palin and The Tea Party are correct. Ron Paul, especially, is correct. Allow the American people and American business to keep their incomes. And, something Sarah is not saying, but Ron is: stop stimulating the economy with the military industrial complex.

On the whole, I must shout to add to their chorus: enough is too much!

The original motivation behind the Income Tax Amendment to the U.S. constitution and its subsequent use by the government was two-fold: first, to in some small measure equalize what had become in The Gilded Age the wide disparity of wealth between the very extremely rich and all too poor everyone else. Secondly, with the money from the income tax from the overly wealthy the government could provide services for the much-less-than-wealthy — everyone else. The idea was that this would equalize not only wealth but equalize to some small extent the opportunities for social advancement for the vast majority of the citizenship who could not afford education and/or health care and/or an inexpensive trip to the wilderness — known after Teddy Roosevelt as "a national park." Listen to those latter day Rooseveltians, Bill Clinton and Barack Obama, who speechify on this all the time: equal opportunity based on government services.

The income tax was a good progressive idea at the time. I am not so sure at all it is a good idea now. Still and all, providing important social services to everyone is important and we should not do away with them. Yet, these services are better paid for without taxes on income, sales, property et al. I shall show you how shortly.

Frankly, Ayn Rand and Social Darwinists and their latter day followers do not care. There are not a few die-hard laissez-faire wealthy and their spokespeople like Newt Gingrich and Ronald Reagan and Glenn Beck and Mighty Mitt who also really could care less about social services or equal opportunity for everyone.

"Let them eat cake and pay for their own schooling and health insurance! Why should I, the very wealthy person, be paying for your education, your health care, your public park, your needs, you, person of less wealth and status? And why should I, the very wealthy person that I am, pay even more in taxes than you who get the services that I separately must pay for because the government services are not good enough for me and my kids?" Rand virtually says it out loud; Beck occasionally says it more or less; and Reagan, I am quite sure, thought it before his thinking turned to addled mush.

Of course, and as a matter of course, Republicans and not a few Democrats have used the revenue from income taxes and other federal taxes to provide not just social services, but regular good old boy boondoggles for the corporate wealthy, make no mistake about that. When was the last time you heard a Tea Partier inveigle against corporate welfare or the military contract that goes out to Halliburton to award government military contracts to their Halliburton subsidies without bid? Who wrote that law and created that boondoggle? Remember this: Dick Cheney was a law-writing congressman from Wyoming before he was head of Halliburton. Hmmm.

So, if taxes are gone, extinct, caput, out of here, otherwise non-existent, how do we fund all those social services we are so accustomed to, those services that Republicans call "entitlements?"

For the most part, no-tax and no-spend obsessed conservatives would privatize everything that previously was the exclusive or partly exclusive domain of the government: Medicare, Medicaid, Social Security, schools, even prisons, certainly the Post Office and so on and "drill baby, privately drill baby, drill, drill here, drill there, on national parks territory and everywhere else, too, offshore and onshore. Oh, heck, maybe we should even sell much of the land the Feds owns and pay off the national debt and drill everywhere until we drill ourselves to energy independence in a country full of drilled holes everywhere and all the way to China and we could sell the Chinese all that energy abundance right through a direct pipeline through the center of the Earth."

In this rush to privatize social service functions and every government public function and every nook and cranny of public land under the sun, I am not with them. I neither believe social services should be in the hands of government officials and their hired hand bureaucrats who know very little about medicine, education and, from our collective experience, even how to respond to Hurricane Katrina. But now the biggest but of all: nor do I favor putting everything and all of us into the hands of big business bureaucrats who are in charge of all the big multi-national corporations that are in charge of much of the economic and social life of everyone here and around the ever globalized globe, whose bottom line is the almighty dollar and every line above that is also the almighty dollar. And all those dollars go to them and theirs alone in no small measure.

Why any Republican believes that a few big private insurance companies are more competent to handle the medical system than one big government insurance company is, simply put, counter-factual. Why buck-hungry entrepreneurs could run the prisons better and why greedy corporate CEOs would voluntarily reverse globalized global warming — the Rockefeller Foundation and the Gates Foundation filling in the gaps everywhere else there is some kind of need — is, well, just as wrong headed as the notion that big and bigger and biggest government could do it. Too-Big-To-Fail corporations are no solution, they being even further removed from any effective public control than a distant government in Washington. Donald Trump building bridges or tunnels in New York? Luxury tunnels, private bridges, eh Donald? He once offered to do it and do it better and cheaper than the government of New York City.

American medicine is the most privatized and expensive medicine in the world and by any measure — except in the hyperbole of those who are profiting ghastly inflated sums from it — not very effective at all. Even poor Cuba and its politically and economically repressive regime has a medical system that in statistical effectiveness, equals our rich country, Cuba being 37th and the U.S.A, 35th in those measures that matter in health care. Mr. Chavez went to Cuba for medical treatment — not to the Mayo Clinic like the Shah of Iran for which compassion the Iranians still hate us, by the way.

Ours is the medical system currently ineffectively and inefficiently run by and paid for by government and private companies. There are arguments that more of one way or the other would be better. The Left Socialists of Kucinich, Sanders and Michael Moore stand up for Single Payer government medicine. The Right Conservatives pontificate that we have the best medical system on the planet under a free market medical system of insurance companies and pharmaceutical companies and hospital conglomerates running that part of the whole show not controlled by the government. Yet both positions are counter-rational, and honestly, just not very accurate. Neither works well and right now.

Do charter schools really do that much better than public schools? Here and there better and there and here not better and in neither case, neither as good as Finland or South Korea. Neither public nor private does very well, educationally speaking, with a few notable exceptions, on each side of the public-private dichotomy.

While I am not for any one, the rich included, paying more for someone else's social services, I am also not for anyone, the rich included, getting out of cooperating and paying. Also, the poor should not get out of paying for social service either. We are all in this together and we should be equals in this together. Maybe "The Poor" should not be so poor in the first place. More on that in a subsequent chapter, too.

There is another way, neither privatized, nor politicized. Here is where I can boast of a NEW IDEA! The functions that Republicans would so cavalierly give away to greedy private enterprise and that Democrats want to keep the government screwing up, these functions, public functions, functions that should be controlled democratically by the public, these functions should not be done away with, they cannot be done away with without mass suffering. We need: education, medicine, garbage collection, postal service, car insurance, the fair use of public lands and resources, good quality of the air, the water and so on.

I am not at all proposing that just because the government or private business is incompetent and inappropriate in conducting these functions that they need not be done. Not at all. Someone has to do the grand societal wide insurance thing complete with grand societal wide preventive medicine, even if it is not Donald Trump or Ken Lay of defunct and dishonest Enron or the oft bailed out Citibank or Barack Obama, the ghost of Ted Kennedy or Nancy Pelosi or the tear filled perpetually tanned Mr. Boehner or the holy ghost of Adam Smith.

Then who? Then how? That is the next chapter, but a quick preview first.

I would like to propose a third way, a real third way, a way you can not only believe in, but vote in: democratic public non-profit monopoly companies. Not government or part of it. Nor private. A public company that the public democratically controls. A company that has the statutory ability to equally bill all members within its geographic realm. Equal citizens pay an equal bill. Equal citizens have democratic control over the societal entity that bills them equally.

We are all in this relationship called society together and while we should not throw out Adam Smith's capitalist style competition when it comes to telephones and 3-D television sets and automobiles and restaurants, yet there are areas of life that are public and handled better by the public, that should not be subject to competition at all, where equality and quality of service should be the rule, not the exception. There should be no relative winners and losers when it comes to health care and education. Social Darwinists, be damned!

Chapter 4
Services 'R Us,
We Be Democratic Earth Mother

Shit happens. We all know it. It happens to each one of us. It happens to all of us. Some of it is our fault. Some of it is the fault of someone else. Sometimes, no one we know is at fault, but someone far away is. Sometimes, it is just a part of the natural order of the natural world, thus no fault of any of us. Sometimes it is a product of a civilization and its systems gone amuck: wars, toxic spills or the sound of the southbound traffic on Second Ave. and 27 St. at three in the morning just after the light has turned to green. Maybe it is a canker on the lip, a tumor in the tummy, a fire that brings down an apartment house, a tree that grows and then keels over in Brooklyn, maybe, but hopefully not, on your dog or you or both. You know it happens. The 9th Ward. Breezy Point. A tornado in Kansas or Alabama or Oklahoma or Oklahoma again.

One of the better parts of civilization and our society is that while neighbors still do help neighbors in person and directly at least part of the time. Yet, when the shit that happens gets serious and especially when it gets costly and the gent next door who might be able to change a flat tire for you or fix a leaky faucet or offer condolences on the loss of the family python just isn't enough, then we all pitch in. That is a wonder and a wonderful happening and speaks, nay, bullhorn shouts oral volumes of happy and cooperative tomes about both our dependence on one another and our solidarity with one another. Indonesian tsunami. Ethiopian famines. Halfway around the world and we ALL pulled together, even elder Bush and The Clinton. Oklahoma and Oklahoma again, too.

We pitch in more indirectly as well. Some examples of a general indirect pitching in are: health insurance, car insurance, life insurance, home insurance, flood insurance, and any of many more insurances under the sun. Of course, there is Social Security when we get too old to do much more than wait around until shit happens or it all ends.

Then too, there is the fire department. There is the police department. There is also our National Guard and Marines and helicopter pilots that guard against foreign intruders bent on doing us harm or track them down if they do. There are doctors and nurses and MRI techs and acupuncturists and chiropractors and Reiki masters — the latter being some of my personal favorite helpers. For that matter, there is garbage collection. We even have flush toilets when shit literally happens.

I really could go on for quite awhile listing all the social services that we take almost for granted until some shit happens but that we in American society, have agreed to help with — especially in the sense of pay for — so that all of us will have our garbage picked up and have relatively clean and non-toxic water to shower in and our children will go to school and learn to read and write and maybe even think adequately.

Ignorance can happen, too; and it too is toxic.

We spread the cost of all this around to all of us, more or less. We require car insurance even if we dispute whether everyone should be required to have health insurance. To my mind, why we readily accept requiring help for your car but not your body seems a bit strange. Well, maybe we simply value cars more than ourselves. I am sure that there are other reasons for this, too, liability from auto accidents among them. But are we not also liable when someone who does not have health insurance uses the free emergency room at the local hospital and the hospital must charge us and our insurance company higher fees?

Not only do we assist each other after the fact, but understanding that the proverbial ounce of prevention being worth a pound of cure and a whole lot cheaper besides, we know it is best to take measures before the typhoid of some errant waters gets into our bloodstream or mass illiteracy creeps up on us or any of a thousand and one or another horrible preventable apocalyptic destructions come smashing, crashing and thrashing down on our poor inadequately defended selves. We prevent as well as take care of — more or less.

Add them all up and whether as prevention or clean up, social services are ubiquitous and necessary — and we are glad we have them. Even Ayn Rand used Medicare, poor elderly non-impoverished Ayn. We anted up for her, too.

What we have had a tendency to do as our American society has become greater in territory and complexity over the last two centuries is to turn over to the greater society and its companies, public and private, many social service functions that used to be taken care of either at home or by the local community. Even early child rearing has been taken more and more out of the soothing and loving hands of mothers and the playful and loving hands of fathers and put in the skilled and loving hands of day care workers.

(Not that nannies never existed for the wealthy plantation owners of the antebellum South, — nor wet nurses for the European aristocracy before that — getting enslaved adults to raise children, but for the greater number of people north and south, this was not the case in bygone eras.)

How we take now care of our infants, babies, toddlers and young children is historically unprecedented and is one more demonstration of the proof that social services have become a central feature in the larger American society — from the house to en masse.

Most of the social services where profit is obviously low, as in taking care of impoverished alcoholics, drug addicts and the mentally disabled or fighting fires or collecting garbage or sewers, these services are mostly given over to the government, be it federal, state or town. Where there might be money to be made on a social service, as in life insurance or medicine or feeding the troops in Iraq, private enterprise has dominated.

Yet, there are reasons why a democratic citizenry should take charge of some of the more important social services that Big Brother-ish Earth Mother-ish government and the vagaries and corruptions of supply and demand laissez faire economics and its corporations both take care of but poorly and with a devil-may-care bureaucratic air.

Neither government nor private enterprise does some of each of the social services particularly well a good deal of the time. There are exceptions, of course. Fire fighting is done well generally by government localities. I rather like my local post office people — both my postman and the postal workers at the Carrboro, North Carolina post office. They are all friendly, helpful and my mail packages get delivered well and on time and I get incoming mail delivered just outside my door as well — which is quite nice really. But then again, my local UPS store does a darn good job as well; and, the local UPS drivers are neighborhood friendly as well.

Like everyone else who has gone to public school, I have had exceptional school teachers and a few clunkers to boot. As a public service, public schools are a bit of a mixed bag. Yet when I went to a private university— New York University — as an undergraduate, I found exceptional professors and not a few clunkers there, too. Private enterprise education is its own mixed bag, too.

Even if a social service like medicine, for example, is done well, say, as in France, rated first in the world, and is government run as Michael Moore has so well and aptly pointed out; and even if a social service is done well by a private company, as in better food for the military brought to the troops by ex-vice president Cheney's company Halliburton; still and all there is the issue of public control. That is, when it comes to services, public services, the public should have far more direct control of the delivery of those services than it does now. Even in France where they have generous social services, they must take to the streets to correct problems, say, in educational services. You should not have to go to into the streets and protest every time tuition goes up.

Now, of course, Right Republican conservatives would argue that individuals have control of services as consumers in the market place. If you do not like the service from one company you pick another. Yes, I would agree that there is some public control there. And, of course, the Left Democratic liberals would argue that there is democratic control of social services because you elect government officials who oversee social services. And I would agree that there is some control there too.

The problem with Right and Left points of view on social services is that they ignore the instinctive public reaction of disgust and fear with large distant bureaucratic organizations, public governmental or private corporate, that while existing and persisting supposedly to serve us, have their very own and separate agendas, not all of which are service oriented — money in the case of private and in the case of government, well, it is always difficult to tell exactly what their hidden agenda could possibly be except the perpetuation of their continued existence.

In any event, both are only under indirect control, often minimal control. Both Big Government and Big Corporation feel — for all that they try to provide and all the good that they do or do not do — Kafkaesque. The locus of social power is displaced on a mass scale from the home and community to distant boards and bureaucracies that appear to tell us what to do and then what ream of paperwork we need to fill out to fulfill some bureaucratic arcane legalistic need for order. The Byzantines would admire our byzantine paper trails. Having personally billed for acupuncture medical services both the government and private insurance companies, I frankly cannot tell them apart.

Especially when we are most in distress — whether from a recent stroke in our brain or a flooded basement in our home from an errant hurricane — and trying ourselves to regain some sense of personal normalcy and control during an out of control situation, then to be forced time and again to deal with a far away and unfeeling entity that is out of our control only compounds our distress when we need less of it, not more. Ask any handicapped veteran who has had to deal with the V.A. on a regular basis. Or ask any number of regular middle class folks paying through the nose for and dealing with their health insurance company. Not that every veteran is in a snit over their V.A. doc; not that every last Blue Cross/Blue Shield patron is dissatisfied. Still, we all know instinctively, if not wholly consciously, that something is very much out of whack and we have far too little influence getting it back in whack.

When the service is done poorly or does not meet the person's need in a given bad situation or simply does not pay the bill and the individual then has to deal with bankruptcy for the part of the medical bill not covered by either Blue Cross nor Medicaid, then: double social service jeopardy: Kafkaesque and inadequate.

Even the care itself, let alone the insurance overcharges and underpayments and bureaucratic issues, is questionable in our corporate-government system. By any measure of adequacy of care, we are not doing well, getting well, nor staying well in our American medical system. Ask any senior spending their days going from test to endless test and put on ten to twenty pharmaceuticals. There are stories by the tens of thousands, the old, the young, the newborn, the diseased, the worried well. They are not only alien to us, Big Government, Big Business, but they do not do an especially good job either.

Sarah Palin's seemingly irrational rant against a government board that would be the one to decide whether to pull grandmas' plugs from coast to coast, despite grandma's wishes or her family's, is not quite so out to lunch as the facts would suggest. Yes, she got it wrong in fact, but look how she got it wrong and why so many of our citizens went along and still go along with her. She is tapping into just that fear and dislike with distant bureaucrats making life and death decisions for us in a distant and patronizing fashion.

Still and all, I do not know why Sarah would believe that there is not the potential for a private medical insurance company, as they most clearly do right here and now and factually so, not just in paranoid political illusion, to make all kinds of medical decisions based more on how much a therapy costs than whether it does you or me any good — grandma included. And whether they are right or wrong about this decision or that is irrelevant. Why and how come a distant bureaucrat, in this case a corporate bureaucrat, makes such decisions is the issue. It just does not feel right. It is not right.

Real local control in general takes place in bits and pieces here and there already around the country. Go to an annual town meeting, The Town Meeting, in the spring in New England where the town budget which includes the education and road services budget as well as the rest of the town budget for the year is thoroughly and systematically debated at length and voted upon. Or go to any elected local school board across the country. Oh yes, school boards can make mistakes and ban Huck Finn from the library, but which is worse, a federal bureaucrat banning Huck or a democratic board? Neither is right, but the board is directly subject to the next election, the bureaucrat not so much.

Townspeople in Vermont and New Hampshire feel like they have substantial say in the operation of their towns. We do not exactly feel the same way about D.C. in the conduct of our country

Of course, democracy is messy and authoritarian bureaucracy is clean and neat. For all her run on sentence Alaskan nuttiness, I believe that what really motivates poor confused Sarah Palin is the grizzly wildness of her native wilderness, nature being part and parcel of her soul, democracy in her blood — or so I hope. It is clearly not obvious. I just wish that she understood that the opposite of a sterile federal bureaucracy is not a sterile corporate bureaucracy. McDonald is not better than the Senate cafeteria. And neither is as good as grandma's home cooking.

Freedom means more direct democracy, not just government democracy, not just free corporate enterprise. Grandma, not Barack, nor Boehner, nor BP, nor Kaiser-Permanente; grandma should be in charge. Elect grandma! Who will pull the plug on her then?

What I have begun to propose in the last chapter and now will fill out in this chapter is the following: the creation of democratically controlled social entities that have the right to bill every citizen within their jurisdiction equally for the social services provided. I think this is far superior to giving all social services over to a federal government charged with everything from wars on the other side of the Earth to how to get antibiotics out of chicken feed, how to fund medicine and pensions for everyone without everyone and the government itself going broke, how to license naturopaths and to how to license marriages. How can a congressperson from a congressional district from anywhere in the country, rural Nebraska or downtown Philadelphia, have enough expertise to know whether a bridge to nowhere is needed in Alaska or whether radiologists should get paid for MRIs without prior approval from an insurance company or whether or not our foreign policy towards Iran makes any sense or at what level the U.S. government should be in debt up to and including its ears.

It would be far better, to my mind, if Congress and the President and all those far away officers of our government just concentrated on a few issues, the issues of law and order and who is polluting the air and poisoning us all and leave the rest to other social entities. No Department of Labor. No Department of Education. No. No. No. Just an Attorney General, a Secretary of State. A Secretary of Defense. I'd stop about there. (By the way, the Federal Reserve is, in fact, a private entity, but that is another chapter.) But yes, no Treasury Secretary either. Let the President sign the money. Commerce, bah humbug.

And yes, these are an extension of Ron Paul's proposals, I must acknowledge. There is wisdom on The Right.

Public Services Generally

So then, how many and exactly how would social services operate and what would be their scope of operation? Already this is now variable around the country. When I lived in rural Vermont, I paid for water and water waste disposal. That is, I needed to pay someone to dig a well and then I bought a pump to pump the water up the well and into my house; and there was a leech field in the field out front so the shit would not hit my fan, but go underground and compost. I also paid for private garbage collection, there being no municipal garbage collection in rural Brookfield, Vermont, population 234.

Now I live in town, in relatively urban Carrboro, North Carolina right next to Chapel Hill, North Carolina, adjacent to Raleigh and Durham and suburbs, all lumped together in something called "The Triangle." Population: about one million and climbing. Garbage and recycling is collected by the town, water comes from OWASA (Orange Water and Sewer Association), the detritus of the land and woods around my house is periodically picked up by the town — whereas in Vermont, you did what you could with detritus, leaves and sticks and pricker bushes recently cut down. I am quite sure that around the country who covers what varies from place to place, depending on geography and historical habit. By the way, the public services in Carrboro are done very well and done with neighborly friendliness. I much appreciate my town, even though my taxes are very high. But then again, I am paying for some very good and necessary services, good schools included.

Law itself varies from place to place around this one country as well. There is federal law and state law and local ordinances, multiple spiders' webs of laws everywhere with multiple governments spending ghastly amounts of time writing and enforcing all kinds of laws for all kinds of things. Every time we for one reason or another, need to interact directly with The Law, we need one or another kind of lawyer to help us navigate the webs.

We have court systems and all kinds of courts at all levels of government for all kinds of laws for all kinds of reasons. Family Courts. District Courts. State Courts. Federal Courts. So that even something as simple as marriage and divorce is handled differently in different jurisdictions. It's okay to marry another adult member of the same sex in Buffalo, New York, but strictly against the law in Montgomery, Alabama; although, I am quite certain that you can do certain other things in Montgomery that might get you in trouble in Buffalo — once you dig out from the lake effect snow.

You might be thinking about now that I am going to propose that we do away with some of these many jurisdictions and sets of laws. Perhaps we should have one set of uniform laws across the nation. Moreover, you might think that I have set opinions and think I can decide here and now which social services should be private, which public and which, as I have suggested, democratically in between. Nope.

Ah, if there were but world enough and type, that there were enough ideas and solutions in the author's mind to wrap around all of that. Whether garbage collection should be public or private in suburban Minneapolis or downtown Boise or rural panhandle Texas I am going to leave these social conundrums to later thinkers and democrats in their respective jurisdictions. One day I think we can privatize most everything; on other days, what the heck, I think, make them all public. Strange for the man who wants to solve all problems for all people, to be this indecisive now.

Still, I might, I would, offer a fairly modest set of proposals in these regards. Yes, we can simply do away with most governments, period. There are just too many of them making too many laws. I would be fine with just federal and state government making laws, even just one nationwide criminal code without state laws. That would cut out an enormous amount of paperwork and save a lot of money. That is, not to do away with zoning regulations, for example; just make them statewide or nationwide, with a statewide or national bureaucracy enforcing them uniformly across the state or country. As with companies that consolidate, this might save a whole lot of money, too.

Moreover, we also have just too many laws covering too many things. Why we have laws, for example, about who can and who cannot call themselves married is simply beyond my comprehension. You want to get married: find a minister or whoever you consider could or should marry you and get married. Why do you need or should you need a license from the state to do that? Why this should ever become an issue of note? Why should "married couples" have extra legal privileges in the first place?

I could go on and on from here of course. And in a short book I cannot cover just how much law, federal, state, county, town I would cut, cut, cut. It makes jobs for lawyers and judges and bureaucrats of all kinds. I am just not sure most of it is necessary at all for social peace and justice. Of course, for the most part, our legislators are lawyers and they make their incomes from the law, so they might have a vested interest in keeping lots of laws around.

As for all the other services that towns now conduct, like garbage collection, water and sewer, and all the rest, a town or county service public entity could oversee those services. The officials of the social entity that oversaw those services, just like town officials now, would be elected. Which really would not change things that much, only take law making and ordinance making out of local control. What do you think? It is not that far from existing reality as it is.

Again, where I lived in Vermont and all over New England, town meetings decide the town budget and other matters pertaining to town government. I think the participatory democracy of town meetings could be extended to cover all towns and then within cities local communities that would decide on local services, whether they should be public or private and all that.

However, I will be more insistent about two major social services that I am in favor of democratizing and placing at a state level. I would like to suggest a couple of areas that I think are far better off using collective democratic means yet neither public nor private enterprise: education and medicine. I believe that medicine and education, being as ubiquitous and important as they are, should take up greater political-social attention. Whether the post office or garbage collection should be privatized and owned by UPS or the garbage collectors in a garbage-person's collective, frankly, just is not earth shattering as an issue, nor can I think of great reasons why it should go one way or another or a third. On the other hand, education and medical care, now these are social meat to chew on — so to speak.

I believe a representative democratic system would be needed at this level. I believe that we can do this together, that these two areas of service need function neither by ye olde free market nor by ye olde government bureaucracy

Education

• Cradle to grave free education for everyone, from daycare to Ph.D. and every technical school in-between.

I will explain what I mean by "free" in a bit. You still pay, but differently; and, to my mind, more rationally and fairly.

The benefits of the extension of free education, not only to each individual but to the whole of society would be considerable. How have the economies of South Korea, Japan, China, India and others lifted themselves up? Investment. And investment in not only machinery but first and foremost in: people. The part that is the investment in people is mostly in a word: education. Each society put their trust, minds, hearts and money into education; they invested in their people. It is paying off. Of course, they did not just do that, but education is at least as great and important an investment as all their other investments, like factories and machinery. Who will work in the factory, set up the factory, engineer the machinery in the factory, invent the products manufactured in the factory? Educated people! And if we look back historically, Europe and the United States can pat themselves on our collective well clothed backs for universal free education. It has meant everything socially and economically.

So, I propose we go one step, two steps further. More education. More training. When you want it, when you are ready, when you need it, education will be there for you at no charge. A post-World War II G.I. Bill for everyone, now and in the future. It helped the United States, its citizens and its economy after World War II. And even now, similar benefits could do it again.

So then, how to we pay for such a thing as universal cradle to grave education making sure it is available in sufficient quantity to fill and increased demand? Same as how we might pay for government making the laws: bill us!

- Bill every citizen equally yearly for the total cost of all education in that state.
- We are all billed equally by a democratically elected state level social entity that oversees the entire education system.

Should this entity, this state entity of education that oversees education have its own schools under its direct control. Should it pay charter schools? Or should it combine both? Should it pay private colleges their going rate or tell them how much to charge? I should not provide the answer to those questions. I do not defer judgment not because I do not have an opinion on such matters, I do; but, you might differ — not on the proposal in general — but on policies within the social entity and those policies can be determined by the elected officials whom you have chosen and who you believe best represent your opinions on these matters. I will vote a certain way, based on my preferences, you on yours, our neighbor, based on his or hers. Then it will be decided. How this goes, one way or another, concerns me but not at the written moment. Another chapter on education will follow giving my preferences.

What is important is the principle that education is free, universal and under our collective direct democratic control and that we are all billed equally for its cost. That is, the social entity that controls the educational system is not mediated through The Government. It is mediated through you. You choose The State School Board — or whatever you choose to call it — the social entity that controls the whole education shebang.

Universal free education. Everyone billed. Everyone may vote. Even if you never use the service, if you do not want more than a basic education, you will benefit by living in a society of better-educated human beings. Given a good education, depending on the quality of that education, our citizenry might well be more virtuous and productive. We should only be so lucky.

Hopefully, we will make wise decisions about who we elect to be in charge of this social entity completely in charge of the educational system. Otherwise, the educational system might not turn out virtuous and productive citizens, but unproductive rogues. We should not be so unlucky.

So, college age students and medical students and career change students will not be burdened by post-graduation debt of enormous size and burden, we collectively hold together and distribute the cost. If the cost seems too great, then we must elect officials to the democratic social entity that controls education who will be charged with decreasing the costs. And if we do not like their solutions to cost savings, we can elect someone else and so on. Still and all, by law, by federal law or federal constitutional amendment, everyone is required to pay. And state boards are required to offer cradle to grave education.

I think that education as universal and free goes far, very far, to creating an equal opportunity society. What we have done already with free primary and high school education and inexpensive state schools has gone far in this direction already. Free and universal would go even further. With universal access comes more opportunity and equal opportunity at that. Family financial circumstance, your financial circumstance, will not be in anyone's way to getting as much education as you want and need. That is real equal opportunity to advance yourself, especially if one puts the time and effort into this opportunity.

And cradle to grave means free day care, too. The cost of present day care is a burden on new families and young child-rearing adults, especially poor ones. This would change in this system.

Universal free education is egalitarian, not in the sense of bringing the top or the middle to the bottom but in bringing up the bottom. Nobody needs to be brought down, unless, by their personal lack of resources and effort they fall down on their own.

This is the ultimate taxation with representation; although, I believe it is more like an insurance policy with representation than taxation. Your governor does not choose your chairman of your state department of education. You do. Your chairman of the state department of education does not pick the members of the board of the state board of education. You do. You and your fellow citizens.

On the other hand, you do not get representation and education without paying the bill. I have heard it said as you have in cliché that "there is no such thing as a free lunch." You pay as part of a collective whole so that the cost does not burden any one in particular — again, like any good insurance. Yet for every citizen an equal bill. Equal representation and equal educational opportunity requires an equal bill. Fair is fair.

Such a system does not guarantee either quality or efficiency of education. But such a system of education does guarantee an end to feeling separate and apart from the very institutions that are so important to the lives of each and every one of us, an end to alienation. It is ours. We own it, for better or worse.

• Research. All state school boards should be required by federal law to contribute a certain percentage of their budget to a National Research Board, say 10%. This board is subject to election by the state boards. The National

Research Board would fund all research. Research that results in business profits should be reimbursed to The Research Board and to the researcher(s) at a certain rate. Research that is more general and of benefit to all need not be reimbursed to The Research Board. We, the general collective we, have already paid for it; and, therefore, we should receive the benefit of it without further cost.

Still, regardless of benefit and who pays what, research is necessary and important and should be an understood and eternal part of the educational system.

Medicine

The same principles apply to medicine as it does to education:
- Free all-inclusive health care for all.
- Everyone is billed equally.
- Everyone can vote for the Board of Directors officers who control each state by state entities that are in charge of the health care system.

This is a single payer system, but it is neither a government nor a private insurance company.

You simply receive a bill at the end of the year, not for your indidivual medical care, but your collective equal share of the cost of everyone's medical care in your state.

And you elect the heads of the social entity that is billing you.

We pull together collectively for the good of us all, but we also have the power to choose the terms that the social entity operates under that provides for us all and bills us all.

It is: free cradle to grave medical care that we all pay for together and control together.

This is a system controlled by neither a distant government, nor a distant corporation. Just as you are a part of the collective in your state in education and, — in a sense —

own the education system, so too, as part of the collective in your state in medicine, you in a sense own the medical system. You might think of yourself an equal stockholder or equal stake holder.

Everyone is respected equally in this type of system. Not only equal rights and status under the law and in the creation of the law, but equal rights and status in education and medicine and in the creation and maintenance of that system that conducts education and medicine. Psychologically, I think this would have enormous effect across social classes and social differences with each citizen feeling more and more a part of the whole. More patriotic, more part of American society, as well as feeling pride in themselves as an equal citizen. I think Teddy Roosevelt would love it for just this reason.

Again, the details about how to run the medical system in any particular state I will leave to voters and those whom they vote for. Will the next health care system be better than the one we have now? If it is not, if it still is the most expensive in the world with outcomes that put the United States on a par with Cuba, then we will have ourselves to blame, not Obama and the notorious "Obamacare" or medical insurance companies or insensitive wealthy cardiologists performing unnecessary and unhealthy surgeries or insurance company bureaucrats. Ourselves and those who we elect will be to blame. And guess what? If it does not work out, elect someone who will fix it in your state.

Yet in this new system the one aspect that will work without any doubt is that everyone will have healthcare when they need it and there will be no deductibles or limits of coverage to force families into bankruptcies. Everyone is covered for it all and the cost is shared equally by us all. Required by law.

Under those terms of agreement, I think too that the medical system state to state will improve under the closer scrutiny of the public. And if the public is not paying attention and education or medicine deteriorates, we will know who is to blame.

As for the law that creates the medical social entity that I have outlined above, the law needs to be passed by constitutional amendment. These kinds of proposals require broad consensus from the general population. Yet, given how these proposals synthesize what appear to be mutually incompatible points of view, I think it is possible that Americans can work together more than they are doing already and do this.

While the laws that created free education and free medical care with everyone being billed equally and voting equally for the administrators of this system should be passed nationally, the social entities themselves should be on a state by state basis. Such a system allows for regional variation and local experimentation. What should not be variable are the principles of free and equal access to medicine and education with democratic control of the social entities that organize education and medicine.

• Research. Again, too, a national medical research board can be created to fund medical research. 10% from all medical boards.

Summary

Let us see where this leaves us so far. On the one hand, you are no longer paying income tax from any level of government, federal, state, city. There are no more sales taxes anywhere. Nor are there any property taxes in any town anywhere.

Taxes no longer exist.

Nor, by the way, are you paying a private insurance company for health insurance. Nor do you have any student loans to pay back. Nor need you pay for your child's day care either. You are clearly going to be making more money, not being taxed hither and yon as well paying for education and health care yourself.

Still and all, as I have said already, since there is really no such lunch as that proverbial free lunch. You will be receiving bills for: education, medical care, local services and the cost of making laws and enforcing them. You will receive a bill for each of these like everyone else and equally so. However, and here is the democratic spin, each of those bills comes from a social entity — call it a company, call it a semi-governmental agency, call it what you will — that you control with your fellow citizens.

I think you might have more interest in these elections than the current ones in which you elect oh so many officers in oh so many governments at oh so many levels that it is hard to keep up. No more elections for judges and sheriffs and county commissioners and all the rest. Those get appointed by the one social entity that deals with laws and related matters, the government — which by the way, you elect, too.

What you will elect will be officials of social entities that will have impacts in any number of ways on your life in ways that you well know: education, health care, local services and the law.

Lest I be misunderstood. I am not saying that everyone is billed for medical insurance and the medical field, hospitals, doctors and nurses, pharmaceutical companies and everyone and anyone and any company is private and for profit. That is partly what we already have.

What I am saying is that there is a social entity — call it the State Department of Medicine or call it simply The Medicine Social Entity or hold a contest and come up with a much better name — that controls medicine, period. However they choose to do it, it is based on you electing them. It is all public, yet it is not governmental the way we now understand government. Nor is it private and for profit the way we now understand companies. Nor is it a private for profit insurance company.

Medicine, then, is at least partly removed from the market place and market forces, yet neither is it in the patronizing boondoggle hands of politicians. Collectively and democratically, we are in direct control of the whole shebang.

Whether doctors and hospitals and all that stays private or comes under the direct supervision and control of the state social medical entity, can be decided by that democratic entity.

Money and Control

There are umpteen books and articles you can read documenting in horrible detail all the problems with our private health care system as it is, as it is in private and government hands. Shannon Brownlee's Overtreated is a fine exposition of the moneyed dimensions of the multiple problems and disasters of our medical system. Take the money motivation out of medicine and maybe we would have, could have a system that is less expensive and serves us instead of pharmaceutical CEOs, insurance company CEOs, hospital CEOs and very wealthy radiologists and everyone else who is supposed to be serving the public, that is, all of us, but are pretty much serving themselves at our expense.

Then, too, if you have nothing else to do late at night and have a penchant for sociological masochism, you can read about the problems of highly socialized medical systems. Not that highly socialized systems are not better than private medical systems, but they have their issues as well. Why will I be waiting for elective surgery in Calgary well past its time? What is Westminster doing about the state of hospitals in Manchester?

After that, understanding the limitations of Capitalist medicine and education and Socialist medicine and education, we can move on to systems that are democratic and might even function better and be less costly — probably worth a try in a state or two before we change the whole system.

I am quite sure, that democratic medical and educational systems will present problems of their own in the short, in the long, in any time. I am hardly proposing a static utopian solution. I am simply proposing that we put important social services back in the more or less able hands of the population, rather than the money grubbing hands of a small elite. The 99% takes over. The 1% goes home. Government as Big Brother social service agency takes a permanent vacation.

The Tea Party has now met Occupy Wall St. They wake up, hug and make up. They go into the election booth and pick who should run the hospitals and schools.

Social Security

Yet, what about Social Security? Do we need another election for that, to pick a board to do our retirements? In this case, I do not think so. I tend more to the Republican Conservative side of this argument and would allow everyone to invest as well as save. Or would I? Here is the problem for me: I have eliminated investment possibilities by eliminating private investment as you shall read in a subsequent chapter, so there is a problem there.

I would, however, adjust the Social Security system as follows, and I do not believe it needs elected administrators. I think it can be administered by our community banks. Ah, that is in a subsequent chapter, too, on banking and what a Community Bank is.

But I can say a little now. I would create:
- A mandated requirement that everyone have a retirement account on file at your local community bank.
- Banks provide a moderate interest rate.
- You are required by law to have this account and automatically contribute to it at an established percentage of your income, say around 15%. In fact, in the Social Security tax, that is pretty much how the Social Security tax works now, except it is held by a federal government that appears incapable of administering it in the longer term.
- You can at your discretion add more money to your account above the required minimum. Again, you receive a modest interest amount from your bank.

However, given the economic system I will outline below, you cannot privately invest and get big rewards or big negative surprises and lose your retirement to market fluctuations and plunges, but you can add to your Social Security privately. More on investment in a bit, too.

What if your community bank somehow goes belly up, where is your pension?

• The entire coordinated banking system guarantees Social Security much as the FDIC guarantees deposits.

Banks in this system are regulated by a banking regulatory body. Hopefully, a bank going belly up would not be a frequent occurrence. Although, it could happen, just not on a massive scale. I think a sustainable banking system, without wild speculating and gargantuan bonuses to questionable bankers of ill repute, would not permit the kind of collapses of '29 and '07.

"Like a rock," as the commercial croaks. And then, too, Community Banks will be required to contribute to a bank insurance system to guarantee all retirement deposits.

This is all not so totally different from what goes on now, but it is different in part. The major difference is that it is a retirement savings account, not a government "entitlement program," with Congress debating whether to increase you retirement amount depending on inflation or how the political winds are blowing at any particular time. On the other hand, you only get back what you have put in.

This has an advantage for society in that the system cannot go broke in say 30 years, as now, because the system never has to pay out more than is put in. On the other hand, what if what you have saved individually in this system is not enough to carry you through an extended old age? And by the way, at what age you choose to retire I would leave more or less up to you with a liberal lower limit.

- There would be a age when you would collect more at 62 than at 66 than at 70. None of that. You have what you have and that is that.
- You cannot access this savings account until a certain age. Maybe it is 55 or 60 or even 70.

Social Security then becomes a mandatory savings account that you can access when and if you retire. And, you can spend it all the first month of retirement or you can parcel it out to yourself over time. You are required to make the call. I suggest you might pay more attention to retirement under those circumstances. This system requires good planning on all our parts.

Still, what if you stop working at say 55 and the money runs out at 60. What do you do now? What does society do now? Does it let you starve to death? Kick you out of your home? Maybe at 60 you must return to work — still with the same requirement that you put money aside for your second retirement.

Or what if you decide at 60 to only work part time and still want access to your retirement savings account? No problem: you have it.

And by the way, if you die before any of these ages, it is a savings account, so that the amount you have saved would go to your estate and spouse or children or whoever you want.

Still, here you are out of money at 60 because you have been entirely injudicious about your retirement savings or maybe at 80 or older and the money runs out even though you have been fairly moderate and judicious about spending your retirement. But the money runs out. If you need to go back to work and are able, maybe you should. Society guarantees employment, (again, in a subsequent chapter, guaranteed jobs) so back to work you go. Or you can either go back to school and get retrained or join the infrastructure gang. (All this in subsequent chapters.)

Still, really and truly, you are 107 and really and truly you cannot work. And there is no money left and all your relatives have died off and cannot take care of you, what is there to do? In a word: disability insurance. You are disabled and cannot work. You are the same as someone of a younger age who is disabled. Therefore, you, like them, should receive disability payments. It is at simply a living wage level and not more, but it should suffice to keep us from being out on the street begging in your and my old age. You might or might not need to leave the mansion for a lesser apartment, but at least you can get by. Which, by the way, is what Social Security was supposed to do, allow us to get by in our old age and not necessarily support us in the golden manner we might desire for our later years. (I shall deal with disability insurance in a subsequent chapter.)

We have taken care of taxes and we have taken care of the major "entitlement" programs. I think by now everyone is very happy, Right and Left, with the society I am outlining. Hmm. Not quite yet. Maybe not at all. But read on. It only gets more … well, there are more ideas and they all dovetail.

All those caveats about "in a subsequent chapter," in this chapter are explained in a later chapter. But first up in the next chapter the topic is: regulation. The Right is about to get uptight. Elizabeth Warren will be sending me political love letters. Love you too, Elizabeth, politically speaking.

Chapter 5
The All Pervasive
Regulatory Comfort Blanket

Make no mistake about it: law is regulation; regulation is law. The law is the rules of the game, the regulation of the society game. You can do this; you cannot do that. If you play by the rules, other people designated by the government, aka the police, will not scoop you up, cart you off and then, after the court system gets through with you, punish you. If you do not play by the rules and you are discovered, there are various consequences and penalties from mild to severe.

There is, of course, a long and interesting history to the establishment of law and regulation and all that, going back many thousands of years, Hammurabi, Roman Law, The Magna Carta, The Napoleonic Code and later the Articles of Confederation, and the U.S. Constitution. We are not required to know all that history to talk about how to regulate society in the present moment. Although, it is comforting to know that human beings have wrestled with these issues of law, what is right, what is wrong, what is permissible conduct and what not, for a very long time and have come up with many and diverse answers. We, here and now, are part of that tradition and we may change the rules of this game if we so desire and hopefully for the better — if we think about it and place a good deal of reason behind us.

Law does not just concern itself with the obvious. Although it does with that, too. There are laws against murder, theft, mayhem and the like. Conduct is regulated by law so that we do not tear each other apart or come into each other's houses and take away each other's prized or puny possessions. Simple and clear enough. There is not, also, a whole lot of dispute politically when it comes to such laws.

There are, of course, disputes over penalty relative to the law. As in, should we execute the murder, that is, murder the murderer, or incarcerate for long periods of time the petty thief or cocaine dealer, that is, instead of cutting off his hands putting his hands in stir, as it were?

There are naturally disputes about the guilt or innocence in particular cases. Was justice served in the Trayvon Martin, George Zimmerman case?

I worked as a vocational counselor many years ago in a government program for "model ex-offenders" who were hardly "ex" and I am not exactly sure what they were modeling. My wife directed the state's Victim's Compensation Program in Vermont in its first years. We were at the two ends, perpetrator and victim sides, within the criminal justice system. Although I have many ideas about the criminal justice system itself — another book for another time — here I would like to write about justice within the economic system.

Here there is far more dispute and hyperbole and nothing is either as simple or straightforward as theft and murder. Although, in another sense, theft and murder are certainly involved. One often hears the complaint that such-and-so company, especially modern banks, are "robbing us blind " — even as we pretty much can see them doing it — or that so-and-so company by spilling toxic this-or-that is murdering porpoises and people. Maybe it is simple, after all. Our experience with obvious criminality may help with fuzzier criminality.

Republican conservatives, including the latter day "severe conservative" Mighty Mitt, but certainly not him alone, scream at the top of their political wheezy lung capacity that the government is over-regulating business and by over-regulating business the government is stifling business and therefore being stifled, business cannot prosper and expand; and if business cannot profit and prosper and expand, they cannot hire you and me; and therefore we cannot ride off into the unregulated sunset of joy and job-filled prosperity. Of course, there are not a few of us and Democratic Party Liberal types who might point out that many an economic collapse and toxic Gulf spill is precisely because large corporations hire lobbyists that successfully cajole and outright bribe governments and their regulators to water down if not eliminate regulation and law and because of over-de-regulation, we are in the economic mess we are now in.

I am all for freedom. I am all for freedom of enterprise. I read my Adam Smith assiduously. Yet, as personal conduct has limits, so does business enterprise. You are free to do what you want except do another harm. If you hit your friendly umpire over the head with a baseball bat over a disputed third strike or fourth ball and cause him cranial breakage, you are over the limit of personal conduct. To my mind, if you dump cyanide or a dioxin or two into the local river that downstream is the drinking water for other human beings, including the umpire, the parents in the stands at the Little League baseball game as well as the kids, you are also over the limit of personal and business conduct. Why do Republican conservatives think it alright to have law for the bat over the head incident but not generally for the cyanide or dioxin incident? Why should environmental law be voluntary, Mr. Bush, and direct personal violence not? Why on God's green Earth would they do away with the E.P.A. and environmental regulation?

Yet how do we in society do this without over regulating and stifling legitimate enterprise? While I think that we err on the side of over-regulating personal conduct, I think we err on the side of under-regulation when it comes to economic activity. Why the heck can't someone smoke marijuana, amongst other personal vices, if they want to? It's their very own brain cells they are frying, and why am I not letting them cook themselves? We permit putrid stuff that gets out into the environment, worse to all our lungs and nervy brains than marijuana. Why can't you now, in New York City, supersize your Coca-Cola? If you want to overwhelm your pancreas with glucose and fatten your midriff and clog your arteries, it is your own business, not Major Bloomberg's. If the City Council of New York does not have better laws to make than this silly and irrelevant city law, they should find another profession.

Universal Business Regulation

• Across the business and societal board all business-es and professions should be regulated. Each and every business and profession, none exempted or ignored. Each and every business and profession is regulated by a board in their field appointed through the federal government.

I have been proposing that we should all pay equally for the creation of the laws and regulations, that we pay equal-ly for our legislature, our president, and pay for those who enforce the law, the police, the courts, the corrections de-partment, the military. We pay for them making the law and enforcing it. This is all the law for personal conduct.

• The price to regulate any given business or profes-sion should be borne, not by the general public as it is now, but by each and every company or self employed individual in a particular business or profession. The fee they pay to the their particular regulatory board should be proportional to the size of company.

That is, if you are an acupuncturist, as I am, I would pay my equal share for the regulation of all the other acu-puncturists. We pay for the licensing board itself. I do now in North Carolina, so no problem for me in the future; and even if it went national, I would welcome it. If I owned a gas station and convenience store, I would pay my equal share for the regulation of my gas station and convenience store and all other gas and convenience stores. All bed and breakfasts. All automobile dealers. All fast food restaurants. All slow food restaurants. All lawn mowers and tree cutters. All banks. All automobile manufacturers. All phone compa-nies. All electric companies. All BPs and Exons. They pay the price for their regulation.

Each board is paid for by businesses in each business category. There is then incentive for businesses to police each other as boards of regulation will be more expensive, needing more inspectors, for example, if certain companies are systematically breaking the rules. If I, a law abiding business, am following the rules and you are not, I wind up paying more to the board, now taking more man power and time for the miscreant businesses' indiscretions. Businesses might very well put pressure on other businesses to be good. Maybe.

Yet, if one company is larger than another it makes sense and would be fairer if larger had to pay more for regulation. Equal citizens paying an equal bill for services is fair when each citizen is a single individual. However, companies consist of multiple individuals and equal financial liability to be fair should be calculated according to how many people work in the company.

- Regulation and regulatory boards are best nation-wide instead of state by state.

I would suggest and it is not a hard and fast suggestion, that these regulatory boards be nationwide, not state to state. I can see no reason for experimenting with regulation as we might with other areas of service, like medicine or education. I see no reason for latitude like that here. I can see, however, businesses playing one state regulatory board off against another in another state for illegitimate economic advantage, businesses moving from state to state the looser and more beneficial to them the regulations, promising localities their business and jobs if they will just give them a break on their laws. There simply is too much opportunity for self-interested skullduggery.

However, while the national government should in a general way mandate law, I do not think the Congress and the President have the expertise to regulate all businesses in detail.

• All relevant regulatory agencies would then need to write specific rules for the relevant specific businesses relative to that law and enforce them. The Congress and President do not pretend even now to do it, but have government agencies that write regulatory rules consistent with general law. The national government could, for example, mandate by law that there is zero tolerance for pollutants and CO2 pollutant emissions that harm both human beings and the environment and muck up the weather that human beings live in. They might even agree with other governments around the planet that carbon dioxide levels in the atmosphere are all too rapidly reaching a tipping point whose consequence is climactic and catastrophic climate change and that we should all, worldwide, regulate just how much we allow CO2 to be put into our limited and precious air. Then we might pass on this regulation to all regulatory bodies that regulate companies that have those kinds of emissions.

Pollution and emissions are no small matter and simply because it is a one or two lines mention here does not mean that our government and regulatory bodies should not expend a good deal of great non-polluting energy dealing with these problems forthwith. The United States within its borders contains 5% of the world's population and is responsible for at least 25% of the world's emissions. We owe the planet and all its creatures big time. If we in cooperation with all the present emissions creators and relatively new big emissions creators, that is, China and India, do not do a lot very soon it will be The Titanic all over again, the ocean liner being the planet, the earthy part of the Earth sinking below waters, literally, as Greenland and Antarctica's ice melts on our watch.

Government, democratically elected government, the federal government, can and should make laws to plan for a sustainable future with ice poles intact, ocean waters close to present temperatures, and air fit for an urban child to breathe.

• The government itself should not be an investor or sponsor research. nor be an infrastructure creator. But it can mandate in law that other social entities, like banks and the educational and health care entities take care of this.

Government and law need not simply become a carping legal nuisance, only scolding us all for not doing right, but never itself promoting a better, cleaner and more humane future. The government, by law, should mandate that at the level of federal banks (see the next chapter on banks to understand what a federal bank would be), that a certain percentage of the bank's investments go towards green investments. Given the present state of the country and the world, that percentage could be as high as 50%, from planting massive numbers of trees — in infrastructure projects (see banks later, too) — to carbon emissions collection directly from manufacturing or energy producing factories — especially those using coal — to reversing ocean mercury deposits and more. And, this means not only money creating infrastructure jobs, but investment capital creating green companies that create green jobs.

Moreover, the federal government could mandate that a certain percentage of research funds controlled by The Federal Education Research Board be appropriated for research into green technology and solutions to environmental problems.

This will not mean that investment in cell phones or toys for tots will not get funded. Yet, law and regulation can also guarantee that capital goes to our better green selves.

The government, too, might mandate a certain percentage to adventurous projects like men and women going to Mars — even if Newt would settle only for the Moon. What exact percentage is not as important as the idea that by law, it can be specified by mandate that a certain amount of investment is in green and a certain amount to big exploratory things. (More on this when we get to banking.)

• For these regulatory boards and the agency personnel they employee, we should create a class of well educated professionals who are expert on sitting on boards of regulation and working for them. They should be paid well, but not exorbitantly for doing this.

University level professional programs will need to be set up to create this profession as a profession.

• Corruption when working for a board or on a board of regulation should be severely punished.

Corruption in this sense is detrimental not only because of the immediate harm done because of the direct consequence of the inaction of the regulator, but the break in public trust is important as well. So this should be severely punished.

• Those who work for a regulatory agency should not have worked in the past for the business they are regulating, nor ever be able in the future work in the business the regulatory board is overseeing.

There has been far too much movement between regulatory board and the same industry the board is regulating; and in many all too many instances this has constituted a kind of informal bribery — and, sometimes, not so informal.

• All of these regulatory boards too therefore, should have a regulatory board regulating them. This board should be appointed by the President and Congress. The regulatory board of all regulatory boards should not only oversee the legal workings of the other boards but appoint it members also. Members of this board, the super-board, as it were, if we are to be consistent, can never sit on the boards or work otherwise on any of the other regulatory boards. The expense of this board of board can come from a percentage or the income of all the lesser boards.

• It should not be possible to lobby regulatory boards. If regulatory boards need information from specific companies they should be able to request it. The companies regulated by the boards should not be able to influence these boards in any way to secure competitive advantage within their fields or attempt to circumvent the public interest.

Political Reaction

Now, Republican conservatives might think this is all rather bureaucratically draconian and not a little totalitarian. They do not like the little regulation that we have in place now. The idea that every business and every profession will be regulated by national boards and then a single board over them might appear to seem like Big Brother on steroids gone viral.

I have no such idea in mind. In fact, I am all for maximum freedom for everyone, including every business and profession.

However, laws and regulations can and must when appropriate encroach on absolute freedom, yes. Once one lives in society, you should not have absolute freedom. Nobody, rich, poor, old, young, whatever the distinction, gets to do whatever they want no matter what. The no matter what matters a whole lot.

Freedom brings a certain degree of responsibility. Absolute freedom means you can kill your neighbor to kidnap his spouse and take their possessions. Absolute freedom means you can extract oil from the Gulf of Mexico and give a damn if a well blows and you kill off all the shrimp therein. Absolute freedom. Law has to do with preventing another person — or a seagull — harm. There is a legitimate limit to freedom: harm caused to another because of your greedy self-interest. Self-interest is fine. Greedy self-interest that harms someone else is not.

Why have any law in the first place if we cannot do this? Law should not be around just to secure freedom and license without responsibility for a small industrial aristocracy, whether hereditary or money based.

• The mandate of the government that democratically reflects the will of the citizenry of the nation is to create laws that permit the maximum amount of freedom, but limits our freedom to harm others. Regulation should reflect that very same principle: maximum freedom, but responsible limits to that freedom.

That is: do no harm. Of course, the devil, as Mr. Perot was wont to wail many elections ago, is in the details, of who is harming who and how.

Arguments come about both in trying to balance out good and harm as well as to decide when harm takes place. It is blatantly obvious in murder or assault. It is not nearly as obvious when it comes to carbon emissions, although not all that tricky either if you follow the facts. That does not mean that we cannot regulate carbon emissions, only that there is more dispute of fact and harm. Yet, once it is decided that harm is taking place, there seems to be no reason why carbon emissions should not be strictly if not absolutely done away with in regulation. If it hurts, get your finger off the stove. If someone is forcing your hand onto a hot stove and you cannot stop them, someone else needs to stop them. If the soot from the stove produced by your now burning hand is harming the whole planet, not only does your hand need to get off the stove, but the stove needs to cool out.

Will it harm the businesses that now cannot discharge emissions? Most likely. Does a prison term or death by electric chair harm the murderer? Most certainly. Yet externalizing costs as polluting industries do onto you and me by harming our personal health and environment is not legitimate. We pay for their lowered costs. We pay in health and environment in a big, bigger, biggest way. I have seen studies that estimate that more than 75% of cancers in this country are due to environmental toxins of an industrial sort. Some business rights are stomping on your right to life. You might drive a cheaper car because they do not have to pay; but eventually you pay anyway and through and in your nose, literally.

As it stands now they do not have to pay to clean up their act and even arrogantly complain that they have to put in for health care even when they are causing big time, big health problems. That Republican conservatives want to close the EPA is just one of many indications that they are for freedom for business and leaving the costs of doing business to the public, not to the corporation where it belongs. It is why all their talk of "freedom" makes me cringe. They want to restrict the freedom of gay couples to marry. What harm is that doing anyone? No hot stove there, except to the sensibilities of the religiously challenged and over-sensibility does not trump another's substantial human right.

• The number of regulatory boards is not final and new boards can be created.

There is one more issue for me as an alternative medical professional especially concerning regulatory boards and that concerns who and who is not under the jurisdiction of any particular board. What is the scope of each board?

The problem with much licensing is that it creates various kinds of monopolies. Only this certain set of individuals can be a "M.D." if they have gone through the process that the state medical board specifies. The medical board, while its mandate is to protect the public from the harm done if quacks got a hold on medicine inadvertently — and maybe not so inadvertently — in the end protects the monopoly of the medical profession by limiting the number of people that get into the practice. Moreover, alternative practices, unless licensed — I am licensed as a North Carolina acupuncturist — can be subject to laws against "practicing medicine without a license." Which unfortunately restricts the freedom of naturopaths and homeopaths and other alternative professionals to legitimately practice and help people. Moreover, there are licensed medical professionals who are themselves practitioners of alternative forms of conventional medicine who are over-regulated by their medical boards and squeezed out of practicing according to their conscience and good works.

That the point of boards and regulation being is to prevent harm and not to create monopolies, nor to stifle innovation and alternative practices and products, the creation of new boards could be and should be ongoing. That is, if you are an M.D. who cannot practice within the parameters of the medical board in your state or you are a naturopath or homeopath, a board should be created to regulate your practice to assure that you are free to perform your service without doing others harm. Of course, you must pay for the operation of that board and because you may be one or just a few, the expense might be high and that would be somewhat prohibitive and make the decision to ask for one a serious decision at that. Still, from what I know of acupuncture and licensing laws around the country, acupuncturists accepted that expense when we were fewer in number.

> • When businesses or individuals feel that a board and its regulations are not conforming to law and regulation, there is that general board to which they can appeal, the board that regulates the boards and that could create other boards when they are appropriate. And, if that is not sufficient, there are courts and legislatures to which they can appeal, as well.

Here is where a technocratic elite of wise and compassionate regulators is called for. No body should be above the law if the law is balanced and fair and protects everyone. We should create a profession of fairly incorruptible regulators that reflect that principle. It is they who are at the center of the yin and yang of freedom and responsibility and it is no small responsibility to know how to balance the productive life of the nation and its people. Training people for such a profession will be no small task, but important enough to do.

   • Regulatory Boards should also be informing and educating the legislative and executive branches of government about their fields and what general laws are required.

This is, of course, necessary to keep the process effective and efficient.

Now, of course, if it were me and I were in charge of regulatory boards across the board, that is, if I were all powerful — which I would rather not be, but just for the sake of argument — some of the regulations, especially concerning the physical environment might seem, from our current political and economic practice to be draconian and hurt business right away. That is, I would have zero tolerance for pollution and less for carbon emissions. Of course, I might not expect the end of pollution and carbon emissions overnight but then again, maybe the night after next.

   • The number of regulatory boards should be limited to one per business type.

That is, businesses should not have to contend with as they do now with all kinds of regulatory bodies. An E.P.A. for toxins, O.S.H.A. for worker's safety, local zoning boards, professional conduct boards and on and on. One board regulates that kind of business, period. That does not mean, because there is no longer an E.P.A. or an O.S.H.A. you can dump whatever you want wherever you want to put it or treat your workers how you want regardless of the safety consequences for them. No. No. No.

It is just that ALL regulation from worker's safety on down the line to environmental effect and every which way is covered for your business by one and only one board. Much simpler, much cheaper, and they know you and what you are doing so ultimately it is more efficient overall and you do not have to deal with umpteen jurisdictions and bureaucracies. I am sure that business would like that maybe even enough to put up with my system of regulation per se.

More Political Reaction On The Right

Now, of course, this is a course of action and organization that the business freedom Right will actually more than likely not like. Any hint that government whether it as law or regulation has any right to do much of anything that interferes with anything any business does is "Big Brother coming after us free and hard working Americans who do not need to be told what to do and if you just got off the backs of the American people, every little thing would be hunky dory." For them, it is Life, Liberty and My Property. Since they own the property, they think its use is their inalienable right to dispose of it and use it as they want.

I think not. Property is not an unregulated right, but depends on how you use it. The murderer using a gun or a knife to kill cannot claim freedom of property rights in the gun's or the knife's use.

Still, it is not the intention of regulation to punish those who do not harm others in the conduct of their businesses, who do not pass on downstream the misery and cost of some ill to others. The vast majority of businesses are not only benign, they feed and supply us all. Still, if you are in business, you get regulated. It will seem much fairer to any particular individual if no company gets a free pass on regulation. It is fair, equitable and understandable.

That said, it is very necessary to distinguish between assigning harm and simply trying to assert Big Brother power and control for the benefit of big brother and his brethren. This is another harm and it is either outright corruption or a subtle form of it. You should not need a permit to blow your nose or put up a house in any way you choose. Whether it is the individual bureaucrat getting a kickback on every nose blowing or house building, this practice being obvious and outright corruption or the bureaucracy itself getting its own kickback for every unnecessary action and is another and subtler form of corruption, neither should it be permissible. These are an overstepping, an excess of regulation and law.

The principle I am enumerating is still maximum freedom, but within responsible limits and those limits are the line that divides benign and harmful. Maximum freedom. Reasonable responsibility. Reasonable incorruptible regulation.

Summary

In summary, while what I have outlined does increase regulation in one sense — that each and every business is regulated by a professional regulatory body — there should be on the whole a decrease in unnecessary layers of law and regulation, as each and every business is not regulated at federal, state, county and town levels, but need answer to one and only one regulatory body. The greatest decrease in regulation will accrue because there will be one and only one set of regulations for the whole country. No federal, then state, then local, then more local regulations overlapping and driving us all bonkers trying to figure out what we can and cannot do on any particular day of the week. In one fell swoop swipe, the many branches of the tree of bureaucracy has been pruned back substantially.

Personally, as I have written in the last chapter, I would not care if all law, too, criminal law as well as regulation was uniform nationally, and state and local governments ceased to burden us with this labyrinth of laws. However, because of the history and tradition in this country and the jealous guarding of state prerogatives, I do not think this possible currently or in the near future. Yet, it would not be a bad idea at all.

As with equal billing respecting each citizen equally, I think that psychologically, having everyone subject not just to law as we all are now, but every business subject to regulation through one regulatory board creates a sense of equality, not just before the law, but before all regulation as well. Equal opportunity. Equal responsibility.

I also think that making each person and business pay for their regulatory body takes the burden of paying for regulating someone else out of the taxation system and would strike most people as more fair. People can more easily swallow the notion of paying for their own industry rather than using their taxes to regulate someone else's.

The Left Reaction

I think The Left will be more sympathetic, but perhaps believe that I am emphasizing freedom a bit too much and things can get out of control pretty easily.

I would like both sides of this divide to understand that the line of balance between freedom and responsibility is where many if not most of the debates in politics originate anyway and this will not eliminate their argumentative careers by adopting these proposals. This will not end discussions and debates. They will still have things to complain about and fight over. They will not be totally lost in a world without politics.

Law and regulation are complex discussions often if not always. For example, and to put this into stark terms, if we establish 0% tolerance for pollution wouldn't this mean the end to the energy that drives all our cars, tractors and factories? We will have done away with one harm only to create another.

As I said, this book is not a utopian exercise. I cannot in a single bound leap tall conundrums and solve all forthwith. But, in creating a more reasonable system within more reasonable parameters within which that debate can take place, maybe Right and Left can debate the divide between freedom and responsibility democratically ad infinitum, but without the current unnecessary and divisive foolish rancor that we are all getting to know all too well.

Neither complete freedom, nor complete regulation should ever win this debate. Complete freedom for some will eliminate freedom for others; and complete regulation will not allow individual creativity and productivity. Both freedom and responsibility in reasonable balance are necessary for a sane and nurturing society.

I pray, if not daily, then perhaps every couple of weeks, that the discourse of our politics changes from accusation to accommodation and seriousness. Considering the seriousness of possible economic collapse and environmental catastrophe, the terms of debate in the United States requires a toning down of rhetoric and more sober and wiser debate. Listening to the Republican candidates for President in the '12 election, you would think that Barack Obama was the devil incarnate and only wanted to starkly impose government control of all aspects of our lives. It is extreme-ism to the extreme. Yet, who knows what a Democrat stands for anymore either, except to exchange tit for tat.

A new government system of national laws and national regulations, making general policy in relation to regulation and choosing who to carry this out makes who we elect an even more serious democratic business. So, I think it incumbent upon us as voters to choose wisely those who are making the laws and regulations in general, even more important in the system I am proposing because instead of regulations in multiple jurisdictions, I am proposing one set of regulations.

And, if ever, collectively, we decided to have a uniform criminal legal code countrywide, it would make elections even more important. It might simplify law to do so. It would then be the one and only election where citizens have an influence on the law. Perhaps instead of multiples of elections in multiple jurisdictions we would take that one big election even more seriously than we do now.

It is difficult to listen to the present democratic debate without cringing in fear, even for this new system. But who ever said democracy was easy. It is just the fairest way of organizing a society — not the easiest way, just the fairest way.

In any event, so far, I have shrunk government and taxes considerably which The Right should adore. I have also detached social services from government without privatizing them, but democratically socialized them and even reasonably regulated business. Which, perhaps, The Left might adore.

So, next up, an even more important set of ideas that change the economic system, modern Capitalism, in a big democratic way. The change is to democratic economics: Democratic Capitalism. Not Capitalism with a democratic government alongside it, but democracy within Capitalism itself. I believe we can keep the best that Capitalism has to offer — which is considerable — but creatively and democratically modify our economic system in such a way to remove it onerous tendencies — which are considerable too.

Chapter 6
Democratizing Capitalism

To summarize again the current political economic stalemate. It is fairly easy to sense a touch of the old fatalism about our joint economic prospects amongst all but politicians who run for office with a silver-streaked and shiny rhetoric shouting "…well, yes, America has all these unemployment problems that I am surely called upon by God almighty and you, the gullible electorate, to solve" while doing their best Reagan- Clinton-Obama- dare-to-hope-best-days-are-ahead-of-us imitation. Even the petulant, smirking, perpetually self-resurrected Newt Gingrich primps, if oddly, in primetime about a golden future mining the Moon. Not to be outdone, rich man witless Mitt amped up his slicked back hair veneer and pontificated, in his unoriginal and uninspired way, how very inspired we should all be, especially if he were President. Humph.

Although they gesticulate away about the best days and some bloody thing called The Promise of America or The Dream of America or some other reason to believe that material Utopia and The Shining City on the Hill are just around the proverbial corner if we elect them the next great Chief Executive Savior or holy-moly Congress-person, it just seems to be the same old way of making a speech and saying nothing. It is the pro forma thing to say. Be sure to say, politician, "God bless America," too, at the end of each and every speech.

Still, even if America as business John Galt Haven or socialized Michael Moore Graceland is not in our proverbial cards under the present reign of these wound up wonders, there seems to me to be no reason — religious, cosmic, practical, rational or historical — why still we cannot have a social-political-economic system that works and works for everyone and does not go through periodic larger and smaller catastrophes. Oh yes, and we can even make it fair and just.

Our current economics-angst baby has gestated and been midwifed by ever promising politicians making promising promises they could not possibly fulfill because their pitiful platitudinous proposals lack any good sense and sensible exit out of economic and ecological stillbirth. Yet, I think there are ways out of our barrel at the apex of Niagara Falls just before the big down thrust splash.

I know as you know that we all feel the barrel speeding up and hear the great big whooshing sound close below — and it could be a depression that no anti-depressant will numb. Or possibly, we will skate on over the thin ice of this one extended recession and hope the next thaw of economic global warming does not eliminate that skinny layer of surface safety.

Our greatest limitation has been our collective socio-political imagination suppressed by the very economic forces that keep this all intact for the greater good of the lesser and richer part of the community. The directors of these economic forces and their media buddies are sure to preach and teach that the current ideology of this version of Capitalism is eternal, necessary and true. We simply retrace the same social lines right off one social-political-economic cliff or another or swerve and miss another Fiscal Cliff and fuss and fight all kinds of futile battles Left, Right and Center without anyone coming up with any solutions that might do the complete societal job now and in the future. Not that we require that shining hilly city — or in a valley or out there on The Plains — but simply a reasonable and rational society that gets on with the business of living and the living of business without this fuss and bother and repetition of futile political gestures and periodic high unemployment numbers.

Imagine a better world we can. We will just need to do it in a new and rational way taking EVERYONE into account, not merely one party or faction or class or group or religion or another. Simply, what will work for US ALL, regardless.

It is also not obvious to me why we should be so very imaginatively innovative in spontaneously generating iPads and Facebooks and magnetic levitation railways while so very unoriginal in our approach to societal arrangements.

Why can Steve Jobs pop out of his one brain those Pods and Pads and Macs galore and there is not one President or member of Congress who has had a decent idea in decades? It just makes no sense, all the political sound and fury signifying more of the baneful same. I believe that we call this, "the same old, same old." And then again.

Yes, we can, Barack, but what can we do? If we wonder why we are a bit fatigued by good Barack, perhaps this is why. He is so likable, so personable, so intelligent, so reasonable, so apt in so many speeches, so much the perfect man for the job. What is it that he and those Democrats and we along with them and maybe one or two Republicans, what are we going to do that is all so great — even if he did not have a recalcitrant and backwards Republican Congress and no more than maybe one, perhaps but not certainly two Republicans going along? A few more percentage points in tax for the few percentage of the very wealthy? Do we think everything will be rosy posy then? Here a tweak, there a tweak and it all works out? More education for four year olds, not just five year olds? Maybe, maybe not. A few less deductions for the super rich and everything is fine? Really?

What would Mitt have done? God only knows, if God knows, because nobody else does. And even when we got a glimpse, he too proposed nothing particularly new either, except to call it new and "severely conservative." Fifty seven empty pointless points? Mitt's is just a different set of the same old Elephant effluence to the Democrats same old Donkey dung.

It is not the case that I believe that what I have outlined next is the one and only way to go. Nor that there are not lots and lots of tangential proposals related to these proposals that could and should be made. There are gaps that need filling.

But I do believe the set of proposals that follows outlines a general way to go and gets us out of all kinds of dilemmas. It will seem to many of you bloody well impossible. It may be. Although you can be very sure that what we are currently doing cannot and will not be any better. I think, of course, it is much worse and a late hour. Is that a snap, crackle, and maybe a pop or two from the ice cracking and crumbling beneath our feet? Literally, figuratively.

I believe that we need to do far more than, as I have outlined in the preceding chapters, adjust education, medicine, regulation and law to get to a better place, a society that is free, responsible, cooperative and compassionate, as helpful as all that would be.

The laws of economics are not written by either Heaven or Nature, but the result of our social practices and laws, therefore and forever subject to our whim and best judgments. There are no Laws of Economics other than what we make or are the consequence of those makings.

The following chapter is where the rubber hits the road, as we say — especially in America where we have so many of them. What I am proposing is not going to redo all of American society and its rules and roles. It will not and should not dissolve the whole societal shebang and make all obstacles and roadblocks go away and then poof, The Next World Millennium, the Second or Third or Fourth Coming, Jesus, The Buddha and Mohammed coming on high with a host of heavenly non-heathens.

We really and truly do much that is good and right already. A complete overall will not bring us an absolutely new and better day, an extreme utopian fantasy of Left or Right or Center. Instead, in our very own conservative-liberal-preservative way, we might — and I think, should — just and justly adjust the societal terms of endearment and organization. Adjust, not obliterate. Use what we have, but adjust it. Reform and big reform at that but not obliteration.

Human beings of the 20th century in one form or another tried to create A New World Order. They and we, got the biggest disorder and odor — the odor of death — of all political and social times. World Wars I and II. Minor wars, major wars. Genocides. Millions and millions killed, maimed, raped, traumatized.

Let me propose one way of going about adjusting, not a superficial adjusting, but a fundamental adjusting. An adjusting that could work and work for everyone of us. I expect you to critique it, criticize it, and even adjust the adjustments, and, perhaps, add and subtract to it. It is an opening, a hole in the fabric of dystopia, a tunnel and a way out of the Hell of our own making.

Workers and Entrepreneurs Unite!

Ayn Rand in Atlas Shrugged writes a what if story. What if the essential productive entrepreneurs of a society got fed up with government regulation and taxation of businesses, took their expertise and entrepreneurial assertiveness with them and left the societal scene. Bye-bye, CEOs and skilled assistants. It is the equivalent in hierarchal reverse of the general strike of the workers; it is the general strike of the employers.

In the Soviet Union under Stalin and during Mao's "Cultural Revolution" Rand's entrepreneurial class was forced to leave, be marginalized — like her father, a small businessman in Lithuania — or, not infrequently, killed outright. In Rand's novel, frustrated and disgusted by corrupt government interference businessmen leave USA America by choice. It was and would be disastrous for society as a whole and its economic well being in particular either way. Ayn is right and Right there.

Yes, Uncle Joe, Chairman Mao, Comrade Fidel, entrepreneurs are an essential part of society and its economics. They know quite a lot about running businesses and serving consumers, that is, other people. Yes, some of them make too much, but certainly not all of them are greedy or even particularly rich. And we even need the ones who make too much — although we could fix that without losing them. Kill Mao's "running dog capitalists" or, as Stalin did, starve them in the Ukraine or put them on boats to Miami as Castro did and your society will suffer and suffer greatly for a long time. How many died in famines that were the result of Stalin and Mao's policies? Millions died, and not just the classes above the workers and peasants. The worst of it was suffered by workers and peasants.

Entrepreneurs have expertise that you do not want to needlessly throw away by, as in Mao's Cultural Revolution, sending them to worthless "re-education" down on the peasants' communal farms, or as in Stalin's exile and murder of factory owners and managers and then peasant kulaks in Ukraine. Entrepreneurs know what products the public wants, they know how to sell them and they know how to organize a factory to produce those products. They may even flat out invent the product.

If an entrepreneur does not do all this, who will? A commissar, a revolutionary guard? And then, who do they become? An autocratic entrepreneur of sorts all over again! At worst, they become a non-enterprising authoritarian bureaucrat who does not know what they are doing and ruins it all. Authoritarian Communism, not just Capitalism, contains its own contradictions and demise.

Yet, dear Ms. Rand and followers, Maggie Thatcher, Ronnie Reagan, Newt Gingrich, Mr. Ryan, essential too are the workers who do the work for the entrepreneurs. They are just as important. When they go out on strike, disgusted with the terms of employment be it with wages or lay-offs, tired of being treated as object rather than as a person, the profit from their work confiscated by the capitalist when it is rightly belongs to them, there can be no production.

The assembly line stops either way as in Atlas Shrugged or A General Strike in Spain in the 1930's. If there is no body available to work for you, entrepreneur, you cannot make any thing and therefore, any or most of or all the money.

Communists and Capitalist apologists alike confuse organizational function with its meaning. You cannot do without certain roles and tasks within productive organizations. This is function.

However, this does not mean that the people who occupy the role space within the social entity need necessarily own the enterprise and keep most of the fruits of the labors of the laborers and the machinery that they labor upon or that they, as boss, get to boss around laborers as wage slaves. This is displaced meaning.

Nor, does it mean that you should kill off or socially and economically marginalize those with the appropriate expertise to create and run productive companies. Nor does it mean that you put all enterprise into the hands of the patronizing and barely competent Communist governments, instead of giving the workers ownership of the means of production and watch the state fade away, as Marx would have had it, by the way. The Marxists in state Communistic power betrayed Marx and the working class in general in a big way.

Marx — and Emma Goldman (Mother Jones) — has more in common with Michele Bachman and Grover Norquist than either would ever believe — with a boat load of Anarchists and Anarchist writers besides. All talk about the "withering away of the state," if for different reasons and in a different way.

It is not, to my mind, the Capitalists nor the Communist Soviets that owns or should own the company and get to do what they want only subject only to the economists' Law of Supply and Demand or the dictates of The Politburo. Companies are social entities, not private or state entities. Companies are not private property or government property. Companies are social property and they should be controlled and governed appropriately.

Companies should be under the direction of the people who work in the company — including the entrepreneur — and the local community within which the company is embedded.

A person, an individual, an entrepreneur may own "the means of production," that is, the machinery itself, but an individual cannot own a company which itself is a collection of people. It is possible to own things, but a company is social organization and that belongs to the collection of individuals who are the society of the company and the society within which the company is irretrievably imbedded.

"Life, liberty and property," yes. "Life, liberty and company," no.

In social enterprises, company entrepreneurs need workers; company workers need entrepreneurs. And we all, in community, need both. We really get nowhere one without the other. The question is: what are good and workable terms of endearment instead of hostility and class warfare?

And then, how can we make laws and rules for a cooperative economy to prevent: stock market collapses, recessions and depressions, or high unemployment or too big a spread of wealth between a small upper class and a mass of poor without trashing the whole enterprise? Is any reasonable arrangement of society possible that wholly works and is completely fair besides? I think it possible just not under present arrangements.

Capitalism, Hero & Villain

We already have laws and rules that structure this version of a Capitalist economy, the multitudinous regulations of economic law, and even the law called The Law of Supply and Demand — that is not a formal law at all but simply the mechanism derived from the establishment of laws and rules that regulate social economics. There are more than a few laws and rules, anti-trust laws and such, sometimes effective, sometimes lax, sometimes overly stringent, that are in place to make sure, make very sure, that The Law of Supply and Demand stays in force in all areas of the economy rather than, say, The Rule of Monopoly.

I would like to suggest here some fundamental changes in the rules to modify the system of Capitalism in such a way that its outcomes are both righteous, democratic, sustainable and palatable to all, even as we get to keep Capitalism's dynamism. While the economic system of Capitalism has been a great boon through its many incarnations since about the 1600's, it has also generated problems of enormous consequence: depressions, wars colonial and territorial, and then, too, exploitation and poverty, even gross stinking poverty and deprivation — Manchester in the 1830's — and, oh yes, not coincidentally extreme environmental degradation and climate change on the way to catastrophe. It is, as we say, a two edged sword. I would like to take some of the bloody bite out of Capitalism's negative cutting edge without cutting out its cutting edge innovative productivity.

I am certainly and hardly alone in reacting and proposing solutions to the up and down sides of Capitalism. There is an extensive literature, a virtual and palpable and readable library of literature, coterminous with Capitalism, in reaction to the Yin and the Yang, the ups and the downs, the productivity and the destructiveness, the winners and the losers, the positive and the negative effect on owners, workers, bystanders and willing and unwilling participants of this economic system. These commentators and revolutionaries and apologists include but certainly are not limited to: Adam Smith, Marx and Engels, John Stuart Mill, Charles Dickens, Matthew Arnold, Bryon and Shelley, Sinclair Lewis, Lenin, Schumpeter, Hayek, Ayn Rand, Margaret Thatcher, Marcuse, Fromm, Bookchin, a plethora of intellectuals and then ordinary non-intellectual types, writing, marching, crying, shouting, all about the outrageous social steam-coal-gasoline-jet-socio-economic engine called "Capitalism."

While Capitalism has had many variations and incarnations, forms and turns of fortune, two other social partners it has been married to from its beginnings are: science and machines. It is not that Capitalism could not survive without science and machinery and that science and machinery could not survive without Capitalism but they have been coupled from the beginning and each has contributed mightily to the other — mightily. While they do appear tied together at the proverbial hip, they are not exactly.

A great deal of the prosperity of the Capitalist system is actually the prosperity created by science and technology, that is, the machines. Not that the Capitalist economic system has not promoted the productivity advantages of machines. In fact, the Capitalist economic machine has been in many ways the engine of the engines.

Still and all, I believe that we can have this grand productivity and reasonably reform the economic-political-social system, keeping the best that machines have to offer, keeping the best that the old Capitalist system has to offer organizationally and motivationally and at the same time, promoting the best for all of us instead of just a small minority of the sometimes silly and frivolous, the sometimes mean spirited and nasty, certainly the almost always greedy and self-centered, The 1%, Mighty Mitt's Multi-millionaire Minions.

Consistent with my radical democratic leanings, I want to make the Capitalist system far more democratic than it is, while still retaining its best aspects. Capitalism's best includes rewarding hard work, innovation, productivity, rationality and ambition.

Yet, what I will propose is not simple and easy reform; it is more than a bit radical and democratic revolutionary. To my mind, it is a continuation of the radical democratic revolutions that began with our American Revolution. In fact, the idea of democratic Capitalism instead of its present mildly authoritarian form — and its even more authoritarian form in China and elsewhere— is a further continuation and expansion of the American Revolution beyond politics, an extension into today's economics.

Perhaps you do not think that the corporations at the center of The System are authoritarian and oligarchic? At least in politics, in government, we get to elect the knaves and fools and the occasional wise Lincoln, Washington, Jefferson, or Obama President. Moreover, every couple of years, we may recall the congressional politician who proves incompetent or worse. Of course, incompetence is in the eye of the beholder, but that is the point. Perceive a problem with your representative and you may vote against them. Not so in corporations. If you are a worker in a company with incompetent management, you are stuck with them.

There is some democracy within businesses and corporations. It is the democracy of an elect and wealthy few, really — elected by wealth, as it were. And even then, if the head of the company controls or owns the majority of stock in their company, there is even less democratic control. With their wealth, they elect themselves. It is very few companies — there are some — that are democratically controlled by all the workers in the company. Companies are medieval manors by other means.

In American politics power flows from down to up and back down again, from the people who elect their representatives and back down to the people in the form of laws and regulations, benefits and services and much else. In Capitalist corporations, there is precious little bottom up. The vast majority of decisions are only top down: the company ordering its staff to do this, do that, make this, sell that. It is either do our bidding or see you later, you are out of a job. "The real world," we call it. They decide what they will pay you as a wage or salaried slave for your compliance with their demands. Bosses give orders, eh?

We may have a democratic polity but we do not have a democratic economy. Only as a consumer do you have some democratic choice in what you buy. As a producer, you have precious little democratic choice. You take orders, more or less, usually less if you are further up the hierarchy, more if you are lower down in the company.

Need you guess who decides what salary you are to receive as compensation? Not much to wonder: someone above you in the hierarchy. And above them, someone decides their compensation and so on. So then, is it any surprise that those at the top of the corporate food chain get the choice and biggest pieces of the best meats, most of the meat, on the corporate profit menu?

As an employee, you are told when to arrive and when to go, maybe how to dress, maybe what to say and with what demeanor, what to do and not do and so forth and on and on. How many employees tell the CEO when to arrive, when to leave, how to dress, how to talk, what to do? You get the idea. I am sure you know the drill although for the most part we try to forget.

This is all not to imply that companies in the future should allow employees to arrive when they want, dress the way they want, say and do what they want and with what demeanor. A job needs to get done and it is the business of the management to coordinate its getting done by telling workers what to do and how.

Still and all, Japanese companies have outdone American companies in the past and even in the present because they listened to worker input about how to get the job done better. It is not only management that understands what is best; employees can as well.

And in the most modern era, there is some leeway for high tech employees who need to be attracted to work at particular companies rather than go to their rivals; and comfortable and congenial work conditions are a product of that competition.

Yet, who is in ultimate control of the company and makes essential decisions, like salary differentials and the terms of work in a company, maybe that should be, as in politics, from below to above and then back down and then back up again and so forth, instead of just top down, period.

I think the Capitalist system is in need of rebalancing and democratizing. So here are my proposals, first in outline form with some of the benefits of these changes and then I will try to explain more fully.

But then, of course, there are those who will think that, "oh no, here we go as with the politicization of social services. Isn't it bad enough that we have to listen to all that political garbage during elections, now there will be more political garbage, more, more even at work..." I sympathize.

Democracy is messy and can deteriorate — indeed, has deteriorated — into shouting matches and irrationality, as we now well know. The alternative is one or another authoritarian way of doing and I would prefer even a democratic mess to a clean and neat authoritarian debacle. Personal preference. After all, I am an American. The brown dirt here is democratic — ask the Iroquois before us.

So now for the next set of ideas. What comes next is the reorientation, balancing out, adjustments of the Capitalist system itself. Here we go out of the frying pan of government, taxes and social services and into the fire of economics. Hold on to your heat shields, citizens. However wonkish and geekish these proposals may be, they add up to a restructuring of society and economics that is nothing less than revolutionary, democratic revolutionary. Democracy here. Democracy there. Democracy, democracy everywhere. I really have faith in us all. And to my mind and I hope yours too, democracy across the societal board is a Human Right.

Companies

• The Board of Directors, the controlling group in all companies and corporations, will consist of representatives:

— from the investors, i.e. the societal Community Bank (see below): 50% and

— from those who work in the company — including workers and management: 50%.

Democratic election by all employees of their representatives. Representatives from the employees may choose their representatives at periodic intervals (one to four years) at a company town hall style participatory democratic meeting. At these meetings, employees may, after open discussion, instruct their representatives as to their wishes for the next period at the company.

- Companies may fail. Companies may succeed. It is the Capitalist way.
- Founders of companies have the right to be the CEO and Chairperson of the Board of Directors of the company for its first 10 years.
- After 10 years even the head of the company is elected by its Board of Directors and need not be the founder.
- Profits are paid out 1/2 to the community bank, 1/2 equally to all who work in the company
- Investment loans are not repaid to the Community Bank. Capitalization from community banks requires no payment either on principle or interest of loan, because capitalization is not a loan, but constitutes part ownership and therefore, deserves only a share of profit (50%) as long as the company exists.
- Wages are absolutely required to be at least at "living wage." A minimum wage for full time work is a "living wage."

A "living wage" should be understood as sufficient to keep a family of four at a reasonable level of well- being. Two adults working should not be necessary to keep two children and two adults solvent. If both adults want to work and have double a "living wage" and more, that is their choice.

- Wages need not be equal. The Board of Directors decides on whatever the differential. Profits are distributed equally; there is no differential re. profit.

Skill and productivity should still be rewarded in pay differences.

- Wage and salary differential from top to bottom may be no greater than a set percentage, e.g, from high to low @100 to one, so that the lowest wage is 1/100 of the top salary. Maximum differential is set by governmental law or regulation. Board of Directors may decide on a more egalitarian differential but not one that is more unequal than the law allows.

• By law, there will be set a maximum salary at a certain to amount, say for example, $1,000,000 per year. Shared profit is not calculated in this figure.

• Smaller companies, say of one or two entrepreneurs and just a few underling employees can be organized without a Board of Directors. They might not require a Board of Directors but could be administered more by direct participatory democracy.

Ownership of company where you work still applies.

Advantages

There are, to my mind, many advantages that if these proposals were adopted society-wide would accrue. I will list just some of these now and then comment in a longer discussion after several more sets of proposals concerning the economy.

I am certain that you can come up with even more as you think about these.

- Far less tendency for companies to relocate to the far reaches of the world for cheap labor, not with a Board of Directors coming from the immediate community and those who work in the company.

- As ownership and the profits of companies is now in the hands of those who work in the company and the community, workers and community are far more committed to company success. This can result in better work from workers and cooperation from communities

- The Free Market still disciplines companies with all its competition advantages: better, cheaper products, greater efficiency and all that. (Read Adam Smith or talk with your local Economics professor for more highlights.) The advantages of competition hold. Of course, there are those among us, myself included, who would wish that competition was not part of the human mix and that if we all out of the goodness of our beings cooperated we could work it out even better. But give Capitalism and Adam Smith and his followers their due. Somehow competition does work efficiently and effectively, even if there are problems and gross flaws too.

- Initiator founders of companies are still rewarded with control of their companies. They cannot be forced out from under their ideas and initiative by democratic shenanigans, at least for ten years. At that point, they will have to deal with it like everyone else. This encourages initiative but then requires cooperation, too. See the Steve Jobs bio and his ins and outs at Apple.

- While this system is not totally egalitarian, the gross inequalities possible in present Capitalist society are alleviated. There is incentive to work harder and more efficiently and effectively, and therefore rise in the company and get paid more, but the tendency of the system to create social strife through unfair distributions of income is alleviated to a great extent.

- Alienation, that is, being treated as an object at work is over. Everyone, in terms of ownership, if not salary, is on an equal footing and receives equal profit. Psychologically as well as materially, there is a difference between working for the company or for yourself. You are now working with others all together rather than under the boss.

Jobs

• All individuals in the entire society are guaranteed a job or a living wage.

• If there are no jobs available, capital from coordinating banks — state, federal, world — should flow into an undercapitalized region to create more companies to create more employment or to create appropriate and needed infrastructure projects.

• If the unemployed individual is unemployed not for lack of capital but for lack of work ethic, lack of skill, or other problem, this individual should be directed to a training center. Funds for these kinds of centers will come from a percentage of funds for this purpose from the community banks and/or from the educational system.
If an employee loses a job through lack of skill, they may simply avail themselves of education from the lifetime free education system.

In either scenario, they should be paid a living wage while being educated and trained.

• For start up entrepreneurs or artists or anyone who need time to formulate an enterprise or career, who are not yet employed or cannot be employed in the usual manner, special funds should be set aside to temporarily fund the entrepreneur while planning an enterprise or perhaps permanently fund the artist bringing beauty to the world.

Of course, such dispensation much be applied for, but that the society should fund activity that is of great benefit, but is not immediately related to work or will never be part of the money economy. Still, as with Michelangelo and his works but oh so many other artists of all kinds — including Ayn Rand's architect in Fountainhead — we would all benefit.

• For the first two years after childbirth, all women should be given two years off at full pay, paid for not by the business but by the banking system, part of the unemployment insurance fund. Their same job is guaranteed returned to them after those two years.

This is pretty much the way they do it in France and I applaud them for it. In addition, they supply child care after two years. In the system as I am describing it, remember: free child care is available for two year olds. Fathers, if that is the choice of a family, could take the place of the mother to care for a child for two years instead.

And remember, too, that if mother or father wants to stay at home beyond two years, the other spouse will still be working a job at a living wage for four people. Although, in this case, a second wage from insurance would terminate after 2 years.

Would a woman who had not been employed before childbirth be given the two years of minimum living wage? How about the father of the child? Maybe. This could be a society wide political discussion.

• If there simply is no way to employ an individual because of lack of ability of any kind, disability funds at a living wage are paid out through the coordinated banking system that sets aside funds for this purpose, too.

• Temporary unemployment that is a function of lay-offs because there is not enough work at a company or because the company has closed compensates individuals at their previous wage until the individual gets a new job at the same or another company. They are compensated at their previous wage.

Again, these insurances come from Community Bank profits.

• If unemployment lasts longer than one year, a public infrastructure job should be offered.

• Those who quit a job because they do not fit well with a particular company or they do not like the kind of work in which they are employed or for other personal reasons, provided they have worked at the company for one year receive unemployment funds at the same rate as those laid off. There should be, however, a limit to the number of times — 3, 4, 5? — in one lifetime an individual may quit different jobs and receive one year of comparable wages. After these number of times is exhausted, they will not be eligible for unemployment compensation for a year, but only an infrastructure job.

• There should be infrastructure construction and service jobs made available when there is no private system work available or the person lacks skills that would be needed by any private enterprise.

Again, these jobs will come from money allocated from the community banking system.

• Those who have left a job because of layoffs or quit and desire retraining of course receive free education. They also may receive full unemployment benefits for a longer period of time if the training is longer than one year.

• If a person does not want to work, but is perfectly able to work, no guaranteed living wage will be offered. Not to let anyone starve, but if you in no way shape or form can hack the world of work, you can always head out for "the territory ahead," and if there is room enough in the wilderness for you, (see chapter on The Four Zones) you are free to be a rugged individualist and make it on your own. Otherwise, everyone is expected to contribute. You must put out sometime to get back sometime. Fair is fair.

• Everyone is required to give two years of service work. One year is required before the age of 30. One year is required after the age of 50. Service work is determined by the needs of society as determined by the national government. All citizens in service work will receive the same wage (but not profit shares) at the rate of their previous year of employment, that is, the same rate as full unemployment compensation. However, money for compensation shall be paid by the national government and factored into the bill that all citizens receive from the government for the cost of government.

As infrastructure projects will be covered by the banking system, the national government will most likely ask for work in: the military – either national or international — and the police, the criminal justice system, i.e. at prisons and in rehabilitation of criminals, the judicial system (e.g. a juror for a year) and other similar positions. Naturally, if anyone objects to any of these jobs, especially the military or police that involve coercion or violence, they will be offered a different position.

Advantages

The jobs problems of recessions and depressions where many are out of work is over. Everyone who can and wants to work has a job or is compensated by insurance. Forget the monthly unemployment figures. And even if you are unemployed you are covered. Everyone is in fact covered.

As advantages go, this is BIG!

This is a kind of ultimate social security and the elimination of fear and anxiety over making a living. You might feel fear and anxiety about where you place is in the social strata or what goodies you can buy, but you need not fear that you will be out on the street and cannot eat.

Of course, you have to be willing to work, but that is the deal living on the planet. Either you secure your sustenance through some means of employment, whether it is hunter gathering, farming or another kind of production or not and you starve. But you are guaranteed to not starve and to be able to afford necessities if you are willing to put out and put up with work.

Society, that is, all of us, do not lose the productive work when some of us — and it could be a high percentage — are out of work. It may not be productivity in a consumer goods company, but infrastructure work. As everyone is employed there is no drop off of production at any one time.

Banks & Stock Markets

• Banks are not and cannot be privately owned

• The fundamental unit of banking is comprised of The Community Banks that are democratically owned, not by the government, but by the general population per community.

• Community Banks have annual town hall style meetings at regular intervals (one to four years) where all members of the community elect their bank representatives — the Board of Directors of the bank — and express their wishes to their representatives after thorough discussion.

• Banks dispense the one and only source of investment capital, either initial capital or capital to fund expansion(s).

• No stock markets and no private investments. No money making on money.

• No bond markets. No government debt whatsoever. (Paying off the present debt will be a pain in the butt for awhile, but then after this is done, there is no more debt allowed by the government, period.)

• No money markets. NO SPECULATION. Again, NO MONEY MAKING MONEY!

• No private investment companies. (Bain is out. Mitt is poor. Poor, poor Mitt.)

• Commodities markets are reorganized: no speculation, only a place for retailers to buy from wholesalers.

• Community Banks are local, that is, by town or county, but there are also coordinating banks that are state-wide and then country-wide and then world-wide whose directors are elected state-wide and nationally and then internationally by vote from the Community Banks' Boards of Directors.

• The function of more general banks is to regulate and oversee local banks and coordinate the distribution of capital over a wider geographic field

• Banks are responsible for all unemployment and disability insurances.

• Banks are responsible for infrastructure project funding and choice.

• Infrastructure is reimbursed to the community banks by rents or other means, from whoever is using the infrastructure either as business or consumer.

Again, Advantages

We are far less likely to have booms and busts and over speculation. There are no stock markets, bond markets, no bank gambling on derivatives — whatever those were, invented by Harvard and Yale physicists for their own enrichment — speculation making money, gambling making money.

Banks are not only regulated by bank regulators but by the public in elections. (As are educational and medical institutions, by the way. There should even be government oversight by a regulatory agency as well to assure the ethical conduct of politicians — not politicians regulating themselves.)

Democratic community control at the center of the Capitalist system gives everyone a greater stake in the whole system. The banking system runs in the interest of everyone instead of a small group of individuals who could try to game the system, as some have.

Wealth is now more legitimate: you can only make your fortune from work and productivity not from gambling. Only money for work, not money making money. Innovation and productivity is then valued more than gambling with money. (I cannot almost say this enough times.)

- Vast fortunes for individuals cannot be made at the expense of the community of everyone. That includes commodities speculators, investment speculators, bond speculators, money market speculators, but also greedy

CEOs who keep it all for themselves and a few greedy cronies. Gone.

- As community banks control all investment and the community democratically controls the banks, the kinds of business that get funding is now far more under the control of local communities. "Bottom lines" and profit motive do not disappear, but communities and community banks might not see only bottom lines and making more and more money at the expense of environments and the community itself as most important. Maybe. At least if a company is guilty of ruining a community in one way or another, the community must take responsibility for facilitating and sponsoring the company.

Of course some communities might collectively lie to themselves and justify miscreant behaviors, putting profit before people. Cover-ups can happen on a larger scale, but I think it a bit more difficult than when it is an individual or a small corporate group of individuals. Would the city of Detroit have put up with the Ford of exploding gas tank fame and its cover-up? Perhaps. But then again, there were workers in Detroit driving Pintos.

A Short Summary

What does this all add up to? We will still have companies. We will still have laws. We will still have entrepreneurship. Everyone is taken care of reasonably well. There is freedom. There is responsibility. And, yes, there is democracy all around. I am quite sure in reading these ideas that you can think of more advantages than I have. Still, let me provide some foundation and more for all this, that there is some reasonable logic and rightness behind it before you either adapt this or dismiss it out of your mind and sights. This is still change and big change at that.

I may not be willing or able to go into detail about each and every one of these ideas, again that is a whole book if not several, but I can give some background and justification now for some of it. I would like to explain though some of the underlying justification for these proposals that translate what I believe is a Capitalist system that is neither democratic nor conforms to my idea of what I believe is a fundamental human right to democratically control all the institutions within which we all live.

THE WISEACRE'S JUSTIFICATIONS:
The Beautiful Beatific of Profit

As William Greider, one of the editors of The Nation magazine, taught me years ago: the genius of Capitalism is profit and profit reinvested. Reinvestment from profit is as important to the full throttled engine of the Capitalist system as the now ubiquitous internal combustion engine is to machinery.

Yet for me, profit is the only monies I believe it is legitimate to regulate; and profit, I think, is the only monies that should be distributed not to individual entrepreneurs and individual investors, but socially. By this I mean: to all employees, including the entrepreneur but excluding private investors and to the one and only Community Bank investor.

Why? And then how does this all work? And why will it work? And then, why is this so important and why is this the change of all changes, the leveraged revolutionary lever of change? Why is how we deal with profit so bloody important?

Profit is a kind of illusion, a grand sleight of hand, a sparkling Midas touch of social magic. When you make a profit in business and put those proceeds in your bank account it surely is not a figment of an un-oiled addled brain. It is not illusory in the sense that it is not there. No. It is clearly there. Yet in another sense, it is a made up fiction as many of society's best ideas are — as are all of societies' thoughts and rules, for better and worse. (Undergraduate sociology at N.Y.U. does teach you that.)

Profit is not equivalent to the cost of the production of some product, cost being the combination of the combined cost of the material of the product and how much workers have labored over and shaped it into a useful thing-a-ma-jig — an iPhone or a food processor, a scooter or a toilet seat, et al, infinitum. If goods were sold at cost, that is, what it cost to simply make them, every last item would be cheaper. But then they would also generate no profit whatsoever.

While in one sense, a sense that is of fairness and balance, selling goods at what they cost to make is just and balanced; in another sense doing business this way has no social and economic dynamic. It is stagnant. As long as, socially and economically speaking, you do not mind walking in place, everything is just fine. You are just not getting anywhere as in what we now call "The Dark Ages." Of course, on the other hand, you are probably not wrecking the planet, nor overworked, stressed out and miserable generally. But then again, would you be able to play Dungeons and Dragons on your new iPad or reheat your quiche in that neato Samsung microwave or wash your clothes in a Maytag automatic washing machine? And even more essentially, would there be enough food, clothing and shelter around for everyone? Perhaps not. "The Dark Ages" were not a gay old time either and not just for lack of light bulbs and the bright lights of Broadway. After the fall of Rome, for hundreds of years in Europe, there was population shrinkage due to, among other factors, lack of food, due to, among other factors, lack of innovation in the technology of plows.

Still, as I have said throughout, I think we can keep our technological cake and munch it too.

By the way, you hardly ever pay for just the cost of just making the goods to begin with. There is the packaging and shipping, advertising and displaying and all those other activities factored into what you pay for one item or another, whether it be a Mazda Miata or a stalk of crunchy celery. If all the other costs were eliminated, that is, the cost of advertising and packaging, and all that was left were the necessary costs of making the goods and shipping them to you, the products you bought would not only be even cheaper, but ghastly vastly cheaper. Pennies on the dollar, as we say.

The method of Capitalism, of supply and demand Capitalism, the spellbinding secretive method is that you will pay more than the cost of production and all that rest of costs combined. Of course, a company that charged you less than all those costs will lose money and go out of business forthwith. Not too many of those around; they are gone.

A company that charges you more than the cost of what it took to get that thing to you will make what we call "a profit." They are still around and some, especially some of the very big ones, are thriving and awash, splashing and sloshing around in the social psychological economic miracle of "profit."

In a competitive system of buyers and sellers, that is, The Market, entrepreneurs and their companies do not simply charge what they please. They may be in competition with other companies for your hard earned buck. And you might or might not be willing or able to spend so much on any one item. So while businesses try to do what is called maximize profits this is not done in isolation, nor are there no controls nor rules on their maximizing and maneuvering for profit. This is called "market forces," or sometimes called "The Law of Supply and Demand," or "market discipline." Ask any salesperson, stressed out on the showroom floor, about "market forces" or "market discipline." They know it first hand and ulcer.

For all the ins and outs of how this system works in detail there are umpteen economic texts and books to fill you in on the comings and goings of Capitalism and markets, supply and demand, from Adam Smith to Milton Friedman and Mr. Samuelson, F.A. Hayek, Mr. Schumpeter, et al. I will not go into all that here.

I just want to point out that one aspect, and a neglected aspect I think it is, of profits, of the very nature of profit itself, that profit is a result of more than the product is worth. It is a quite lovely fiction, my dear. Profit is accrued from what I can get from you for it, over and above what it cost me in time and labor and every thing else to make it and get it to you and get you to buy it. Amazing. Genius.

Looked at from a different and more jaundiced perspective, one might call "profit": theft — sly theft, but theft, nonetheless. We do not talk about this too much, if at all, because quite frankly it is a bit of an embarrassment. It need not be. It is the fuel for that robust engine that moves a dynamic economic system. Andrew Carnegie does not retire to a golf course mansion in Northern Scotland without it. There is more than likely no iPhone without it.

And now, here is where the real engine of Capitalism, the real genius rocket ship flying to the monetary stratosphere and beyond of Capitalism gets it fuel. The entrepreneur takes this illusion, this fiction, this "profit," this quasi-theft and reinvests it in more machinery, more company and produces more goods and tries to make those goods better and then makes them more and more efficiently, lowering the cost of production and then again and again selling this increase in production as goods — are goods, a good thing? — to you and making more and more "profit," which in turn, theoretically, gets reinvested and reinvested in more and more production. We are ever so inundated in cheap goods in great numbers and the entrepreneurs who make more and more "profit" get richer and richer, skimming off some of this now great big "profit," not just for more production, but for themselves.

Hence, from horses and buggies to planes, trains and automobiles, from the Gutenberg Press to Kindles, from shouting at the top of your lungs to be heard across a field to iPhones heard around the planet, the Capitalist world, according to its present ethos, is sheer productive genius. Phew, it is exhausting just to think about it even as we breathe the exhaust of its machines, even as the owners of the means of production skim a greater and greater percentage and absolute money amount from the profit system.

As Adam Smith wrote: it works. Capitalism produces.

Capitalism grows. Ah, and it is from such beautiful creative fictive theft! Business takes the money that you pay for things, more money than it takes to bring you those things, and then tries to make more and more things and then more and more money to make more and more things to make more and more money. Gorgeous.

Yet, here is the fly in the richly oiled ointment. Profit is only a social fiction, not eternal veritas. We must all in some sense agree to the system of "free markets" and "supply and demand" and" profit" for it to work. We agree to the story, the fabrication, the illusion, the mythology. It seems of benefit.

Yet, think about it. Think about this: it is your money. Your money, spent on a product, is going to enrich a small group of entrepreneurial individuals because you accept the terms of The System, however unconscious you are of the terms themselves. It is a social contract alright, albeit one you never sign or are all that aware of.

Why is the profit theirs and not yours? How do they get to sell their products for more than they cost to make? Again, in some sense, we all agree to this — but only in some sense. Your money gets invested into more productivity, which, in the end, you may benefit by, too. Of course, those who make the profit, then reinvest that profit — which is, again, your money — they will reap even greater benefit than you who give your money over for this.

And they, the entrepreneurs, are very proud of it all. Ask Ms. Ayn Rand, flaunting her diamond bat broach. Ask the ego of Donald Trump. Quite proud and not a bit overly self centered — and congratulations to me and mine. To my mind, more than a little bit too proud, and then greedy too. With your money! It is your money that enriched Ayn and Donald and Mitt and the 1%. It is your money and their use of it that produces the profit that grows The System; and yet, they are the one's who benefit the most by far.

It seems far more rational and far fairer to me if given that the fiction of "profit" is a social fiction, if "profit" went to whom it really belongs: to society, that being that collection of individuals that make up society, that being all of us who paid in excess for all those goods and, also, and especially to those, not just the one entrepreneur, the actual people who worked to make the product. That is why I believe the one aspect of the economic system that society has a right to get its hands on is "profit" but "profit" only; and why, I believe, the factual producers, the workers, deserve some of the profit as well as the entrepreneur.

Profit through The Community Banks still gets reinvested in more enterprises and production. We get to keep the growth genius of The Capitalist System. And profit distributed to all those who work in the company gets spent by more than a few at the top. That would increase consumer demand which would grow the economy even more. We keep the genius of profit, Capitalist profit but make it fair.

I do not think society or government has a right to tax your work or your property. I believe in Locke's formulation that you have an inherent right to "life, liberty and property." Yet, work and property are not a social fiction the way profit is. They are yours and you have every right to keep them. Society may have a right to bill you for services provided to you, but it has no right to take away part of your work or part of your property in taxes.

"Profit," though, a social fiction, a wonderful lie and theft, now all of us have some rights to that. Yet, why do only the entrepreneurs get to keep "profit," our money? In a sense, we have agree that they do. By law they do. By now, after several hundred years of it, it seems quite natural, as natural and eternal and right as slavery did a couple of hundred years ago; although, both are social fictions and artificial, — if quite real, that is, in the sense that it is real social practice. Drowning in all this material productive fecundity, we seem to agree to it forthwith, maybe even with enthusiasm of varying degrees.

Yet, I believe we can keep the productive forces of Capitalism going and Capitalism itself going but with a set of substantial modifications that will allow it to be fairer and more sustainable. I think "profit" is too good a fiction to give up. I really do believe it is worth it to keep it. Still, a little change in the rules and maybe we can keep the entrepreneurial spirit without many of Capitalism's downturns and downsides, its injustices and excesses. Entrepreneurs will still get to keep some "profit" and some "profit" gets to get plowed back into more productivity, as it should, but "profit" itself, as itself, given that it comes from the collective us, should also in greater part be returned in part to all, workers and community and not just an entrepreneurial individual. The workers made the product that the community paid too much for. Workers and community, with all fairness, should get back what is rightfully theirs, even as entrepreneurs get to keep what is rightly theirs.

Of course, the first step onto a righteous Capitalist sidewalk is to get up and over the bumpy illusion, to see "profit" for what it truly is; and then, understanding the nature of "profit" we may use it usefully rather than as now oppressively. It is our creative fiction; we can do with it as we please. If God or Gods or Spirits gave it to us the way it is now, well, that might be another thing entirely. If it were part of the order of the Universe, the way it is now, well, I might think differently about it. But the idea of "profit" is from us, not from Heaven or from the heavens.

Everyone in the company, all workers and managers as well as the entrepreneur, and then the investors in the company, the members of the community represented in the bank that does all investing, The Community Bank, I believe, truly own the company. This is not the current paradigmatic manner of looking at companies. I am proposing a new way of seeing ownership, a new paradigm of Capitalism: Community Democratic Capitalism — if you want to give it a new name.

We are not returning "profit" directly to the consumer who has made profit possible by paying more than the cost of production. We are not doing away with "profit." "Profit" is simply too valuable to do away with. We are not Communists, heaven thank goodness. But we are distributing "profit" in a much fairer, righteous and more socially conscious manner.

In the new Community Democratic Capitalism model, 1/2 of profits are distributed equally to the workers of the company from top to bottom, including management and the entrepreneur, 1/2 goes back to the Community Bank. The Community Bank, whose directors are elected by the citizens of each community, can expand and create other enterprises so that everyone who wants to will have work and the means to support themselves and their families.

Not only does this seem far more fair to workers and the community than our current system of privately owned companies with private distant individual or private distant bank investors, but it provides for those working in the company more incentive for the company to do well. Everyone in each company has a stake in the company.

And, beautiful energizing "profit" still goes for expansion of enterprise, right back into investment, instead of to excessive compensation to rich investors and profligate CEOs who live a lavish lifestyle out of all proportion of decency and economic justice.

Are Tea Party-ers groaning and grumbling now? Is Ayn turning over in her grave? What would Newt and Perry and Romney and Bachman and Cain and Mr. Ryan, et al, say now? They could well say, "the company is mine, we own it, it is private property; you are stealing our property! Thief!"

I believe contrary to Republican conservatism, that every worker in every company has a Human Right to be a part owner of the company they work in and as much right to just compensation for work as anyone else in the company and a share of the profit of the company. I also do not believe that companies and corporations are private individual property. Nor do I believe that who consider themselves to "own" the company and in their greedy little minds believe that they own the rights to your labor, have a right to decide for themselves to take what is yours, not theirs.

Why is it that a select few own the company and give themselves the pick of the fruits of the labor of everyone in the company? What right do they have to "own" the company and then possess in turn the product of the labor of others? It was not just Marx who pointed out that this might not be right. "Property is theft," was not first declared by Karl, but by Pierre-Joseph Proudhon; and the cry was taken up by many — many! Just as I do not see or understand why the government thinks it has a right to your labor in the form of taxes, neither do I see why a select group of "property owners" in a company has a right to decide the compensations in a company or to whom the profits accrue. It is a theft that, unlike the productive genius of profit theft, creates many problems. There is theft and then there is theft.

Companies are social entities, not material property. Therein lies the difference. You should be able to own material property, a machine, a couch, a child's toy. Owning a social company though means owning other people, the labor of other people. NO!

Of course, there is disagreement about all this. They are still screaming "thief" and perhaps even now throwing this book against the nearest wall.

Any conventional economists worth his academic and Adam Smith-ian salt will tell you that the basis for ownership of companies is a kind of gambling. One works hard, accumulates a little or a great deal of extra money and then invests that money in a new enterprise, a company, a kind of gamble that through invention and hard work and the entrepreneurial spirit will turn into ye olde "profit" and money will multiple. So it is not like lottery gambling with long odds and no social benefit or productivity whatsoever, but it is productive gambling and one is hedging one's bet with economic intelligence and the spirit of Capitalism.

Capitalist myth contains the following items: saving, judicious gambling, enterprise, inventiveness, productivity, profit and on and on and again. And some of the time, as with Bill Gates and Steve Jobs in their respective garages, it is true. And some of the time, as in three generations after John Rockefeller made his gargantuan fortune in Standard Oil, his great grandchildren are not gambling in that same sense on new and innovative enterprises nor are many CEOs of major corporations.

Still, left out of this myth and equation are those who work for the gambling innovative entrepreneur. They might not gamble with their money on the new company; they might not have any extra money, neither born into wealth as the latter day Rockefellers, nor do they possess an excess of wit and a certain kind of intelligence as Jobs or Gates. Still, they gamble their time, their labor and their lives on working at the Rockefeller or Jobs or Gates company and they have as much of a right to own the company as these others. They gamble with their very lives; and, I think, that they deserve as much for that as someone who gambles their money and wit.

Moreover, the society all around all of them has done more than Rockefeller, Jobs, Gates, and any entrepreneur could ever imagine. The myth of the rugged capitalist entrepreneur individual who pulls himself up by the boot straps — whatever they are —somehow in splendid isolation from the rest of society, is not only a myth, but an untrue myth at that. Nobody. Nobody does it alone. Not even close.

It is not that Ford or Edison or Ted Turner or Jobs or Gates or Rockefeller or Buffett are not great men. Each in his own way is. Yet, without their parents, without the teachers in their schools as they were growing up, without the scientists and thinkers that had gone before them, without all the technology that preceded them invented by other people, without roads to deliver their projects, without the automobile of Ford that allowed Rockefeller to make millions in energy for cars and on and on and on. Not only is no man an island, but no entrepreneur works alone.

We are all dependent on each other. In a sense, nobody owns the factory as much as everyone owns the factory, not only the workers in the factory, but the community and not even merely the living community, but many people and communities that have passed away and leave their legacy of expertise behind for others to pick up. We all stand on the shoulders of those who have gone before us, too. We stand on the shoulders of history and community.

Yes, Edison's inventions come from his inventive mind. And Jobs conceived of iPads and iPods. And they should get much credit for that. And, as far as I am concerned, they should live and die wealthy. Still and all, fair is fair and society should get back as the workers in the factory should get back what is theirs, too, as they are not working for Mr. Gates or Mr. Rockefeller or Mr. Ford but with them. They all and society, too, has a right to own the company, the corporation.

Where would Steve Jobs be if he had to single handedly pull himself up by the iBoot-straps and in rugged individualistic isolation had to produce each and every iMac and iPhone by himself? He would not and could not. Give the production line and all its workers credit where credit is due; and Mr. Jobs hosannas where his hosannas are due.

I believe that if you work alone, then you own your own labor and your own company. As soon as you employ someone, as soon as you hire someone to work, your company cannot be your private property. It is not your private property; it is now social property, group property, community property. You cannot own either another person — called "slavery" — for their labor, or treat another person as a "wage slave." There is a difference between your private property purchase of your home and its furnishings and your private possessions and owning, as Marx said, "the means of production" — although I think, more accurately, Marx might have said, not "the means of production" as in the machinery of the factory, as much as the social arrangement called "the company" which is "the means of production" in a slightly different sense. You actually may own the machine, you may own the physical factory and its floor, but you cannot own someone else's work and the product of that work. You are working with someone; they do not work for you.

Again and to emphasize, owning someone else's work is called "slavery." You are owning part of them, their productive activity. It might not be the slavery of the Greeks, the Romans, the antebellum South of the United States, the French in colonial Haiti, but it is a form of slavery nonetheless, again "wage slavery."

Ah, "but they signed a contract" the Capitalist apologist says. "So it is OK. The worker freely signed a contract to work for me." One issue is how exactly free that signing was. You sign on so you can have access to money which gives you access to the goods that sustain your life, but someone else has a kind of monopoly on "the means of production," so you have, really, not that much choice — it is still a form of slavery. In this case, slavery that was signed for. It is very similar to the "indentured servitude" that brought many to this country from Europe and elsewhere, which was a kind of modified slavery, slavery of limited duration.

A different social fiction, I know, is still a convention, a fiction, but I like the one I am proposing better than the story of the lone wolf entrepreneur competing against the crowd and deserving of ostentatious diamond broaches. I prefer a wolf working with the pack for the benefit of all, even the wolf.

The quintessential Capitalist wolf — was Mitt a wolf in political sheep's clothing? —exploits and enslaves others and then dishonors them as being dependent and lazy. The 47%, in fact the 98%, are the ones who produce the wealth for Mitt's 1%. Looked at objectively, Mitt was dependent on "the 47%,"not the other way around.

I am not against anyone becoming rich. I am all for creative hard-working entrepreneurs making a bundle. The problem is one of proportion and fairness. It is not that the talented and conscientious should not be compensated justly. They can make their big bucks in top salary in their company because they work well and hard and inventively they get a share of profits because their good work produces profits for their company.

The question is: what is just compensation? Distributing "profits" in the manner I have described is far more just without substantially decreasing motivation. In fact, it distributes motivation around the company itself and everyone in the company can benefit from being more motivated. Moreover, with everyone a partial owner, there is far more incentive to make sure one's fellow compatriots as well as one's managers are doing a good job. The overseer watched by the overseen. How is that for justice?

Wages

Society also has an interest in the limits of compensation, both top salaries and bottom salaries within a company. This applies to both ends of the salary spectrum, the top salaries and the bottom wages. It makes no sense that anyone should not make a living wage from full time work. What is the point of work if you are not able to do what we call "making a living." At the very least, from a full time amount of work, one and one's dependents should be able to live. If the economic system does not provide a reasonable minimum for a reasonable amount of work, a living wage for full time employment, then the economic system is without fundamental morality and reason.

If the wage is not a living wage there must be money flowing in from somewhere to allow the worker to live. We now see the government in that role providing services to those who do not have the means to keep up life with their current wage. And, the government runs, financially speaking, by taxing everyone who does make a living wage to make up for what Wal-Mart is not paying its workers. Food Stamps should really become a thing of the past. If you work you have enough money to eat. And a place to live. And clothing. And all that for your kids, too.

We would not need the government trying to equalize things this way and taxing us to smithereens if all wages were living wages and all those in one way or another disabled or unable to find employment were covered elsewhere. If we say that a living wage includes the bills that the worker is required to pay for social services, then government need not do what I believe it not designed to do: provide social services. Then and only then should we, could we, allow Grover Norquist's nostrum "to shrink government until we kill it" come at least mostly true — although not until then!

Moreover, if there are no income taxes and sales taxes and property taxes then the income of most wage earners has just about doubled and become a living wage. Companies might not have to raise wages at all under this new system. They must, however, pay a living wage that compensates enough so that everyone can foot the equal bill for their services and government.

Society and its government can also mandate by law what the maximum compensation for top wage earners can be within all companies. I am not here to argue for egalitarianism within companies. I believe in a differential between those who are more skilled and those less, between those who work harder and those who do not work as hard, between those more valuable to a company and those less. How any company chooses to differentiate salary and wage within a company is their business, for the most part. Steve Jobs and Bill Gates and Ted Turner should still get rich, just not as rich. Reasonably rich. Ayn could still have her diamond pendant, okay? Maybe a few fewer diamonds, but still, she could flaunt her broach and her bat cape on Broadway and West 135th Street. Donald Trump. Well, maybe not The Don.

Society has an interest in setting a maximum salary, just as it has in setting a minimum. It would be quite simple for those who are greedy in even a system that returns profit to all employees and recycles profit through the Community

Bank for further growth to compensate themselves in salary what they would have given to themselves in profit taking and bonuses. There are not a few so-called "non-profits" that operate this way now, having the advantage of not being taxed, as they are a non-profit corporation supposedly acting for the general welfare and doing good deeds, but paying their CEOs exorbitant salaries and doing less good because their monies are going to their bigwigs.

A minimum wage is a living wage; a maximum wage is, perhaps, say, $1,000,000 per year. That would cut a few professional athletes salaries, but also the compensation for the owner of the sports franchise, too. Still, the hot dog vendor would be doing better and the grounds crew, too.

Is anyone in the country worth more than one million per year in salary? Anyone? Even Jobs? Even Walt Disney? J.K. Rowling? Well, maybe Rowling.

In this way, profits could not be completely siphoned off into the greedy pockets of a few in any particular company, as there are maximum limits to salary. Moreover, as control of the Board of Directors of companies is under the control of Community Bank representative and employee representatives, the likelihood of such a skewed differential is less likely. It is against the interest of the Community Bank to give all the profit to a few bigger wigs in the company as salary and starve themselves and the other employees of revenue from profits. Although, some particularly good and creative executives, like Jobs, could threaten to leave their company if they did not receive 10 million per year in salary, for example.

But if there were an absolute maximum for all companies, where would they go? So that would not be such a big issue.

If they, the Steve Jobs-John Galt entrepreneurs, are more valuable than just their salary and thus their company is getting filthy rich, well, they will be sharing in the profit of their company and make untold more money above their salary, too. But their additional wealth is dependent on their company doing well. This is the reverse of the golden parachute that GM executives in particular and other company and corporate CEOs received even when their companies were going to the proverbial dogs as we well know GM did — and then got rescued by Take-It-To-The-Bank Barack.

Of course, in a free market system, companies that are doing well will attract more competent employees because of profit sharing and then they will get even better and make even more and attract even better employees. But that is progress and completely fair, to my mind. We all benefit from better!

A complementary legal method of controlling maximum salaries fairly is to establish a maximum differential econo-my wide so that the top earners in a company can only make X times more than the bottom earner in a company, say 100 to 1. So that is the top earner makes $1,000,000 per year, the bottom earner makes no less than $10,000 — although $10,000 now is hardly a living wage and they would neces-sarily be paid more.

If there were no absolute maximum of one million, again for example, then if the top earner was coming in at $10,000,000 per year, the bottom would be taking in $100,000. Or combine the two ideas: no more than one mil-lion with a 25% differential, so the bottom salary is $25,000.

Profit sharing is egalitarian whereas salary is not. Both exist in the same company, but I think there should be maxi-mums on salary absolutes and differentials, lest, as I said, the greedy simply shift their greed to salary instead of profits.

I do not want to prescribe exactly how this should work or what the amounts should be, but to my mind, and in all fairness, a better society is one in which there is not such a great and grave discrepancy between top and bottom. I do not think we have to be draconian like the twin evils, Stalin and Mao, and level society both to the detriment of everyone by equalizing everything, the ultimate race to mediocrity and worse; but neither do we have to have an unfair differ-entiation that breeds resentment, revolution and poverty — and then similar draconian solutions.

Justly compensated rich is OK. Filthy rich is not ever. Rich that shares fairly is sustainable. Filthy rich that is unfair is rotten and will rot the social fabric. Rich that produces more wealth works. Filthy rich that drains the society does not.

I believe that instinctively and in our hearts we all know that a society that contains only a few wealthy and a mass of poor is unfair and unstable. The 1% versus the 99% is a prescription for societal upheavals of many varieties. Frankly, it is not really the case, as Mitt Romney and his "47%" speech would suggest, that there are only a handful of superior people and they deserve all the wealth they can lay their entrepreneurial hands on and that the vast majority of humanity is a bunch of wimpy beggars who are always looking for handouts, and therefore, there really is justification for an elite of vast wealth and a mass of the impoverished.

Should ours be a society of the rich and shameless and the poor and shamed? Still, could it be that the philosophy of Republican conservatism is true, that the super rich get what they deserve and all the rest of us do, too. However, it is simply and frankly not my experience in life and of people. I have personally know people from all strata in this society and for the life of me I cannot say that what Ms. Rand and Mr. Reagan and Mr. Gingrich and Mitt and Paul experience of competency and incompetency, of superiority and inferiority plays itself out in laissez faire economics in a completely fair manner — far from it.

Some of the rich who become rich may be special, but they are not that special. I know very many people who are creative, intelligent, productive and quite frankly morally superior to some of the wealthy people I know, and deserve more. I do not think that society need be totally fair. Yet, I think it needs to be more fair than not for the good of us all.

Marx saw this problem back in the 18th Century and thought that the gap between "The Bourgeoisie Capitalist" and "The Proletarian Worker" would grow greater with time and that eventually the working class, the collection of all those working for less and less and more and more squeezed by the Capitalist dynamic would revolt again the owners of the factories, the entrepreneurial class. It did not happen for the most part. What Marx did not foresee was the ability of the Capitalist system both to change and reform, distribute its great productive wealth more equitably and ameliorate the conditions of the working class. In Europe and America, the working class became, in white and blue collars, the new middle class, of hard work and moderate comfort.

Successful Communist revolts did not take place in more advanced and evolved capitalist society but in nascent ones, Russia, China, North Korea, Cuba and others. These were societies that had not reformed because they were not yet full blown Capitalist systems — despite what Lenin believed — and the gap from rich to poor was not only great but the societies themselves were in various degrees and kinds of crisis before their revolutions.

Yet, if the Capitalist societies of America and Western Europe had not reformed and become consumer societies with a fairer distribution of wealth but had remained a few of the gilded wealthy ruling over an impoverished populous, then Marx's International Workers of the World, the old IWW, the Wobblies, would be ruling the world. Revolt would have been everywhere — it almost was. The Capitalist class is lucky they had reformers around however little they supported them to pull their irons out of the fire — so to speak.

Yet, the trend in recent times is a return to the Capitalism of the Gilded Age and the politico-economics of fat cat McKinley, fat-bellied Taft, corrupt Harding and colder than cool Coolidge. The rich get richer. The poor get poorer. And the middle class is, as we know and politicians inveigh, on the ropes. If the trend worsens and continues, Occupy Wall Street will eventually become Take Over Wall Street. Given the murderous history of the first half of the 20th Century, the workers revolts and then the fascist and Nazi reaction to the worker's revolts, this is certainly not a bombed out genocidal highway that anyone should want to repave. Real class warfare would not be a good choice.

Republicans pontificating that any change in the current

economic-social system to construct a fairer and more equitable system is class warfare will lead to that very conflict. Conservatively returning to the 19th Century, as many a Republican reactionary would have us do, and gutting the social buffers and reforms of Teddy and Franklin Roosevelt, Woodrow Wilson and The Liberals would give us the same set of social problems a reformed Capitalism so handily got around.

Unfair is in the heart and mind, but economics stresses the body, having everything to do with life and limb. Thinking that one is poor or in a poorer class is one thing and not very good for one's ego — just as being in the upper crust inflated Mr. Bush II's. Yet, when no jobs are available and you are thrown out of your repossessed house and deprived of your repossessed automobile and your repossessed furniture and you cannot buy food for your babies, that is another and more fundamental story. When 8.1% unemployment becomes 15.4% or 25.9% and this story, bad enough as we know at 8.1, becomes more and more frequent, then all kinds of social consequences and miseries besides revolt becomes inevitable. In shielding themselves from more and more misery, the super wealthy 1% live in more and more highly gated communities with more and more gates and guns and the poor and poorer fight amongst themselves for less and less. Greece and Spain may only be a prelude and a mild one at that; think South American Banana Republics and military dictatorships like Pinochet.

This is only a trend and a beginning warning. Yet if the trend turns from a trickling brook to a river to a raging river, the misery flood will carry away not only social peace, but all of us. It is not necessary, but the trend is in the down direction, not up. It is not necessary. I am hopeful, but certainly not sure that the mild reforms of Barack will get us far enough, even as Mitt's would turn back the societal clock to the 1890's.

Investment

Within the current system, besides the too-large-to-fail banks being the source of investment Capital, there are those who are rich or filthy rich who invest their money in the stock market or the companies of friends or relatives so that they can keep a good return on their money, so they can profit not on providing goods but by loaning out money. They are making profit; they are making money on money. In a sense, the are very private banks.

We have stock markets and other social means for money, too, to make money in this manner.

For middle class individuals and workers in their pension funds, the way to retire, too, is to make more money on the limited money you have but have saved over the years. I have not a few friends who are planning to stop working in their old ages based on a combination of money on hand and Social Security but also money invested that keeps money coming in after their work income stops because they have stopped working.

My proposals do away with making money on money. The only investment allowed is by Community Banks. I do not believe that money should make money. To my mind: work creates wealth. If you do not work, you do not deserve money from someone else's work.

That does not mean that I do not understand the howls now coming from my friends. I am not saying that we should do away with Social Security or pension funds. Savings for retirement is a good thing. Moreover, in a more equitable system, everyone should be able to save more to put into their retirement. Perhaps, if you are very sensible and work for a good company, you will take all the profit sharing and put that into your pension monies.

Still and all, you will not be able to make money on money, to make money on someone else's labor, just as someone else cannot make money on you by skimming profits from your company because, in stocks, they own your company.

You are getting your well deserved profits, not some distant wealthy person or an insurance company or someone else's pension fund.

What happens in this new system if you run out of money and your forced pension amount — called Social Security — is insufficient in your retirement and you are unable to work? In addition to Social Security, there is still unemployment insurance for the disabled. You are not disabled because you lost an arm and a leg or because your IQ is insufficient to do any job, but because you are old and feeble. You are unable to work. You receive disability insurance money if you have run out of Social Security pension.

Otherwise, as always, in this society or any other it is a good idea to put aside some savings for a time when you are old and unable. You just cannot bet on making money from your money. You just have what money you have and disability is equivalent only to a minimum living wage.

Doing away with private investment of all types means that nobody can make money on money itself, except for the general community — which is all of us. This ends any number of possible abuses, abuses we have seen time and time again in a privatized Capitalist economy. Some of the rich can get even richer, not by doing anything useful, but simply by being good gamblers on the stock market.

Some of us even do investing for a living and a too lucrative living it is. Sometimes, as Warren Buffett, they invest their own money and sometimes, as Warren Buffett, as they are such good investors, other people hand them money to invest for them. You invest in the very good gambler who is good at the game because they know the game so well. They do their research. Of course, sometimes, you can be taken for a ride on a side road — as we say — and the gambler investment fund is a fraud, as in Mr. Madoff who made off with everyone's money.

And, what of Mr. Romney and Bain Capital? They bought, owned and sold companies. They were not entrepreneurs. They did not invent. They did not work in the company.

They used money to buy, own and then sell companies. They had much investment money and they would suck the profit from companies for their very own. Sometimes in owning the company they would reorganize it for the better; sometimes they would dissolve it. They made money, not from actual work, but from speculation and manipulation. And a whole lot of money they all made! For what? Again, sometimes they were good for companies; sometimes they just sold the company in pieces, not for the good of the company and its employees, but for the good of themselves and their investors. The present system not only allows this but encourages it. Mitt got rich, filthy rich.

This kind of gamesmanship, though it has its place in a Capitalist system does not have a place in Democratic Community Capitalism. I do not at all believe that society's economics should be in the hands of the productive-work-phobic greedy. As individuals or as individual companies they do not, in my mind, have a right to someone else's profits and labors. Playing the Capitalist game, instead of actually and materially working, is not worth what we pay for it. To be blunt about it, those who take the profits of others are leeches, sucking the life blood of others. Some of us are more leech-like than others, and Mr. Romney and big bank executives and stock traders are the biggest leeches of all. They are unnecessary besides. Ayn Rand, bless her greedy little soul, at least, exalted producers in her novels, not Mighty Mitt's many manipulators. Mitt Romney fundamentally had a lot of nerve calling 47% of the population blood suckers when he is the ultimate one.

International Capital & Democratic Companies

There has been a problem in some European countries and particularly in the United States with companies moving parts — if not more — of their operations to China, India and other countries that have lower labor costs. The United States has lost a good deal of its older manufacturing base. While this may make consumer goods cheaper and helps American companies stay competitive in the world market, the overall effect is higher unemployment amongst those who would have had those jobs in Ohio, Michigan, North Carolina and elsewhere.

For these workers, we see the beginning of a more generalized misery. Work is the basis of making a living. If you cannot make a living or if your living standard is reduced, there can be suffering for you and your family — to a greater or lesser degree depending on the rest of the circumstances and the economics of your life.

What is little noted is that there is no such exit of companies out of Germany. Germany is still, with China, a net exporter. Germany has no balance of payments problem. The German government is not in debt even though they have many social services including medicine handled by the government.

In no small part, this is the positive consequence of a societal policy initiated by the victorious Americans after WWII. Those who work in large companies in Germany are given 49% representation on The Board of Directors of those companies. Companies where the employees control virtually half of the company's Board do not ship their jobs to Shanghai.

Not only am I proposing that those who work in a company control 50% of The Board of Directors but also that the other 50% of that Board consists of representatives of the local Community Bank. Will companies be outsourcing or moving to Manila or Vietnam or Nanking or Mexico City any time soon under that system? Highly unlikely. Workers will not want to see their companies outsourced overseas; communities will not want that either as they would not want their population on the dole and searching around helplessly for work that no longer exists.

However, there is a danger here, too. While companies may stay put, they can be at a competitive disadvantage in global market place when companies in other parts of the world can pay their workforce less across the board. If companies can get away with lower labor costs and still produce products the equal of American goods, wouldn't that put American companies out of business, creating unemployment and jeopardizing Community Bank investments anyway?

The answer is yes, that would be a problem. Capitalist competition is what it is. Adam Smith foresaw just that. And his answer was: become better and more efficient or lose the company. Even, he might add, in the case of workers, you will need to take a salary cut to preserve your company in order to compete with other companies. The strong survive in this system; the weak go into another business.

What I am proposing does not preclude companies failing or, if not failing, losing substantial parts of their markets to better run companies in other parts of the world, as GM and Ford lost market share to Toyota and Honda. A competitive system may always have winners and losers.

Yet, the point Adam Smith was making was: the less able companies may die off or they are forced — if they want to remain in business — to get better at what they do. GM and Ford need to make better cars or they go out of business. Without a government bailout GM would have had to. Have they learned their lesson?

Yet, there is another problem here as well. What if the only difference between a company in China and the U.S.A. is that Chinese companies are able to pay their workers extremely low wages because a previously impoverished working class will accept extremely low wages; and there are no labor unions or other means of negotiating for higher wages? The latter is, to my mind, an unfair advantage for Chinese companies; the former is not unfair, but just unfortunate and will change in time. How does a company that makes a perfectly acceptable if not superior product compete with companies that make the same product but can get away with treating their productive workers poorly?

There are any number of problems with free world trade, the human rights of laborers being only one. Environmental regulations are another. It is simply cheaper to manufacture goods and pass the cost of environmental pollution and degradation on, literally, downstream or across oceans if you are not required by government regulation to do otherwise. Countries with higher standards are at a decided disadvantage. Or how about government subsidy of industry against countries that do not subsidize industries? The list goes on.

In a competitive global economy, all things being equal, the best and the most efficient should survive. The less best and not efficient need to get a move on. But all things are not equal. Toyota makes a better car than GM. Sony made better TVs than Motorola. Fair competition. But does China make better children's toys than a factory in Marietta, Georgia? Not with all that lead in the paint on those toys. Are Chinese bedroom sets made better than those made in North Carolina? They certainly are cheaper, but not better. Those bedroom sets from China have devastated the domestic furniture industry. But was it fair and free trade with all things being equal?

As President Obama has opined and I agree: we should not be in a race to the bottom, giving up our environment or relatively high employment standards to compete with anyone, including and especially the Chinese with wage slavery that is closer to real slavery. I would modestly suggest that it is everyone's interest, the interests of the citizens and workers in China, as well as the citizens and workers in the United States to level a few proverbial playing fields.

That is, how much Chinese companies pay their workers as well as their environmental standards should rise. This will advantage everyone as Chinese workers will be able to buy more and more products made in both China and the United States. In the long run, it does the Chinese no good if American companies go belly up and discharge their workers. Who is going to buy those Chinese goods? Not unemployed former workers.

The worldwide Capitalist competitive system works only with some degree of reciprocal fairness, otherwise what should be a world wide growth of prosperity will instead be that race to the bottom. In no small part, the current recession in Europe and the United States is a consequence of productivity moving to areas of the world where wage slavery is more obviously a form of slavery. It is Authoritarian State Capitalism.

Ultimately, if China does not change, it would be possible, for example, to refuse to trade with them unless they recognize the Human Rights of their workers to organize into unions. We could also refuse to trade with any country that did not agree to a certain set of environmental standards. Hopefully, solutions short of economic war can be negotiated.

The alternative to these kinds of trade wars is a World Government that would make world wide rules of fairness in business across the board; and what is on board that ship is everything from worker's rights to environmental protection. More on that in a later chapter.

Banks

Now to the issue of banks. Ah, banks. Ahhh, sigh.

We now have some kind of idea after all the problems created by mortgages and banks at the start of the latest Greatest Recession, that banks can be a problem. So, in the same way we looked at Capitalism and profit let's look at the essential scheme of banking — apart from all its mind boggling complex complexities and ambiguities.

Whereas banks make a profit, they do not manufacture anything, like scissors or toe nail clippers or Viagra nor do they provide a service like stylishly cutting your hair or toe nails, nor writing a prescription for a statin drug. They do provide a service, but it is rather an interesting service. They promise to make you money on your money, and they in turn by making money for you on your money make a profit.

It is all a bit odd, but it adds an essential layer to the Capitalist system, a currently abused layer. In fact when banks goes awry, when big banks gets mucked up or bigger banks screw up in royal fashion, well, the whole bloody system creaks, groans and just about falls over and dies — or, at least, is very very sick. Call these: The Great Depression or Greatest Recession since The Depression. Banks can be too big to fail because when the whole of world Capitalism fails. Oops. Big oops!

To make a long and complex explanatory story short, banks solicit savings deposits, that is, the money that you put in the bank for the bank to hold for a rainy day and a hole in your roof, in return for a small rate of return called "interest." Now, everybody likes "interest." I am interested in "interest" like everyone else. The best kind of "interest" is "compound interest," a force stronger than all those forces in physics combined, as Einstein acknowledged — but that is another and mathematical story altogether.

So, in a sense, a practical world real sense, "interest" on your money is profit you have made on money by keeping it in the bank. A very nice social fiction, indeed. If you are wealthy enough, very wealthy indeed, you can live well not by working at all, but by your money being in the bank. You make money without doing anything. You money makes you the money. Now that is truly Capitalist genius, at least for the very wealthy.

Why will the bank pay you "interest?" Seems a bit on the fishy side. Percentage wise, these savings "interest" rates are quite small. Investing directly in companies or in other ways could make you a lot more money as Mr. Romney knows well. But these ways of trying to make money on money are riskier and bank risk is far lower, at least most of the time, until, God and Ben Bernanke forbid, the whole shebang goes bang, imploding or exploding.

Still, what is the banks' interest in paying "interest?"

Simple: they invest in companies and mortgages and loans of all kinds; and, the bank believes that those deposit monies they can invest or loan wisely enough to make even more money. They do the gambling for you and for that take a slice of your money pie. The banker believes that they can make more than the pittance of "interest" that they will pay out to you by their investments and loans. There are investment firms that do essentially the same, the difference being that instead of just loaning out money to companies and the companies do as they will with the money, Mitt's Bain and other such entities actually own and control the company they invest in.

Banks make money on money. Banks make a profit on money. Banks pay out interest money to get more money to invest and loan out. Banks profit in this manner.

For example, with this accumulated money on which they have promised to pay out "interest" at say 5%, banks will loan this money out to companies as capital or to someone wanting to buy a house but they provide this loan service at a higher rate, say 10%. For the home buyer, this may be fine, because on their own they do not have the accumulated dollars to buy their house, so they are willing to pay the "interest" rate so they can be in their home before the end of their life when maybe they will have saved enough to completely buy a place to live. And the business person, thinking that their profits will top 10%, needs to buy machinery that they, too, do not have enough money right away to buy, so they are willing to pay the bank that 10% so they can get started.

The bank's centralized accumulation of money based on interest is turned into more profit which is, in good Capitalist style, invested into even more investment and loans that make more money profit and so on. It is a wonderful and sensible social fiction again. And, of course, of course, there are big and bigger bonuses to the executives of banks for such a wonderful and middleman service function.

Banks are at the heart and soul of the Capitalist system because it is hard and now harder to accumulate enough capital yourself when you are starting out to then get to the stage where you are accumulating more profit from productivity to be self generating. No entrepreneur is an island here either, each needs a bank and bankers.

In fact, as the service banks provide is so essential to the system itself and its businesses and the people in those businesses and everyone who requires shelter and automobiles that are too expensive to buy outright generally and so much more and as the service banks provide is doubly socially fictitious, that is, profits that are a social fiction are being accumulated and then redistributed to make more social fiction profit, I believe that it is the community of individuals that make up society and community that should have far more control over banks. Banks should not be in individual greedy hands. Banks should be only Community Banks and their derivatives. Banks are making profit on profits and then generating more profits for themselves. Still and all, ultimately, it is our money, not the Borgias or Rothchild's or Goldmans and Sachs.

All that money in that bank is your money, one way or another. It is either profit or deposit. You have not only paid more for goods and services than their cost of manufacture, now your are paying again when you take out a loan. It is some kind of ultimate Ponzi scheme, if one that works marvelously well.

Well, even if you agree that it is A-OK that profit is made on profit, money on money, even so, you deserve more control over the whole banking process. Banks, to my mind, as the quintessential Capitalist institution of all institutions, require democratization. You paid for it one way or another — you get control. The bank should be ours.

So, I have proposed that all banks should be as Community Banks, not "nationalized" banks controlled by the government. Trading in your greedy too- big-to-fail Citigroup banker for a control freak government banker — much as I admire Paul Volcker — does not seem like progress to me. Commissar or corporate tycoon, I would rather think of a different social role model. Call it "socialist," call it "communitarian," call it what you will. It is putting all of us back in control of the economy and its money.

I call it: Democratic Banking. Democratization is simple. Everyone owns the banks. Each community elects the Board of Directors of each Community Bank. How large is each area where there is a Community Bank? I would suggest one Community Bank per county. Yet, I do not think the size of the area that the Community Bank entails is as important as the principle that all banks are owned by everyone. And decisions and the election of the Board of Directors at the bank can be decided at community wide participatory democratic meetings at regular intervals.

I also think that there should be coordinating banks, that is, state-wide, region-wide, country-wide, world-wide that regulate the flow of capital where it is needed. Lest democratization lead to so much voting for so many offices that citizens become overwhelmed, election to these coordinating banks could possibly be by ballot from local community banks' board of directors.

Community Bank profits could be distributed one-third to the coordinating banking system, one-third to invest in new businesses or to expand local businesses or to consumer loans — whatever local investment is required — and then one third to the unemployment system, including the infrastructure building employment system as well as to disability insurance.

A county-wide Community Bank would thus be sending one-third to a state bank. The state bank in turn would be able to send capital to Community Banks and communities where it was needed, where businesses had failed and unemployment was increasing and there was need for business investment when the local Community Bank did not have enough capital on hand.

These coordinating banks in thus sending capital and money to local community banks could also be sending one-third of the funds they were accumulating from local community banks to national and then international coordinating banks, so that capital could flow everywhere it was needed and profit could serve everyone everywhere, rather than be overly concentrated in particularly prosperous areas only.

Moreover, larger banks, these coordinating banks could distribute one-third to large multi-county companies and projects that cross state and county lines, and one-third to larger infrastructure projects, e.g. N.A.S.A.

Of course, along with capital to capitalize depressed areas, expertise and education would need to flow as well. Coordinating banks would need to coordinate with local educational institutions to increase the capacities of local businesses and their personnel so that future enterprises will succeed.

I believe that banks are such a central institution in this society that elections for bank officers will become more important and be better attended than current government races. It is very important to choose well when designating those who will be making the decisions about what to invest in and influencing how to run companies. It is also very important what infrastructure projects get funded. As they say, "follow the money." Communities need to follow the money and control those who handle the money.

Democracy would then be far more than a formality. It would be more meaningful because it would have essential consequences.

Democratic banks would be the government of the economy.

Personal Economic Security

If God or whomever or whatever granted each of us "life, liberty and the pursuit of happiness," then each and every one us requires the means to sustain "life" and limb. In other words, each of us has a right to work, a right to a job. No job = no money. No money = no food, no house, no means of supporting your life and the life of your family. To my mind, what The Almighty powers grant, no society has the right to take away. If you have a right to life, you have a right to sustain life, period. You have a right to "the means of production."

That does not mean you have a right to any old job you want, especially the ones you are not qualified for. Nor do you have a right to make as much money as you want. Above sustaining life, as in a "living wage," I do not believe you have a right, as Marx put it, "to each according to his need." Of course, you need to have a good enough salary to keep your life going, but over and above that, just saying you "need" this or that, well, that just does not fly, nor should you be given a free societal plane ticket to what you decide you need. We will all need to do a little better than just saying we need a newer than new computerized gizmo paddy to get it. "To each according to his need," is, to my mind, simply childish, in the negative sense of childish.

Here is where Capitalist motivation should rule. It should not be the threat of starvation and gross deprivation unto death that motivates getting up early and trudging off to the computer widget factory. We will accept that if you show up and do a reasonable amount of work you will receive a "living wage." Society will guarantee that a minimum amount of work will be available to you.   You need not fear if you only want to get by, that you will have to scratch and claw your way into a job. Give the minimum and you will get the minimum. That is OK. There are those of little ambition who still have a right to their God given right to life — as long as they contribute enough energy, an amount of output to justify that input.

Still, if you desire more than minimum subsistence, you will have to put out a bit more. Want more? Have more wants and needs? Well, it is only fair that if you want more, you work more and better.

Given my proposals, on the one hand every citizen is guaranteed some kind of job. And if they become better educated and work harder, being then more skilled and more productive, they can earn more in their companies, assuming companies reward such skills, which they should. If companies do not reward well, the company will not be as productive and make as much money and their skilled employees will go to some other company who will appreciate them more and pay them more and, in that way, the chintzy company will lose their workers and their income. Ah, the free market. It does work, doesn't it?

On the other hand, if you do not want to do the kind of work that your society requires of you, if you want to be a rugged individualist like Ms. Ayn Rand's heroes and heroines (like herself, she thinks) and go off on your own, what is an independent soul to do?

If you want to do your own thing within the general parameters of the society you find yourself within, the superior individual with superior ideas need apply to the local Community Bank for funding to get their superior sole person enterprise off the ground. Particular local community bank not into this set of ideas? Not unlike what would happen to you in this society, you would need to find another bank, another bank in another community. Somewhere in the vast expanse and given the number of community banks, well, I am sure if you and your ideas are a cut above, talent will win out in the end. The society I am outlining is not all that different from the one we are in, only fairer — a fair Democratic Capitalism.

Yet, what if you are not at all superior or spectacular and you just cannot abide by the choice of work and employment available to you. Yes, no work = no money = no means of support = means, the end of your life. If you are in no way disabled, but just very disagreeable, you are in trouble. You have a right to life, but not to a free lunch or free house or free sweatsuit.

What should we do when there is really no work around? Maybe there is a gap between the time that a business closes and the time when a new business opens or between the time you lose your job and the time you need for retraining. There should be, as we do now, for at least limited periods of time, unemployment insurance money, available until another business or factory is up and running and you get retrained for the new job in the new company.

The money for all that comes from the community banks putting into a working person's unemployment insurance fund. Unemployment insurance still exists, but it is not in the hands of a politicized government; it is in the hands of a democratized banking system This bank will be quite interested in finding you work, of funding good new businesses so you can work, instead of paying out money from its insurance fund.

Then there is disability. What if you cannot work due to injury or a physical or mental handicap or extreme old age? Well, worked into the system, as the system at present, is disability insurance too. All these are paid for, as now, at least in part, again, by profits recycled through the community banks. Disability insurance still exists, as it should.

Yet, I think we might want to consider also some means of productive work beyond unemployment and disability insurances. Here is where infrastructure projects kick in. No good businesses created and new work found, then there is always and should always be made available infrastructure projects.

And then, there are those who need time out because they want to start up a business. They are entrepreneurs and it takes time as it took Bill Gates or Steve Jobs or Thomas Alva Edison time to get it going. There can be funds put aside by all Community Banks to fund start up time.

There should also be funds set up not just to fund infrastructure projects but art projects — another kind of infrastructure project — as well. As with entrepreneurs, artists and musicians and others — maybe spiritual leaders — whose skills are valuable to society but whose line of work is not either immediately or ever matched with a money economy should be able to apply for a regular stipend from the banking system so they can pursue their art or music or enterprise. This can be done at all levels of the banking system — local, state, national, international, so that we have artists of all kinds at all levels.

Difficulties & Such

How are we doing? Does this all sound too good to be true? Or does it seem a bit ridiculous given the state of The World?

Could there be recessions, depressions, stock market crashes, governments in horrible debt in this system? Could there be mass unemployment? Could the system break down or is it infinitely sustainable?

With these proposals, we could still have recessions, even depressions and the system could break down. There could be mass unemployment. Nothing is infinitely sustainable. There is no equivalent of a societal perpetual motion machine. However, and this is a big: it is far less likely that recessions or depressions or mass unemployment on a massive scale would happen to this system. Of course, there being no more stock markets, we would not have stock market crashes.

Yet, what if on a large scale banks invest in the wrong companies and what if, even if the companies were good in a past economic environment, in the present or a future environment their products become all outdated and what if this happens to all too many companies? And then where is the money going to come for getting up and going with new companies when the banks have loaned out all their money to existing companies?

What ifs are plentiful, but there are features of this system that are a bit better at handling bad times — some are inevitable — that buffer against such massive losses. Some of these are the same buffers that keep our present system going and going. A crash on a massive scale would have to be a perfect bad storm and everywhere. Could happen. Community banks across the country could invest in poor enterprises everywhere. Yet, this is a bit less likely than a few big banks making a few massive errors as in the last Great Recession of banks making and gambling on the housing market. The buffer in this case is on the community bank scale. And, even if a bank or two failed, the coordinating system of banks could and would come to the rescue.

It is not at all different than in agriculture. Large mono-crops can be dangerous. Plant only one variety of corn or potatoes everywhere across the country and a single infestation of a single bug that is not killable could be disastrous for food production. Large mono-banks are not much different. Diversification of crops and diversification in banking is far more resilient and sustainable.

Could a famine happen with diversified crops? You bet. It is called massive drought. Could an economic collapse happen with diversified banks? You bet. A far-flung drought of fiscal responsibility could bring the whole system down, yes. But I would rather play the better odds. The odds are far better in a Democratic Capitalism if we improve on the present Plutocratic Capitalist system that in the past has had wild swings of optimism and pessimism, prosperity and crash boom — and where did all those trillions go?

And then no taxes! And all the education and health care we all need whenever we need it. And everyone is taken care of. And freedom. And democracy. And responsible limits. How can we resist? A way out of dystopia. A road paved with better intentions not going to Hell. Democratic. Democratic Capitalism. Fairer than fair.

I understand that in the social economic system I have outlined that the banking system, at the center of the Capitalist system now, would have even more control and power in the future. If what I am outlining were a private banking system I think this would be extremely problematic. However, democratic control at the very center of the system could save us all. Instead of Mitt Romney or Warren Buffett or any of those anonymous billionaire private bank executives, as good or bad as each of them are, instead of the 1/10 of 1% with their hands on the reins, their feet on the accelerator, their mitts on the throttle of the Capitalist jet engine, I believe we need far more control of The System by those of us who live in The System. That is, all of us. We could elect Mitt or Warren to a Board, but they would be subject to our whims, not their own limited financial interest.

I think it past time when power, real power, should come back to the people. Yes, "Power to the People, Right On." Right on the money! This is real and genuine Democratic Capitalism. When the real power in a society is the money then "Power to The People," means control of the purse strings.

Chapter 7
Infrastructure Green

You would not know it from the continuous federal government debate debacle about the federal government debt, but historically and in no small measure, American business and American Republicans — and Federalists and Whigs before them — have loved infrastructure projects paid for by, yes, the federal government. Not that Democrats have not, from time to time, fed and oinked at the same budget troughs. In reaction, many muck racking journalists and the public have used the derisive cliche "pork barrel spending," giving some linguistic alert to just how pervasive and long lived is boondoggle coming out of D.C. — oh, and by the way, many a state capital as well.

What government is out and about doing — going back to Romans, Persians, Chinese, Mayans, any civilization of any size you can name — has largely been building bridges, roads, Roman aqueducts, The Great Wall, wide boulevards in Paris and this list goes on and on.

The United States governments — federal, state, local — have built post offices and D.C. government buildings in imperial Greco-Romanesque style, the interstate highway system, a monument to monumental water delivery systems bringing good drinkable water to New York City from the Catskills or that other great diversion of water into Southern California, the military industrial complex and on and on.

In this country infrastructure brought to you by our governments, and of course, you tax dollar or government debt that you will eventually pay with your next tax dollars. It is what civilization and especially imperial governments do. It is what this government has done from its beginning or at least since The Constitution was ratified and Alexander Hamilton was first Secretary of the Treasury.

No modern infrastructure? Then you are virtually automatically what is called a "Third World country." (Who the first and second are anymore is not exactly clear.) Not actually that you have no infrastructure, just you do not have the right modern kind. The roads are dirt and bumpy; the phone lines extend at best to a small part of what run-down city there is; and transporting goods, even goods you might sell, well, it is hard to get you and your stuff around. If you want to be part of modern world prosperity, it behooves your government do what European and American governments have been doing for the last couple of hundred years which is, one way or another invest in modern infrastructure.

And education. You can build all the factories you might to produce all kinds of goods, for sale and for consumption, but if you do not have an education infrastructure, there may be no workers of any skill to work the factory or even set it up.

Despite the known importance of maintaining our existing infrastructure, e.g. bridges and roads, the U.S.A. is grossly behind on this count. And, the creation of a new green infrastructure and better educational system will require ongoing and much increased expenditure. Just because in the 19th and 20th Century a transcontinental railroad system, a water way system of harbors, ports and canals, an intercontinental road system, a public school system, telegraph, telephone, internet systems, drinking water and sewage systems and so much more were built at great public and private expense, does not mean that in the immediate and the ongoing and hopefully much greener future that we do not need to continue fixing the old and then creating the green. In truth, in order to save our planet for ourselves and future generations, we will need to redo our infrastructure systems green forthwith and into the un-foreseeable future.

Without a doubt, a whole book could be written just outlining, not even planning anything in any degree of detail, about what a good and sustainably green infrastructure would look like. Magnetic lev trains on magnetic lev rails. Solar panels on every building in the country. New public transportation systems on a vast scale. New waste disposal systems that more completely recycle.

If we want jobs, jobs, jobs in the United States, in Europe, everywhere and anywhere on the planet, we might consider requiring of ourselves a countrywide, even a worldwide equivalent of that old development project called The Marshall Plan that got Europe back to modernity after World War II, except apply it to green infrastructure. As we might say now: The Marshall Plan on steroids, green steroids.

Not only would there be many jobs created, but as any good Republican who knows history knows, it would be great for business. I think that a very good case could be made that the great prosperity for the wealthy of The Gilded Age in America was a by-product of the infrastructure products that the federal and state governments undertook and that some businesses lobbied and swindled their way into. The way to get rich was to bribe congressmen or aides to Republican Presidents, especially Ulysses S. Grant and Warren Harding among others for infrastructure bucks. Railroads. Roads.

Yet, I have in my proposals already taken infrastructure projects out of the direct hands of government per se and imagined paying for infrastructure from the banking system, the new democratic economic government. So, community-wide projects would be funded by community banks. Projects appropriate to wider areas would be funded by state banks and larger projects still by a national bank. A local water purification system would be funded locally. A hydro-electric dam, statewide perhaps. Wind farms off the coast, perhaps nationally. Streets in the town = local. Roads connecting towns or jurisdictions = state. Interstate highways = national. I think we could fund trips to the moons of Mars and Jupiter's moons internationally.

Banks should have a certain percentage of their money designated for investment in infrastructure. If there is unemployment in their area and someone or many individuals cannot find work, they should be the first hired on infrastructure projects. I cannot imagine that there would not be some infrastructure work that could not be found for anyone who is out of work. I do not mean make work either; I mean genuine essential infrastructure creation work. We have enough work in infrastructure creation, I believe, to keep us all busy for a couple of hundred years. Rome was not built in a day, or a weekend, or a century. We should be in the process of building a beautiful sustainable Earth home for ourselves, our children and our children's children for a while.

In these proposals, the banking system is the primary, in fact, only investment tool of the society. Community banks, state banks, national banks, and an international bank invests in business and sits on the controlling body of all companies, the Board of Directors, to the tune of fifty percent. In addition, all these banks invest in all the infrastructure projects of the society. They decide what these should be and they invest. They pay for the project.

Do the bank investors get paid back or do they just pay out? We all may get the benefit of all that infrastructure; although some of us will benefit more than others depending on the particular project. People who drive cars benefit by concrete roads. Those who walk on sidewalks and take the train benefit by investment in sidewalks and rail lines. Still and all we all benefit from some of the infrastructure. I do think it would be feasible to just leave it at that and not have anything from these investments paid back in to banks. Or not.

I think it better overall if, dissimilar to the education and medical system (that are themselves more similar to insurance, everyone putting in so everyone is covered, regardless of whether you break a leg or need coronary bypass surgery or you would like to be retrained because your company failed to keep up with the latest in technology) I think it better if the banking system was reimbursed, paid back on most but not all infrastructure projects.

Let me give a couple of examples. Roads for automobiles. Would I require toll booths on every last road, some run by your local bank, some by the state bank and, every time you get on I-95 or I-295 you ante up another toll? No. On the contrary, I would remove every toll booth we have now. Yet, how to pay for the use of the roads by car and truck and motorcycle and RV? I would charge the users of these roads not through an annoying toll system but through an energy charge. That is, not dissimilar to the tax we put on gasoline, a tax on gasoline consumption. Or, if we at some future time have an all electric system, a tax on electrical consumption. The heaviest users with the heaviest vehicles pay more. Fair.

That money, collected as a Road Transportation Charge, yes, I know looks like, sounds like, smells like, not a duck but a tax and, I said I was ending taxation across the board. Well, I see what you mean, but it is really not so much a tax, it is a bill, a bill for using the roads. It is a toll rather than a tax. OK, a duck by another name still comes out of my pocket quacking. Fine. But I think if this is an exception, this may prove the rule.

So, the banking system gets that money back on its investment for your use of the road and with the money that the bank will be getting from the quacking toll, the bank can then further maintain the roads, build more roads or, even lower the rates that are being charged. The money from the road transportation charge does not go into a general fund for the government to spend elsewhere.

Another example are phone lines, cable TV lines, electric lines and internet lines and all other lines that above and below ground bring us all kinds of communication and energy services. I do not believe any of these should be owned privately. These are infrastructure; and their creation, maintenance and expansion should be part of the infrastructure obligation of the banking system.

However, the banking system should not be in the business of owning the TV companies that produce TV shows, nor of the cable companies that bring you TV and internet service. The electric company should not own the line, but they should be responsible for the electricity itself. Cable signals and electric energy are products, not infrastructure.

Banks can then charge companies line rental fees, appropriate to that business area. There might even be several companies competing to send you your TV signal. I have no problem with competition. Each of those companies would be obligated to the owner of the infrastructure cable TV lines — one or more banks — for a certain amount of rental fee.

What if your local Community Bank did not want to invest in fiber optic cables lines and you want the services that fiber optic cable lines bring? I just switched to a company that convinced me that fiber optic internet, phone and TV would be better than my old Time Warner cable service. But what if my local community or even my state bank did not want to make the investment? Well, I might want to, in the next election for the board of the bank, elect a team that wanted to invest in fiber optic cable.

Where is that decision made now, by the way, whether to bring fiber optic cable to your neighborhood? By The Board of Directors and/or the management at A.T.& T. You have less access to affecting that decision than you might if you had democratic control of the investment banking system.

I do believe that one way or another the banks that are investing — whether in private companies or public infrastructure — should receive money in return in one way or another, if not always. After all, it is your money that is being invested and investment, to my mind, should not be giveaways, unless for one reason or another it is neither feasible nor desirable to collect back, like sidewalks and parks.

When railroads were being built, the federal government gave away land to the railroad companies to build the railroads upon. Now, in a new system of infrastructure projects, I think all rail lines are infrastructure and funded by the banking system. Trains should be run by companies, not by the federal government's Amtrak.

When the railroads were first built, it was not only the land right under the tracks that were given to the rail companies that never paid money back to the generously bribed government. Not only did the feds give away that narrow bit of land, but 50 miles on each side of the track. Mega-fortunes were made not just on the railroad system itself; far more was made in real estate speculation. No such boondoggles should be allowed.

The great advantage of pay back on investment money to the banking system is that more money will be available for future investment, whether that investment is in more public infrastructure or private productivity. And, it is fair! Tracks should be rented to railroads, not given away.

Caveat Green & The Physics of Entropy

Nature, with its bubonic plagues killing 50% + of the Mediterranean European population, 20% further North, in the late Middle Ages, smallpox plagues here and there, famines here and there and everywhere at one time or another, droughts, Ice Ages, heat waves, Vesuvius wiping out Pompeii, that Tsunami drowning many a citizen of Japan — Nature, the source of all nourishment, is also the beginning and end of sorrows. Science and technology fulfilled the dreams of many to control, even conquer, something called "Nature." We have tried to rid ourselves of the downsides of It All.

With science and technology we even defeated some of our apparent, if not so real limits. We travel at 65 miles per hour in our automobile for long stretches of time, an unprecedented rate except if you are a gazelle on steroids and even then only for short dashes away from the lion's jaw. We air travel 500 or so mph sitting in the pressurized cabin of our da Vinci imagined airplanes. Only an ill mountain goat falling off a cliff in the Alps plunges downward at the pace we safely cross an ocean in the air.

Smallpox is history.

We live in climate controlled layouts we call "houses" and "home," oblivious to all but the most severe of severe storms.

Gross famines are in isolated pockets for now, poor isolated pockets in northeast Africa. We seem to be getting somewhere, somewhere better, in better control. Maybe with a few more inventions we shall live happily ever after and forever, a perfect iFuture.

What is the payback, the blowback, the Yin for this Yang extravaganza? The signature epidemic disease of the modern industrial era, cancer, may spookily parallel the out of control growth of our populations and our use and consummation of the flora, fauna, rocks and minerals, air and water of the planet. We keep growing in numbers; we keep growing in prosperity; we keep metastasizing to every corner of the planet. In my absolute worst clear headed moments, my time of despair, tears inching down my red cheeks on the banks of the Mississippi in St .Louis, I think perhaps we are a disease that the Goddess Gaia, when her immune system kicks into full gear, will kill us all before we kill all of her. In point of fact, if we do her in, we are done for.

There being, as Sir Isaac taught, for every action an equal and opposite reaction. For every action, for every up in the ante of growth, for every increase of our power, for all our increase in the use of energy, I think there must be a time of reckoning when we perhaps should acknowledge as "an equal and opposite reaction" to our success. For every upside there being a downside, for every increase in energy there being a concomitant increase in entropy.

For all the control we have exerted, for all the victories we have won, for all the wonders we have done, for all that has been accomplished for us and us alone, not for the birds, not for the bees, nor the trees, nor the tomatoes, nor the prunes, nor the cows and pigs and chickens, for all that we had better watch out, beware, be virtually paranoid about what the "equal and opposite reaction" will be. We had better watch our proverbial backs, rather than, as we now say over and over again, doubling down, forever growing, prospering, defeating nature. It is dangerous, all too much so. We have more to fear than fear itself. We should fear ourselves and our fearlessness. We should fear what we are doing to our home planet, Earth.

I would suggest that in prosperous parts of the world, we do not keep growing, neither our population, nor our gross domestic product. I suggest that we spread the wealth around, that we do not go to a totally egalitarian system, but that we moderate inequality so everyone is taken care of, but overall we do not need to grow further. There is enough for everyone at this rate, in this country, if not around the world. Enough is already too much, here. Just as there, in what we derisively call "The Third World," there seems to be never enough.

Yet around the world, especially the non-prosperous parts of the world, "growth," that is, "growth" that will still have its ultimate limits is necessary, to bring those in dire straits or just miserable poor straits up to a decent life.

Still, in the bargain, we must GO GREEN — in The First, Second and Third Worlds — and back to harmonizing instead of demanding from and controlling Nature We must end the war with Nature, becoming bosom buddies with our Mother Earth. Not only will leveling off growth in prosperous nations and then leveling off "growth" when all nations become reasonably prosperous be necessary, but beginning immediately and sooner, we simply as a species need to create a sustainable world, a much greener world. The direction of growth should be aimed away from the same old same old way with all its negative consequences of equal and opposite reactions, called climate change, a polluted unhealthy environment and conflicts of all kinds between the haves and have less and have nots. That is unless we want to pass on no more future generations, or a population shrunk to almost nothing on a miserable used up world.

We can have our cake and science and technology too, if that technology, those businesses, put back as much as they take out, so there will not be that natural backlash of endless inappropriate "growth."

What would such a re-engineered world possibly look like? How much would we have to give up of the modern world to keep the world intact?

The main issue is energy. The next issues are recycling and sustainability. I know there is enough work and enough jobs for us, for the Chinese, for every last job seeker in Africa and South America and New Zealand. Why? Because we need to retool the world. We do not need to continue "growing" the way we have grown, a blight on the planet, a blight to ourselves, a blight that future generations will curse us for unless we change and change quickly.

The first rule of ecology for the future will be this: if you cannot return the consequence of the burning of the underground fuel — coal, oil, gas, nuclear uranium—into the underground, do not take it out in the first place. It does not belong in the above ground, in the air, the water, in our lungs and in our livers, nor on trees or killing off the bees.

We must deal with this. We must do this forthwith! The transition to above ground energy, water, wind and solar must begin now. If there is not enough energy from all that effort to use above ground energy, then we must cut back across the board in our country, in all countries, with that reduced amount of energy fairly distributed around the planet. Not "drill baby drill" and more and more "growth," but shrink back, baby, shrink back.

If electric automobiles need to be confined to 30 miles per hour, so be it. Sorry, for otherwise the consequence of you wanting to go 75 is bad news for your grandchildren and everyone else now alive. If you do not want to pass along government debt to your grandchildren, neither and more importantly do you want to pass on this world odor. Debt can be resolved in bankruptcy court at worst and so what? This malodorous dystopia cannot be resolved in any court of law as it is ruled by The Laws of Nature and the Court of Nature's Consequences. The penalty is dystopian jail forever.

Maybe it is the end of the gas driven internal combustion engine. Maybe that needs to happen. Sorry. Electric lawnmowers are in our future. And that electricity comes off your roof, not from a nuclear or coal fired plant. So does the energy for the slower car.

Maybe the absolute plethora of consumer goods that clog our every step in our clutter-filled houses needs to be less. Maybe we need to get out to a park or a pub, instead of playing with more and more consumed toys at home. Less may be more in terms of life and what we flippantly call "lifestyle." We need not give up everything and race to the bottom, but simply moderate. It would do us, our next-door neighbor, our far-flung neighbors and the planet better if we, in our pursuit of happiness, headed for The Golden Mean instead of mean gold.

If homes and offices need to be redesigned so that they require less energy, whether it is a rich person's mansion or a reasonable hovel in a reasonably poor neighborhood, then they all need to be. Lots and lots of work there too.

We need to take this seriously and rethink how we are doing and energizing our civilization. Maybe food needs to be grown in New Jersey and New England for those who live in Brooklyn instead of being transported from the San Joaquin Valley to Brooklyn. It just is not energetically efficient or sustainable to feed everyone from the artificially hydrated parts of California. It does not mean you need to stop eating, only eating relatively locally most of the time. Buffalo burgers may need to come from the Dakotas (see the next chapter) but potatoes, maybe from Long Island.

I could go on and on with this and on and on. There are so many changes we need to make. And even the ones I have mentioned seem radical and impractical for now. And there are so many more. Greening cities and greening cities to the maximum. And restoring lots and lots of wilderness. And …. and …. and.

GREEN INFRASTRUCTURE PROJECTS. We need to retool, re-engineer, reorganize the planet with GREEN IN-FRASTRUCTURE first and foremost. And, of course, green building structures as well.

Yet the consequence of not turning the Titanic away from the icebergs, the consequences of not turning our society from heading straight for disaster, the result is an Armageddon not from God, but our very own four machine horsemen. To say the least, our thinking must turn radically

Green. The current conventional, The Ship of Fools conventionality that passes for discussion and debate, needs give way to a higher rationality and more complete and real reality.

Barack Obama may be the most reasonable man alive, but here is the problem even with Barack. The times call for creative drastic measures, drastic measures by which not only is no body hurt, but a better world is created by our abilities to do what needs to be done when we need to do it and everyone contributes and everyone has an appropriate degree of say and control. Being all too reasonable and compromising within the parameters and restricted diameters of the current political and economic and ecological paradigms still may result in going off the cliff or sinking beneath the stinking polluted ways in an empty theatre in your end of times neighborhood.

Wake up and save the roses because before long the bees will be gone and there will be no more roses to smell, unless we all get off our collective high-living horses, our sense of privilege and get on with getting on, retooling and accepting less.

It is not necessary that The Mayan Prophecy be true and the man carrying the poster down Lake Shore Drive boasting that it is the end of times and repent should be prophetic. We have choice. We always have choice. We need to take responsibility for our world, instead of slinking back into some burrow of self centered, self interested, complacent freedom and consumption.

In the 60's, in my hippy days, they said, "Do your own thing, man." How about if the new hip slogan is: DO THE RIGHT GREEN THING. Otherwise, bro', entropy is going to take your old lady and your butt right out of here.

I cannot emphasize enough how GREEN we must become. Republicans appear to get completely bent out of shape concerning federal government debt and taxes that will drown the finances of our children. I would like them to be as apoplectic about the future of their children and grandchildren and the consequences of environmental debt. And stop believing that the right to private property means that you can do whatever you want with the land and waters that God or the Gods gifted to you on loan. It is not yours.

In this chapter I have had few if any specific proposals. There are thousands that need to be made. So here is the one in summary that desperately needs to be done:

- GO GREEN ALL OVER THE PLACE. NOW!

Chapter 8
The Four Zones

Driving through Spain out of Madrid airport to the country's northeast corner, the Basque area in the Pyrenees, and then along the north coast, staying at bed and breakfasts in towns and small cities, it occurred to my wife, her sister and brother-in-law and myself, that these wise and friendly Spanish had arranged their space temporal and physical for sociability, unlike us Americans who in space and time, confine ourselves to home boxes within which we watch Home Box Office.

The Spanish congregate together in the evening, in city, suburb or town, in a central town gathering space where people get together at tapas bars with tables on the sidewalks and candy shops for the kids. In some of their cities, while there is parking on the street generally, in some parts of other cities the parking is put underground and the central square area is devoid of cars and this may even extend down the street of shops — what we would call an outdoor mall. It is in most places child, pedestrian and community friendly. We go home to our houses and TVs for a virtual social life of situation comedies or police dramas while the Spanish hang out together, participating in an actual social life.

But even beyond that, they had, if not uniformly but for the most part, zoned the countryside ecologically. When you left a town, there was a sign denoting that you had left that town. Beyond the limits of the town, in the countryside, there was no urban or suburban or any other kind of sprawl, box stores, Mickey D's or Kentucky Fried, or much of any kind of commercial enterprise other than wine vineyards and almond or cork tree farms. In many areas, there were not even farmhouses. Land, I suspect, being valuable in a small country with not all that much good farm land, farmers came into town in the evening to have a glass of red or white at night with some thin sliced ham and hang out with family and friends while watching a bullfight or soccer match on the TV in the tapas bars' corner, then to a bed in a high rise apartment. Can you imagine that? Farmers in apartment houses in small towns is not the American Way but it is the Spanish.

I will not be urging that we adopt or adapt the Spanish model to an American geography and society that is very different from the Spanish. Yet I would suggest that we could rearrange our physical space in a different way that would serve us far better in the short and especially the long term. The shift I am proposing will take a few generations to implement, but I believe, would be well worth the effort. How we have arranged and zoned our physical space in America is a dystopian disaster. The Spanish are onto something and they are much the better for it in lifestyle and ecology. They may have other financial and social problems and depression level unemployment, but ecologically and socially, they are, frankly, our betters. I know the idea that America is not first and foremost in everything is not to be spoken — being less that #1 is our equivalent of saying "Voldemort" — but frankly, it is true and truer in more ways that we want to acknowledge.

I will propose that we divide our physical space into four zones: urban-suburban, farmland, ranchland and wilderness. I would also suggest that we be as strict as, if not stricter, than the Spanish in thus zoning it this way. What I mean by strict is not only that the zones are well delineated with fair and clear boundaries, but also that we do not change the zones as population changes, and grows. Once we have restricted cities and suburbs to a certain amount of land and space, that is it. The way for cities and suburbs and towns to grow is up and not out, higher buildings to accommodate more people not urban sprawl to accommodate more stores and new condos. Moreover, I think it not a bad idea at all if we pushed city and suburbs back a ways even now so that farmland, small towns, ranchland and wilderness could have a greater overall space and population than they do now .

For the good of the planet and us all, the area I am calling "wilderness" needs to be expanded greatly. This is not just to accommodate the people who will then people the wilderness areas, but also to expand natural areas that will buffer and transform the carbon dioxide and other carbon emissions from industrialization that is choking us literally to the childhood asthma bottom of our lungs and building a great big earthly greenhouse, warming the air and oceans to the tipping point of a mass global warming that will have multiple devastating consequences for all of us, rich, poor, over there and back here — goodbye East Coast, hello warm and tropical Ontario.

It is not only wilderness that needs expanding, but ranch lands and farm lands as well. Urban-suburban can be pushed back maybe just in the nick of time to get us back to a good balance of land use and conservation and stop the coming ecological climate catastrophe. Of course, it will take time to do it all when time is scarce. It may take a generation or more, but I think, from the perspective of many generations to come, this is a necessity. We need to start right away, big time even as this will take time to complete.

What will this all look like and what will people be doing in each of these areas and how will they interact personally and commercially with each other?

City, Suburb, Town

For now, it is the truth that the urban rules. As little as .6% of our population farms. Considering that in 1900, about 40% of U.S. population farmed, and that one hundred years before that, most everyone farmed, that is change I do not believe in and, I believe, a change that has many negative consequences. One of them is that when push comes to shove and cities and suburbs and towns want to urban-suburban develop further, making way for the bargain-hunters dystopian blight known as urban sprawl of gross and ghastly shopping centers full of the same set of Walmarts and KMarts and Radio Shacks and any other of the Retail Fortune 500 out to the foreseeable horizon, the farm is on the way out, corn crop and chickens be damned and "let 'em squawk."

Not that the farmer might not pocket — if rarely — a mighty healthy profit from the sale of land that has been handed down in the family for generations, a farm that has become more and more marginally profitable if at all and, by the good graces of developers paying for that land with big city big bucks, the farmers can have gobs of Orlando fun park fun in the Florida sun and pay for the education of their next generation of kin, now off the farm and part of the urban masses but with the cash that allows that next group of progeny to prosper as non-farmers and urbanites and suburbanites. Actually, the scenario is much poorer that this.

The externalization costs are two, however. One, in the short and the other, longer societal run. Urban sprawl as we know it is not only, to my aesthetic and environmental sense, ugly — "ugly" being a single word not even doing much poetic justice to what seems to me the crime of despoiling and deflowering a beautiful continent — but also, by the way, horribly inefficient and unhealthy. When shops and stores and restaurants were in town and you could walk to them as is done in much of Europe to this day not only did everyone walk, but it was not necessary to use the gas guzzling and polluting automobile to get to the places of shopping and out for-a-change restaurant going. It is not entirely coincidental that the walking French, although enjoying to a diet high in unhealthy saturated fats, do not nearly have the heart attack rates of sedentary Americans who do very little good old walking for the most part.

Then there is the long term effect of using farm land for condos and Wal-marts, and using land to produce fast food Kentucky Fried Chicken whose fried and grilled chicken comes from factory chicken farms that proportionally pack more chickens into a tighter space than the over populated packing of human beings in Calcutta. The squeezed, squelched and squawking chicks are fed hormones and antibiotics for good measure because so close together they neither grow nor stay healthy. The long term effect of taking away more and more farmland, well, we have enough land now to feed 300+ million people now. Yet what happens in say, 50 or 100 or 200 years when our population is like India or China today — one or two or three billion? It is, as we say, not "sustainable," in the long term. Short term, it is miserable. Long term, it is not possible.

I was one of those when I lived in Vermont who commuted into work from the countryside. Since the distance from where I lived in the countryside was great, I bought a car, a 1980 Honda Civic HF that revved up at over 50 miles per gallon. My car print, as it were, was not as great as if I drove a GMC gargantuan SUV 4 wheel drive. Still, either way, I think that in hindsight I was irresponsible living as I did, as nice as breathing pretty darn good air was after living in a putrid part of gentrifying Park Slope, Brooklyn.

Unless we have a business in the countryside, like farming or cheese making or dog breeding or we have a home office that logs into a satellite for internet connection and work, I do not believe we should be living out of town. It is a waste not only of gasoline but also of land. Certainly, we should not be taking farmland away for another set of buy-all-you can-at-low-prices shopping centers.

Frankly, I would make it against the law to build stores on farmlands as well as prevent living on good farm or grazing land and commuting to work. Not that I would evict those who are already living in the countryside from living there, but I would not allow the next generation to do the same. Yes, all those countryside dwellers will need compensation for their land and house and woodshed. Then, when we pay them off and dismantle every last center of urban-suburban sprawl and confine Wally and his Mart to their proper place and time, we need to turn the land all back over to the farmer and rancher and wilderness naturalist dweller.

As the population of cities and large towns and smaller towns grows, increasing the densification of urban areas —

growing up instead of out — is better than killing the countryside. And then within the city: more sidewalks for pedestrians, more bike paths, and especially, more green space.

I never walked so much as when I lived in Manhattan
that itself had been built up, not out, by necessity, given that
it is Manhattan Island and not the vast plains of Manhattan.
While Manhattan Island is not my idea of an environmental
kingdom of heaven by any means — with the exception of
Central Park, which if it stretched the whole center north
to south in Manhattan would improve the city immensely
— still, cleaned up and greened, it could be a good place to
live and work and shop. Perhaps even to be emulated, that
is, after it greens up. With some inventiveness and entrepreneurial spirit New York might actually be even better than
we think.

What to do with industrial production, factories and
power plants and all the business and buildings of a machine civilization? Those, too, should be integrated within
urban areas; they are there for the most part now. They
should be both pleasant to the eye and non-polluting as well.
If an enterprise cannot do its business without externalizing
its costs, its pollution costs, its environmental costs, it should
not be in business. Even factory ugliness costs. Although the
monetary costs are not obvious, the cost, in terms of our sat-
isfaction in life, is great, having little to do with money but
everything to do with life and its better aesthetics.

Another way must be found to create products that are
environmentally non-hazardous, both in its production and
in what it does. We should all do without that product if it is.
Sorry, it is just not worth the cost to ruin our world, just so
we can have every last toy imaginable and so someone can
get rich off the general ugly unhealthy misery. This might
take a bit of time as most negative addictions take time to get
over, whether alcohol or drugs or pollution or consumerism.
Detox programs, physical and psychological, will need to be
in place to wean us off all unwholesome destructive production.

Urban areas, however, should have more trees in areas of the country that were more forested to begin with, more desert-like in areas that are notably arid and grassier through the grasslands. If we are keeping the city out of the countryside, we can at least bring the appropriate ecologic to the cities according to climate and topography. No green lawns in Vegas because it is a waste of water. Cactus gardens would be fine.

In the farmlands, ranchlands and wilderness lands, we can bring manufactured goods, including all those nice new communication goods like iPads and Googles and such out to there. Out in the countryside, out of urban areas, we can build or expand towns that are appropriate as centrally located exchange points, with farm and livestock produce going towards the cities and machine goods in the other direction. The same with people: city dwellers to visit out; farmers, ranchers and hunter-gatherers coming in.

We should have a free flow of goods and people in both directions at the same time that we are preserving each area. Not that a good amount of that exchange is not in place already. On that account, there is not all that much to do. Towns are there already, if a bit run down and out of shape. What if all the processing of food stuffs done now in big cities where done in small towns? That would go far to bringing back small towns.

The greening or desert-ing or plain-ing of our cities will take considerable effort and imagination, even as urban areas increase in population. How do you green Manhattan? Since I have lived and worked in Manhattan and even drove a taxi cab and a delivery truck in Manhattan during my youth, I have imagined a different set-up with some variations many times.

I would, first, ban private automobiles from Manhattan. Now for those New Yorkers who want to keep a car because they want to, on occasion, get out of town, a system of garages lining the city where private cars could be kept and, of course, the East Side and West Side highways as get-out-of town routes, along with bridges and tunnels to get off the island would not be banned to private autos.

Nor would a new system like this ban delivery trucks or taxi cabs or public buses or trains; just private automobiles are out. In time all vehicles would be required to be electric and non-polluting. I would also close off to any sort of motor transportation all streets that are not major thoroughfares. All the north-south avenues stay open. And the wide east-west roads as well, 42 St., 34, 14, 59, 72, 79, 86 and others. Still, Broadway would be an excellent pedestrian street, complete with outdoor cafes. Everything else becomes free to pedestrians, period. And parks can be built there and out door cafes and _____ . Fill in the blank and use your imagination, from tulip gardens to water slides to green-houses. It would even be good for business, not just people. And above? Greenhouses on roofs; walkways in the sky between high rise buildings. Build up and build green. Only our limited imaginations keeps us limited.

What to do with Brooklyn and Queens, the Bronx? Take a day off New Yorkers and think about it. There are ways to do this and make it a livable city instead of a monstrous stressful environmental debacle — which it pretty much is now and sent me, in my instinctive youth scurrying for rural New England and a decent non-dystopian environment in which to live.

Think utopian ideal, act practically, but not so practically that you forget that this could work out much better. How about you out there in Cleveland, Albuquerque, L.A.?

Suburbs, for their part, are really just extensions of cities. In population, the towns and suburbs around Boston ac-count for more people than the city of Boston proper. New York City has more residents in the five boroughs than its suburbs, but combine the suburbs in surrounding counties and 8 million city dwellers becomes 12 million urban-subur-ban dwellers. While, there certainly is a difference between living in Queens and Scarsdale, the difference is not as great between the suburbs and "The City" as between life in the suburbs compared to rural New England or the sparsely populated towns in North Dakota. The same building up and greening and idealization can and should inform growth in suburbs as well.

Towns, especially those placed in farmland, ranchland or wilderness areas are different. Towns, as I have said, are two-directional portals, bringing city manufacturing and entertainment to the hinterlands while the fruits of the labors of farmers, ranchers and others — literally fruit — but also vegetables, milk and meats back to urban areas. In towns, rural produce can be processed into different products — Ben & Jerry's of Waterbury, Vermont producing some very good ice cream from its factory from the milk from cows of rural Vermont. Buffalo burgers from the Dakotas; orange juice from Florida; and so on. Grown and processed in the countryside towns.

Countryside and town were the nutritive backbone of America. To a great extent, they are still today. Respecting and revitalizing town — and farmland — would go far to creating a healthier and happier human environment. Not totally different from what is there now, but consciously and ecologically reinvigorating small town America, the real Main St. America, might not be a bad idea at all. Small town life could be a welcome choice to harried urban-suburban dwellers; and those who already live the small town life, the small town reenergized, might welcome not only the newcomers refugees from the city, but the more central role played by the small town.

Farmland

The farmer feeds us all — along with the fisherman and grocer, of course. Personally, not only am I thankful for farmers and their farming, but instead of venerating and paying exorbitantly for the services of banking executives on Wall Street, or retail merchants like the Walton family of Arkansas, personally, my heroes are all those not as well paid farmers and cattle ranchers and fisher-people. As much as Bill Gates has done for computer software and as much as I admire the Apple entrepreneurial Jobs and the iMac I write this book on, still, if nobody was willing to furrow a corn field in Iowa, or herd a long horned steer in Texas or snag salmon out in the ocean Pacific along the Alaskan coast, there would be none of the rest. Maybe we should be exalting and paying them much more instead laying down billions for Rupert Murdoch and his band of merry sleaze artists posing as Fox news anchorpersons.

Little by little, the family farm is being squeezed more and more, going out of business more and more, becoming more and more corporate farming, very large scale. Even when the very large farm is owned by the family and farmer in residence, sometimes the chickens are owned by Perdue and chicken neck Mr. Perdue tells the family farmer what to do and how to coop up chickens.

Chickens are cooped up in ever bigger coops, as are cows and pigs and other farm animals in industrial size and strength factory barn-warehouses, the animals fed hormones and antibiotics with their meal because hormones help them grow and antibiotics keep them well under poor environmentally unnatural conditions.

When you come down with a wicked flu and head off to the ER at your local hospital ten years from now and you have eaten lots and lots of chicken breasts laced with antibiotics and you cannot kick that bug and the hospital does not have any antibiotics for you because you have been, under your radar, taking antibiotics for years and the bugs have mutated and maybe you survive and maybe you don't. Maybe your daughter or son lives through a nasty flu or maybe not.

Do you know what percentage of the potato crop is genetically engineered? Far more than 50%. While those big old farms in Idaho need not spray for potato bugs for a few decades as the genetic potatoes that Monsanto is servicing them with is resistant to that bug now, what happens when that bug mutates, and all the potatoes from Idaho to Maine are eaten by that monster beetle that just loves to munch genetically modified potato innards right down to nothing and there are no French fries from coast to coast? Monsanto will, of course, promise another potato resistant to that particular new monster beetle but they won't have it for awhile, say, a decade or two. Steak and potatoes for dinner, sir? Sorry, no potatoes, sir, for a decade or two or maybe three. (And corporate Monsanto might just sue you for saying so, by the way.)

How many steaks did the English forgo when it turned out that many a cow of England and Scotland was bonkers with mad cow disease. No potato. No steak. What will happen to that poor beefy couch potato?

We will then seemingly all be eating mercury laced fish for a generation, except for the uncomfortable fact that due to factory ships fishing out waters everywhere — and around Cape Cod where the cod are pretty much gone for ever and a day — and everywhere else, there will be not enough fish around anymore either, for anyone, let alone, everyone to eat. Famine is not all that unusual a phenomenon in human history. While we are extremely productive agriculturally as a society in America and feeding 300+ million of us — and on the planet for now, feeding more or less 6+ billions — but how much would it really take to tip it the other way? Less than you think; dystopia followed by hungry Armageddon. We may believe we live in a "post-scarcity" world, but that could change very quickly.

In the name and practice of making a buck, with the only motivation that some small percentage of us gets to be filthy rich, why we put up with all this? It really is very irresponsible on a very grand scale to not do the right thing and arrange our world and its farms in such a manner that it works and works for a long time. I believe we now call this "sustainability." Don't you want to keep eating? Sustainable eating, I am all for it. Nothing that we do in this generation may be more important than how we manage our lands and our farms. No bread and then the proverbial circus in "bread and circus" is not very amusing. In fact, the circus is gone too as not only can we not feed ourselves, but the lions and tigers and dancing bears, oh my.

When, as an earnest if innocent and foolish hippie, I made my way out of New York City and into the semi-civilized wilds of Vermont in the early 1970's about 10% of Vermonters were farmers. By the time I left 20 years later, having parted with my hippy-ish ways and innocence as well, 1% were farmers and I am not sure of that small percentage how many were part-time or faking it.

On my wife's mother's side of the family are the Bascoms of New Hampshire. The Bascoms trace their lineage back some 600 years to the Basque area of Spain and France. Break the name "Bascom" down and it becomes "Basque homme" or, to translate from the French, Basque-man. The land of the Basque region looks a lot like the land of New England. It is not only how it appears, but how it functions — a certain kind of cool weather farming. The Bascoms have farmed in New Hampshire for about 150 years. One of my wife's Bascom 2nd cousins is in the Maple Syrup Hall of Fame and still has a large maple syrup operation pumping out and boiling off jar after thousands of jars of superb sweet syrup. However, other Bascoms who were dairy farmers are going extinct as farmers. They are out of business and off the farm, not because they were incompetent as farmers, but because the economics of small farming in New England pushed them out of the farming they cherished — and which was feeding us down country city people, the "flatlanders."

I lived in a ski area of central Vermont in the town of Waitsfield that contained in its vicinity The Sugarbush and Mad River Ski areas. A couple that dubbed themselves and their business "The Mad Men" cleaned houses and condos. They had a good business and worked hard. They were used to hard work; they used to be dairy farmers in upstate New York. They had gone to agricultural college to learn the latest and the best in farming methods and machinery. They were smart and hard working. They went bankrupt as farmers. Why? They listened to their Ag professors and their government agents and the local bankers who all convinced them to buy the latest and greatest farm equipment so they could farm on a grand scale. They did. They went bust. Now they cleaned condos. They were good at it. They were doing well. Yet, I assure you they would have much preferred to farm and feed us all.

So, I have a few ideas here too to put the Mad Men and my favorite Bascoms back on the farm.

I believe there are too few of us on the farm. And, I do not think this is by free choice. I think many more of us would like to live the hard labor but good life of the farmer. I believe that:

- Not only should the farm be owned by the family that is working the land, but that any one working on the farm should be a part owner of the farm. Farms are a business and the same rules that apply to industrial businesses apply to farms. 50% profit to those who work on the farm. 50% profit. to Community Banks that lend money for equipment. Board of Directors, 50%/50% as well.

- Farmers should be among the most prosperous of us all.

- Farms should generally be smaller and family owned — and if small is not appropriate in a particular geographic location, still family owned. Maybe one family, maybe, as in a co-op, several families.

- In order to farm the land, the farmer needs to live on the land and farm it. The farmer — and the Community Bank — owns the farm and its animals and it buildings and its equipment, but the farmer and family or families or individuals live there and not elsewhere and cannot hire others to do the work at a distance.

- Land itself should be free. Land cannot be bought or sold. Still, the farmer(s) and farm families have a right to farm land without ever being thrown off the land.

- All farms should be organic. By law and regulation.

- All the livestock should be under the control of farmers and not distributors.
- The life of livestock should be relatively more humane.
- No hormones. No antibiotics. Unless absolutely necessary.
- Farms, like any other business, should be regulated by a regulatory board.
- Farm prices might need at times to be regulated by the regulatory body for farms. Otherwise, free market.
- Farm Insurance is required of all farms.
- Community Bank loans should be available for failed or failing farms when necessary. Farms cannot go out of business and liquidate as industrial businesses.

That is, just as I am proposing that the workers in factories are owners of their factory — with the community and its bank that support their efforts — similarly, those who work on the farm should be its owners and profit by their enterprise. Either, a farm is worked by a single extended family or farming is done cooperatively with several families farming together. Or if not the farm family and another family, one family and one or several individuals who have an ownership stake in the farm. There should be no disenfranchised and land starved farm workers who do not have a direct stake in a farm that they call their own.

What if the family farmer and their farm need seasonal laborers, say, to pick crops? Again, the rule of living wage and profit sharing and sharing ownership and control should apply. Cheap migrant labor or even just cheap farm labor below minimum living wage should not be allowed by the farm regulatory agency and the banks. And, if a farm laborer — and maybe the farm laborer's family — is a full time hired hand, well, that full time person should be considered as the farmer is, part of the farm company as well. They own the farm — not the land, but the farm company — with the farmer. The same scheme from industrial and service businesses applies here as well. Boards of Directors for very large farms with lots of employees. For smaller farms, another arrangement and simpler as is appropriate. Either way, control of the farm is democratic.

Both Stalin and Mao decided that all farms should become communes. Forced communalization. Who owns the farm? No one, except perhaps the government that dictates where the wheat should go — to Moscow or Peking. The farmer could not even feed their family and they starved, their families starving by the millions in the Ukraine and the Chinese countryside. The greatest failure of Communism was not in its ability to industrialize — as bad as that record is and it is pretty bad — but in its effect on the farm. In the Ukraine and in the rice paddies of China, it was a holocaust. People died. People died en masse by the unfortunate millions.

Cooperatives and communes themselves may be fine. The kibbutz worked out very well in Israel. There are communes in the United States going back to the 19th Century that still function well too. The Amish in Pennsylvania using a family and cooperative model of farming are among the most prosperous and stable and productive farmers in the country.

Still, forcing everyone to use one model, that it all must be a cooperative or commune or even small family farm, any model forced on unwilling farming families and workers is untenable, especially where control is in the hands of larger political and economic elites that do not have the farmer's best interest at heart. Stalin's and Mao's hearts were ruled by their personal ideological fantasies. Purdue and Monsanto are ruled by their personal greedy fantasies. Neither totalitarian government, nor vampire-ish corporations should rule. The farmer should be in control.

A distant corporation should not own the chickens in the factory warehouse coop. There should be no absentee landlords and tenant farmers. There are no migrant workers exploited by gigantic farms that cannot harvest crops themselves. Many forms of farming would be permitted in this model. Yet, certain models would be prohibited. No absentee farming. No hiring of farm workers without shared ownership.

As for ridding the farmer and us of corporations that own the land or the chickens a la Purdue, maybe those corporation are compensated in some way or perhaps not, for their loss of property.

Land and farm reform will help us all with better food, the farmer with a stable way of life and those who want to be farmers with more opportunity.

Land itself cannot be owned. God or Spirits or The Laws of Physics and biology and ecology created fertile land and I do not believe that anyone can own land. So, to my mind, land cannot be bought and sold.

But land can be farmed. And, the family or groups of families or groups of individuals or individuals have a right in perpetuity to the farming use of the land they are on. Unless grossly negligent or totally irresponsible, you have a right to farm your land and farm it with whom you please, as long as you farm it together. Your family has a right through the generations to stay put and farm the land. Think of the Amish. Think of Iowa — although even Iowa is changing to the corporate.

If the next generation in the family wants to leave and live in the city or go to ranchland or wilderness that is their right too. Their place in turn can be taken up by someone from the city who wants to farm or someone from the ranchland or wilderness land who wants to farm. There can be movement between areas as each generation chooses where it wants to live and how it wants to work, just as those within an area, say, the city, can choose occupations and work within that area.

Now, naturally, social issues could arise such as what if too many people want to farm or be ranchers or wilderness hunter-gathers (see below for these) and it is beyond the capacity of the land to accommodate that kind of reverse migration? What if, in fact, a future "Back To The Land" movement become too popular? From .6% to, say, 60%, a one hundred fold increase. Unlikely, but what if?

The tendency over the last several hundred years, if not a whole millennia has been from the countryside to the city. And then, what if, in fact, that trend continues and nobody wants to do anything but city life. Who shall feed everyone?

I would modestly suggest that if we make each mode of life practical and attractive, whether it be city, farm, ranch or wilderness, that it might work itself out. Maybe. I would like to see what would happen if everyone straight up were given a choice, the education to make that choice feasible so that they would have the skills to survive, nay, prosper, with their choice and then we shall see. If it does not work out and everyone wants to be a rancher on the lone prairie and sit in the saddle from sun up to sun down, well, maybe we shall have to expand the lone prairie. Or if everyone wants to milk cows, well, we shall be awash in Land O'Lakes butter, Stoneyfield yogurt, Haagen Dazs ice cream and the best organic milk ever. Heaven help our clogged heart arteries.

Then there are those who might want to farm for a decade, ranch for two and then do biological research at Harvard. I think it would not be a bad life. Of course, it complicates things a bit, but then again, when was freedom and responsibility simple and easy?

I think it more possible than we can work this out. It seems worth trying rather than going along as things are. I think about 20% of the total population on the farm as opposed to the present less than 1% would be feasible, indeed, preferable. It would make small scale highest quality organic farming possible. Fifteen percent give or take on ranches, perhaps. Five percent in the wilderness. Sixty or so percent in cities. I think some arrangement like that would be about right.

If it did not work out this way or these kind of percentages are not practically possible, what should we do? Can we begin to solve an imaginary problem caused by my imaginary system? Difficult enough to know how to solve problems that are known, let alone problems that are possibilities.

I will try one possible solution though. What if there are too many people wanting to farm and not enough open farms? A evaluator lottery system could be created for farmland that is not in use by other farmers. That would take a social entity, a kind of Farm Bureau — elected by farmers in an area — to evaluate of those who want to farm and either pick among those who would be best at farming or if there were many able candidates, hold a lottery. Still, whatever the system chosen, farms stay farms. They do not get sold so that the farmer can get out of town and retire to Tampa Bay by selling off the only thing the farmer has of value left: the farm land itself.

In this new system, land is free and can be neither bought nor sold. So what happens if the farmer and family choose to end their good earth days and slide on down the road to town or further into the countryside? What if milking goats or tending tender broccoli shoots no longer provides a thrill? Well, you cannot sell your land since you do not own it. One of two things happens: either the land is not farmed or perhaps there is that waiting list of people from another area who would like to farm and the farm land is then entrusted to them, having become available.

Still, farmers should make enough money farming so that when retirement comes up, farmers are not so impoverished that either they must get back up on their ornery tractor or sell the farm. One advantage of the system I am outlining is that the farmer does not have to spend decades paying off a mortgage on land. Instead, the money can go into retirement savings. Besides which, like everyone else, they must put 15% or so into Social Security. Farming is still part of the money economy.

Of course, if the farmer simply inherited the family farm and there was no mortgage to begin, then that farmer and farm family did not have this burden to begin. This brings us to the issue of farms making money, as perhaps even without the land mortgage burden, farmers are not making enough to get by and, as in the present, sell their smaller farm to a bigger farm and then the bigger ones gobble up the smaller ones and the big corporation owns them all.

How can farms be made financially stable and keep families on the farm and allow them to prosper and retire if they desire? And how can we get really good and healthy produce from our farms.

Regulations, as for industry, would take the form of law as provided by government and then regulation as provided by a regulatory agency of regulatory professionals. In planning the future of farming and keeping farms prosperous and productive, and productive not just in quantity of food, but in quality.

Law and regulation, I would suggest, should emphasize farm methods that require the end of artificial fertilizers, chemical insecticides, DNA altered crops and the warehousing of animals. Not to totally do away with innovation, like new styles of irrigation or new varieties of more productive seeds or a better tractor. The idea is not to rid us of good practices that make more and better food, but to eliminate practices that increase quantity but decrease quality and give us less than healthy, nutritious food. All organic should be a regulatory requirement. Food that is non-organic might contain exactly the same nutrients as organic food, but they add on poisons that are not only non-nutritious but simply poisonously unhealthy. Harmful. They do harm.

Of course, if famine is threatens because of a particular bug in a particular year and chemical extermination is the only way to go, it should be permitted. But this should be the exception and not the rule.

Although the transition from our current farm system to one with smaller organic, more diversified and humane farms will require at least a generation and probably longer, but for the long term healthy survival of our grandchildren and great grandchildren in this country, it is necessary.

Overnight, the disruptions might be too great and jeopardize the whole enterprise. We are as addicted to the current methods of farming as we are to oil. We cannot kick these habits overnight, and we will require more than a few Twelve Step Farming Programs of one sort or another.

Why would you want to eat a genetically altered potato when you could eat an organic beauty? Would you rather eat a steak from an antibiotic hormone fed obese sickly cow or a gorgeous rib eye from a chemical free and free roaming contented cow? Why settle for the artificial when you can have the natural? Which does your natural body understand better, real stuff or laboratory stuff? Which keeps you healthier and happier? Do you know how toxic those pesticides really are? You would not want to know.

Yet, what happens if there is a drought or a disaster like hurricane or tornado or locusts digesting the broccoli crop? What happens to the family farm then? The family farm might still have debt, having bought a new tractor last year. Or, even if there were no debt to speak of, how is the farmer in a severe drought area to feed their children without income or a crop? And what if farm prices are not high enough to cover expenses and the farmer loses money, what happens then?

Simply making farms organic and run by families and those who live on the land is no guarantee that bad things could not happen. Given how good smaller organic farms might be as natural quality producers and how abundant the land of the United States is generally, would it not be possible that too much production would lead to prices on good farm goods so low that the farmer's free market system could become a problem for the farmer and put them off the farm?

As for the first set of natural disaster problems, there should be insurance, in fact, required insurance. As with health insurance, every farmer pays into a fund each year to cover the expenses of disaster relief across the country. That's that. Then, of course, no farmer and family can be put off the land anyway. That's that doubly.

Still, paying for the new tractor or barn or new seed or any of the multitude of expenses for the continuation of farming is all important. Answer: covered by insurance if the old one is ruined by a flood or a new loan from the Community Bank when the old one just plain too old.

As for poor farm prices, that is a more difficult issue. We have dealt with this issue since The Great Depression with farm subsidies and payments for not planting and other means. While for the farmer — but especially for the corporate farm — this keeps prices profitable and for the consumer, farm products are relatively inexpensive. Yet, in the end the cost of all these farm subsidies is higher taxes which means that while you do not pay more for your food at the grocery store, you do pay more for your food in your taxes.

On the one hand, I would, as economists say, "unleash the markets." That is, forget the subsidies and forget the subsidies for not planting. Maximum farming is fine. Good quality organic food in vast quantities is fine. Still, again, what if there is too much? What if prices fail? For a country of such vast and productive land, this is not an imaginary fear.

Yet, if you truly want goods to export, we are the perfect land and country for exporting food. Take China, for example. Population rich with about a billion and a half people. Land poor, actually. China has one-fifth the arable land of the United States. They are not alone, nor alone in their fear of future food shortages. Korea, North and South. Japan. England. England imports food! Given the expanding population around the world, the United States could do worse than maximize its food production and sell its tomatoes in Norway or its rice and soybeans to South Korea.

And for those areas of the world that are starving: ship it free. Buy it from the farmer and send it for free. Who would pay for it? Take it out of the military budget. Or put another way, make it part of the military budget. What country is going to attack you if you are feeding them? Have a hostile enemy in Iran? Offer them free food, food they cannot grow themselves — not, of course, food that would compete with their producers. See how long they stay enemies then

Still, it is possible for farms to fail in a free market system, just as it is possible for industries to fail in our Capitalist industrial system. Yet in this case, the farmer and family is not thrown off the farm, as an automobile manufacturer who failed would have to sell off the auto plant and its equipment. In this case, instead of bank loans for new entrepreneurs in areas where enterprises have failed and left people unemployed, in the farmer's case bank loans would be sent to failing farms to start over again. The only caveat to these loans would be the requirement by the loaning bank that the farmer seek education and training in whatever areas they are deficient so as not to fail again, if that is the problem. (Now remember, all education, including farmer's education is covered already!)

Of course, if it is not a question of training or personal failure, it could just be markets. More training or more capital might not be the solution as the farmer is competent and has enough capital to begin. The problem is that the farmer cannot make enough money from a successful season to make ends meet. In that case, the body that regulates farming has the problem to deal with forthwith.   Now, of course, I do not have the solution to problems that from here and now to treat there and later, again. I will leave that problem to future regulatory bodies to consider. In any event, the requirement for mandatory insurance for farm business failure need not apply to only natural disasters. It can apply to market disasters as well and farmers need not starve or lose the family tractor and hay baler. It is the equivalent from the industrial sector of unemployment insurance. But for now, I will leave the questions of with failing farms or farms that do not provide enough income for the farmer to retire or for the farm bank to take in some profit to keep the system going to be hashed out at a future date.

Yet, we should allow future regulatory bodies for farming the option to regulate prices when they absolutely need to so that farms and farmers are protected. Farms and farmers should be prosperous and protected when the free market goes awry for one reason or another.

There are other methods of salvation a regulatory board might use, but I will let them deal with it in time.

Totally negligent farmers, of course, are subject to the rules and penalties of a farm regulatory body appointed by the government. The right to farm is not absolute. While throwing a farmer and family off the land for gross negligence or criminality is possible, it would be the last resort for a farm regulatory body. Still, if a future farmer decides against the express regulations of the farm regulatory agency to spray DDT on the land and cause physical harm to others, what should the penalty be?

Grazing animals should not be grazing on farmland that is better suited to growing crops appropriate to their locale. That is, cows, except for milk cows, should be grazing on ranchland. Pigs, chickens, all those barn-yarders could and should stay put on farms, but, good land should not be going to raise animals better ranging free and easy on land that is better suited to them.

Next: ranchland, cowboys and cowgirls.

Ranchland

In the U.S.A., we now sometimes feed our herds of cattle harvested crops — corn and grains — that farmers have grown on their land. Yet the newest trend at the local co-op health food store is "grass-fed beef," just as the chicken meat and chicken eggs are from contented chickens that are "free-range." The practice of husbandry by which many of us eat our meats is slowly changing back to the good old days. It needs to.

Farmland is becoming and will become even more precious as not only the population of the United States increases — to feed ourselves we have many years of margin before this is still problematic — but also as the population of the planet increases and increases beyond the ability of its land to feed all 8-9 billion of us by 2050. If, as we have seen over the 20th century, oil is the source of wars and dispute, do we want to leave shortages of food and water to power politics and military solutions? Powering up your automobile and lawnmower may be one thing; fighting over food and water, quite another. The disputes that follow from that are difficult to even contemplate. Think Somalia, but on a world wide scale.

We in America are rich in good farmland and not only can we produce enough food into the immediate future, but if we are wise and generous, we should be able to feed ourselves better and healthier and feed a good portion of the world besides.

Yet, we need to make some changes in how we farm and ranch to become ourselves more efficient and, at the same time, increase our quality of farm and ranch goods. The job of regulating and planning should come from our democratically elected government by way of laws and regulation, as I have said. These laws and regulations should not only be in the interest of the vast majority of citizens who now live in cities, but in the interest of farmers and ranchers. Given the dependency of city, suburb and town dwellers on farmers and ranchers, the promotion of the prosperity and happiness of those who feed us all, should be paramount. Farming and ranching are honorable professions, and those who take on this work should be among the most honored and prosperous among us.

It is not only the farmer and rancher who require support and respect. The very animals who we eat and depend on for milk, eggs and half and half, morning bacon and rib eye steaks, turkey breast at Thanksgiving and baked smoked ham at Christmas, should be treated with greater humanity and dignity as well. This is not only good for them, but good for us too. A contented cow produces more contented milk, a chicken free to walk about sweeter eggs and a happy hog better barbeque.

I would request as a citizen of the country, that government and regulators plan and organize our ranchland as follows. (Again, this will be a long process and probably take several generations to implement so that farmers and ranchers will not be put out or put upon. Yet in the interests of us all, I think we can reorient our land use and food lives.)

Land Use

Driving west through Iowa, then heading for the Sand Hills of Nebraska and then the oddity of the Badlands of South Dakota — God's sandcastles, poking up and out of the plains — it was difficult not to notice a shift in the nature of the land and land use. Whereas Iowa was seemingly all corn fields and windmills, and eastern Nebraska not much different, as we drove west Nebraska transformed bit by bit from miles of cornfields to the wind whistle whispered plains of ranchland, steers munching on grass and then, the Sand Hills that resembled Cape Cod without the ocean.

Some land is just better for ranching; and some land is better for farming. Just as the boundaries between city and farm should be better differentiated so too, it would benefit everyone greatly if there were a greater and better differentiation between farm and ranch.

Not that there are not areas where farm-ranches would not be appropriate and the best use of land, but farmers and ranches already know by what they are already doing on the land, that one is better than the other. Drive Nebraska to see it. If we do this right, there is a way that all livestock will be grass fed and those corn fields will be feeding us or our automobiles or sold to our south in Mexico for corn tortillas only. It is not quite natural for cows to be fed corn. It is quite natural for cows to eat grass and clover and digest it all through their multiple stomachs.

• Open up The Plains. Open up federal grass lands. Open up federal lands to the cow and the buffalo.

As Ted Turner is wisely doing in North Dakota, bring back the buffalo. By the millions, bring the buffalo back! Let the cows and the buffalo eat side by side, rump to rump, over vast areas from north to south across the grass lands and plains in the West. Vast lands that are not especially good or necessary for farming are fine and dandy for ranch farming.

- Tear the fences down. Let the deer and the antelope, the caribou too, alongside the buffalo, the cow and all; and all could roam freely. Let the rancher, no longer beholden to endless fence repair and fending off wolves and bacterial infections, safeguard the land.
- Ranchers herd as many free-roaming steers and free-roaming buffalo and free-roaming caribou to market as good sense and The Ranching Board allocates to each rancher.

Animal harvest total numbers and numbers for each rancher should be established by that government agency that regulates ranching.

The fences gone, the number of ranchers needs to be established by that regulatory body that regulates the profession of ranching. Again, no rancher or rancher family that now ranches should be un-ranched. No. No. No.

Ranchers would have the right to herd into designated central locations as many animals as allowed by regulation. And this allotment needs necessarily to be sufficient to allow prosperity on the ranches!

The allotment may or may not be by areas of the countryside; although, the rancher should be able to range fairly pretty far and wide, as long as they have enough access to fulfill their allotment. In a sense, all ranch animals in the entire herd are open to ranchers.

And if the whole herd prospers, all the ranchers should prosper too. That is why all ranchers, in this system, will be interested in the health and well being of the whole herd as well as the territory that they live on.

Even so, for good stewardship of the land and its herds, there are limits to the harvest and, therefore the number of those doing the harvesting. This benefits not only the sustainability of land and animals, but price as well. If many ranchers become greedy for income and overharvest, the price of meat will fall and then more and more ranchers will want to harvest more and more to make ends meet and that cycle will devastate both herds and prices. This is not entirely different than fishing — fishermen and fisheries really are in a very similar category and should be regulated this way as well.

The lifestyle I am suggesting for ranchers is somewhere between wilderness life (as I shall explain shortly) and a farming life. It is clearly not as settled as farming, being a herd-person on the open range and not possessing a particular herd of one's own, but simply hunting-gathering in some part of a herd. On the other hand, it is clearly not as wild and nomadic as a wilderness lifestyle as the rancher is only semi-nomadic while a wilderness lifestyle can be entirely nomadic and have little to do with city civilization. A rancher is still making a living relative to the general civilization of farms and cities.

Still, ranching in this version is a far freer lifestyle than farming. No crops to tend, no fences to mend, no barns to build; no cows to milk. Simply: bring in the herd and collect your money. Saddle up and ride and be a steward of the range.

It is entirely reasonable to imagine that instead of being the lone lonesome cowboy or cowgirl free and lonely on the prairie with only the prairie dog and the buffalo for companions, ranchers might, like farmers, want to ranch in cooperative communities, in herder groups. And again, ranchers will not be hiring hands to do their ranching for them. Each member of a ranching co-op or company is as much an owner as the rest. And again, it does not mean that all members of the co-op or ranching business are paid equally, only that they share in profits equally and have an equal say in picking the members of the Board of Directors that oversees their particular ranching business — along with the Community Bank bankers that has fronted the ranch business the money to buy the horses and lassoes used to conduct business or herd doggies.

I am, as with farmers, not sure that there would not be an excess of those who would like to live like this. I probably would be one of these. I think it would be a wonderful way to live, free and easy on the open plains or grasslands or semi-arid southwest. Again, it will require planning and coordination to make sure there are not too many ranchers and not too few. As with farmers, I believe that once a right to ranch is established with a family then the next generation has a greater right to stay than a city slicker with big ideas.

What happens if all members of an extended and large family want to stay as well as there being a high demand for farm boys and girls wanting to be cowboys and girls instead?

Again, we will have to cross that bridge when we come to it, too. For now, it is enough to begin to set up a system where people and cows and buffaloes are happier and healthier and consumers in the cities are healthier and happier. Right now, we are short farmers and ranchers, not overpopulated with them.

As for all businesses, ranchers should not be overly regulated by the rules created by the government regulatory body that controls the number of herd animals the rancher is allowed to bring to market. Again, the rule of law should be free within reasonable limits. Ranchers, as farmers, should be prosperous, prosperous indeed.

Still, I must add one caveat to this plains rosy idyllic. Animals — and we amongst the animals on this one — excrete methane. That is, between flatulence and manure, methane is put into the air. Add that to all the carbon based pollutants from industrialization we are putting out and all the trees we are cutting down and not replacing, well, the consequence is global warming.

It could be that government planning and policy passed down to the regulatory body that oversees ranchers and ranching could mandate that herds be smaller. Now, initially, ranchers would be bringing in more cattle for slaughter to shrink the herds, but eventually fewer and fewer and then at a level that is appropriate and healthy for the planet and ultimately all of us. For price, this would mean that at first with a glut on the market, we would pay less, but in the long term, much more for meat.

If our political and social doctrine is "do no harm," and "do not pass on costs down the line to someone else," then these policies make sense. Cheap farm products pass on the cost down the line to global pollution and warming whose costs are known and felt by many. It is unjust, unfair and destructive not to plan and regulate.

Again, if there are ranch problems and ranch disasters, an insurance system needs be in place, as it is for farming.

All and all, I think for rancher and ranch hand rancher, the way of life will be better. The grazing animal harvested from the lone prairie, having led a more natural, a better, a wilder life, will be healthier and give us better and healthier meat.

Cows that do not get to roam free are fatter. There is more fat in their meat, lots of bad Omega 6s. We now eat some pretty fatty beef. We have lots and lots of physical problems, including heart attacks and death, as a result of eating fatty beef from couch potato cows – or in their case, corn fed couch cows. If you ever had a Ted Turner bison burger you can taste that it is less fatty. Ever have wild elk meat in Gunnison, Colorado or Maine venison during hunting season? Not much fat if any at all. Not only are they meat lover's tasty but healthier! What if all meat could only be that?

Wilderness

The devastation wrought by Western civilization to native tribes around the globe is maximally painful to contemplate. Genocidal invaders, including Europeans in North America who brought devastating disease as well as predatory ethnic cleansing and murder — even having the hubris and chutzpah to call it "Manifest Destiny," a whitewashing doctrine exalting imperial ambition— have murdered off to a point very close to annihilation native people and their nations. Those few groups remaining are hard pressed to resurrect in useful form a past tribal civilization superior in so many ways to that of the conquerors. There are simply few tribes that are not economically marginalized left in North America. They are not all gone, but neither are they flourishing by any means.

Ask the Dalai Lama how the native population of Tibet and its culture are doing under Chinese rule. Why can't the Dalai Lama and his group go home? They might well be killed or, at best, subject to a strict oppression. And the Lakota Sioux back home to The Black Hills or the Cherokee home to Northern Georgia or the Iroquois? Some survive better than others, but overall not well.

American Indian tribes are impoverished and still in the throes of a recovery through casinos that is slowly and minimally successful. Native Americans as a group are going through an extended, perhaps endless, post traumatic stress over many generations.

Native people are not the only losers, but those — and their descendants, e.g. you and me — who traveled from around the world to take over native lands and the wealth of the continent are much the worse as well. An inferior civilization through force of arms and disease was able to conquer and virtually wipe out a group of nations superior to the interlopers. And since most traditions in North America were passed down verbally, we cannot even begin to know what we, too, have lost in the ability to live off this land well and sustainably — in philosophy, in wisdom, in common sense. Was there a Dalai Lama equivalent among the Iroquois of northern New York State; was there a culture among the Cherokee the equivalent of Tibetan Buddhism? What would it mean if the culture, wisdom and spiritual practices of Tibetan Buddhism were lost to the world? What does it mean that the wisdom of the Lakota barely survives on this continent? Or the horse riding skills of the Cheyenne? Or the sophisticated astrology and astronomy of the Mayans?

The least we could do, the best we could do, what we can do for the great great grandchildren of native tribes, what we can do for ourselves and our civilization — and our "karma" if you believe in such ideas — is restore native tribes to their lands, allowing those who are interested to choose a way of life in what we now call "wilderness" or "national parks."

> • We should give substantial — I mean, really substantial — land back to the ancestors of native tribes and let them live on and off the land. We should give them enough land to allow their way of life to be viable and vibrant again. Tribal lands should encompass not only most of what we designate as national parks but also a good deal of all federal land, as well as some lands that should be bought up and turned over to the new wilderness population.

That does not mean that those of Native American ancestry in whole or in part cannot live as ranchers or farmers or city dwellers, that we will kick them out of any land that is not wilderness and take away all their civilized possessions and force them to return to hunter-gathering when they no longer remember the skills of their great grandparents, nor are particularly interested in learning them.

No, this is a choice and a chance, not another forced ethnic cleansing. I believe in time that not only some from among the ancestors of Native Americans, but many others who come from other parts of the world who, too, had ancestors from tribal societies will want to return to a wilderness lifestyle.

Our families, too, going far enough back in time all come from tribal societies. Not only the blood relatives of those closest to tribal life might want to return; any of us might desire to return to a way of life that human beings have lived for tens of thousands of years before farming agriculture, towns and cities.

The lands in the U.S.A. that should go over to a new wilderness living population should not be limited to the severe limitations of the apartheid Bantustans known as "reservations."

• Wilderness populations should be able to hunt on open ranch although their catch should be limited to what they need for their personal consumption and is not for sale and trade as it is for ranchers. Other items may be, but not food.

Given that tribal populations will be proportionally smaller than the more general population, allowing ranchland hunting should not degenerate into a competition for good meat — as long as ranchlands and the herds are healthy and numerous. Both ranchers and tribal peoples have an interest in keeping the range land and its herds in good healthy shape.

Again, there will be a regulatory body that will oversee the wilderness lands, as there are regulatory bodies overseeing all farming and ranching and industry. Ranchers and tribes as well as farmers and fishermen and industrial workers are all of us subject to law and regulation to assure everyone that everyone else is not destroying the environment for selfish ends.

A wilderness life means a wilderness life. While there can be trade between wilderness areas and the other areas, whatever it is that the wilderness tribes are trading to the other areas, say, for cell phones, should not deplete natural wilderness areas in an unsustainable way. In very early trading days, Europeans were fond of trading for North American furs, to the point where the tribes depleted their supply of animals that grew the furs on their bodies. The same applies to natural gas or diamonds in mines in the West. Whatever it is, trees or herbal medicines, when coming from wilderness areas, great care should be taken to assure the preservation of wilderness in all, in ALL its glory and abundance.

While tribal societies and its peoples might want to indulge in the amenities of industrial and farming society, the disposal of wastes from non-wilderness lifestyle goods as well as their use on wilderness lands should be carefully and judiciously monitored and controlled.

TVs and the Internet in the outback of Wyoming or the desert wilderness of Arizona? There is no reason why that cannot be. However, when does wilderness life morph into modern city life and is the end of a wilderness existence? If one wants all the gizmos and toys and entertainment of the cities, maybe that person or tribe should live in the city. Why bother living on the Alaskan tundra watching National Geographic specials on life on the Alaskan tundra and a situation comedy of California beach life? Move to L.A. if you want to spend your days watching sitcoms or virtual wilderness.

Migration in reverse is possible, nay probable. Someone born in L.A. who does not fathom sit coms might want to ride their dog team sled across central Alaska and live out there.

The tribal societies should become the caretakers of the wilderness, not unlike farmers the caretakers of farmland and ranchers of ranch land. It is in their long-term sustainable interest to do so. Although if they do not, there is law and regulation. Still, given a lifestyle that for very many generations was sustainable and rich in life, I would anticipate very little need to regulate and much reason to admire.

The details of all these divisions of land are to be decided. In small part if not in great, much of this division has already and quite naturally taken place. Farmers corn farm in Kansas. Ranchers herd cows in Colorado. New Yorkers keep building tall buildings all over the city. And Indian tribes live out in what city dwellers call "the middle of nowhere" whereas the tribe calls it home, however limited a home on the range it is. The lines between city and farmland or ranchland or wilderness require fair delineation, and then what is and is not permitted on those lands must be outlined as well. Ah, details, devilish details!

Still, decisions in the near future and in the distant future will need to be made and made democratically and justly for all the city dwellers, farmers, ranchers and tribal peoples involved.

Leaving decisions about land use and livelihood and style of life to the so-called "free market" will not and has not worked out very well. Urban areas encroach on liable farm land; perfectly good dairy farmers go bankrupt; ranchers scratch by and are frustrated by federal government grazing policies; and tribal life is simply barely if at all supportable. The "free market" has its positive sides and within each zone and even between zones "free markets" should apply. Still, without due planning "free markets" unfettered, "free markets" gone wild, "free markets" have taken over the wild and are wrecking the environment, the climate and oppressed those who do not want any part of this kind of Capitalist system — especially tribal societies. Read: Lame Deer.

The devil may be in the details of this plan; yet, does this mean that the angels are on the side of the big picture? I believe they are. Go angels and we shall deal with our devils on the morrow. This will not be easy; and, it will take time. Yet, it needs to be done, for the next generation and 7 times 7 generations and 7 times that after.

One more time to emphasize it: the extent of wilderness lands should be increased, greatly. For us all!

A Little About Other Divisions

We might also want to consider that instead of states as we have them now, across the four divisions, each containing city-suburb, farm, ranch, wilderness, that we change the division. Of course, as I have suggested, too, instead of states and state governments making laws, we might consider adopting uniform criminal codes for the whole of the U.S.A.

There could still be jurisdictions that are state-like in size to govern social services, and perhaps we could still call them states, but I think overall the divisions might be different than the states we have now.

Nor on the other hand, need all of the wilderness area be one state-like big state covering a too-wide geographic area. Nor need a state-like government apply to all ranch land or all farm land. Nor for that matter, all city-suburban land. Maybe nine divisions for wilderness, nine for ranches, nine for farmland and then however many seems feasible for city-suburban states East, Central, West. I think we can all fantasize and work out a reasonable way of doing this.

The principle of governments appropriate to geographic area I think might work better than state government controlling city, suburban, farm and wilderness areas. As I have said before, it seems to me that the city-suburb complex rules now. The city rules The State. The city-suburbs make the rules; and farms, ranches and wilderness are much the worse for wear. Separating them might tip the balance of power and influence more fairly.

Wilderness Service Problems

The wilderness areas that are not nearly as much a part of the moneyed economy as the other three regions might pose service problems, especially with regard to education and health care. I still believe that education and health care should be cradle to grave free for everyone and that everyone should be billed for these services. However, wilderness peoples may choose to not participate in the general money system in the first place; and I think that is very much their right; so, how could they be billed?

Frankly, I am not sure I have a very good answer for this problem; although I might suggest some tentative solutions.

To get funding in for social services, one possibility is trade, of course. The other is tourism. This could secure what funds are needed for resources from outside the wilderness area. While individuals or collectives or tribes in these areas might have a life that is mostly non-moneyed, they might, even as a group, create a tourist trade that exchanges guided forays into the wilderness for some of the costs associated with education and health care.

Or there is always, instead of money, the contribution of time, working in education or health care, equivalent to what you might be billed in the other zones. This perhaps, instead of money is where wilderness areas might go to meet these needs. Everyone is required to put in a certain percent of their time into service, instead of a certain proportion of money, money being itself simply an abstraction of work time. If there is no money going around, one could contribute their work time. But, I think the wilderness peoples will need to work this out appropriately.

I think it is workable but a bit trickier than the other areas of the country.

For Us All and
Other Critters Great & Small

Again and again, I think the land mass of "wilderness" should be large, not just for the sake of a wilderness lifestyle, but for the good of the planet and us all. We need more trees! We need more natural areas left alone! A life and planet without plants and animals — animals squeezed more and more out of their natural habitats and species going out of existence or shrinking precipitously — will soon become a planet without people.

In a sense, we are killing ourselves in consuming the planet. The consumer-based lifestyle of the United States and Europe applied to China and India and then to Brazil and everywhere else would be even more disastrous and is now, itself, fairly disastrous. Endless economic growth and population growth of the kind we pursue and promote is, as scientists and anyone who has a shred of consciousness and conscience tells us over and over, "not sustainable." On my gloomier days, I do not want to think about what not sustainable means.

So, what I am proposing here is not just righteous land reform although certainly it is that, too. Resurrecting and enshrining the family farm and the family ranch and the family tribe and changing urban sprawl from the horizontal to the vertical is not only a way to neatly organize our world, it is essential to cleanly organizing our world.

Access

Dividing the country into zones should not imply a lack of access from one zone to another. This does not mean that as a city dweller you cannot perambulate around and across the cornfields of Kansas or that Yosemite is now closed to tourists or the Florida swamps are off limits to anyone who is not an alligator or a pesky mosquito or of Seminole ancestry. In fact, I think fairly unrestricted access across zones is a very good idea. Of course, by unrestricted I do not mean that you can drive your auto up into farmer Jones' front yard and set up your tenting operation, nor that you can drive a seven room RV through the pristine desert of White Sands, New Mexico. Nor does this mean that we should be constructing roads up and down every last bit of wilderness and thereby destroy it by other means.

In fact, the one way I think tribal societies in the wilderness can earn good and clean money and buy manufactured goods is by running an ecologically sound tourist and wilderness experience industry. The same applies to ranches and farms. There is already a small and sound industry doing these kinds of tours already, e.g. Dude ranches, eco-tourism, etc.. And, of course, walking and non-damaging biking trails and campgrounds of all sorts should be plentiful throughout, funded, of course, by infrastructure money from The Banks.

Just as, by the way, there are now tourist opportunities for farmers, ranchers and wilderness dwellers to be tourists in cities.

Which brings me to my pet peeve, beaches. I love The Beach. I love the ocean. I love Ocracoke Island, part of what is called The Outer Banks of North Carolina. The special thing about Ocracoke, partly national seashore, is that the town of Ocracoke surrounds a bay at one end of the island, but the narrow 12+ mile stretch of island is all free of houses and any development and you can walk for miles along the beach next to the dunes and only experience ocean and beach, not houses and restaurants.

I think houses need to be taken off beaches all along the coast and beaches left to return to sand and ocean. That is not to eliminate tourism to the ocean. I love the ocean. I love the beaches. I am a tourist every time I go. Yet, the same rule that we have applied to cities and countryside could be applied to beaches as well. Concentrate development up and not out. That is, not unlike Ocracoke, confine condos and restaurants and tourist amenities to a smaller geographical area. Let the beach be the beach. As for getting out to a beach that is away from the crowd, if you want that, we should build either less intrusive access, i.e. very light rail or even golf cart style small roads made for small electric vehicles. Like ocean fishing? Instead of riding your big-ass 4 wheel drive truck onto the beach, how about a little motorized cart?

Chapter 9
May All Human Beings Be Peaceful & Prosperous

It is difficult enough to watch news about the American domestic unemployment numbers or the European-Greek debt debacle or the Spanish Depression. Yet even worse listen to American news about the democratic revolutions in Tunisia, Egypt, Libya — the successful if fragile ones, let alone the ones still in the making, especially the murderous repressions in Syria as peaceful demonstrators, asking for an open society, were killed and tortured, children put in jeopardy and women raped. And this is just the news watched in America. Tune into the BBC for the genocide in the Congo or the humanitarian and political travesty in Zimbabwe. I need not belabor the point. If you turn on some news that is not entertainment or sports news, you know; although even then, there are murders and scandals ingloriously galore. Even if you do not watch it, you may know what is going on anyway, perhaps from the internet and that is why you are turning off the news.

Sometimes NATO and the United States can bomb their way to preventing one humanitarian catastrophe or another, as in Libya with Obama as Savior Commander-in-Chief or in the former Yugoslavia when Bill Clinton around to fill the role. On the other hand, as in Iraqi, we, by the Bush-Cheney-McCain military intervention, precipitate a civil war and make matters worse even when we have disposed an oppressive genocide-prone dictator, The Insane Hussein. Many times, for one reason or another, we do not or cannot intervene, even when the blood of innocents is on the streets for all the world to see on TV, on Facebook, all over the internet. Obvious, brutal, heart wrenching and heart breaking.

All this murder and repression is not right and in no small way. This should be stopped completely and forever. John McCain who never saw a war, potential war or conflict into which he did not want to send American troops, at least seems to care about the poor Syrians. The pain and suffering may be half a world away, but who does not feel a deep pang in one's chest when a young teenage boy is tortured in Syria or a young woman carrying a placard is murdered for all the world to see on the streets of Teheran? I have cried and cried watching the news. And cried and cried, too, for the unseen news, the starvation and disease in African or on the streets of this slum or that around the world, the suffering of women, of their children, of poor husbands, and on and on. I do not have enough water for all those tears, given the violence and depredations of the day-to-day life of fellow human beings, fellow members and citizens of our species. And here in this country, Newtown. Unimaginable; actually, all too imaginable. All too actual.

This seems even more real than reading all those books about the most murderous half century in history, the first half of the twentieth. Murder by the tens of millions. Repression, torture and rape on a scale that is worse than today, still, ever so slightly more distant being the past, even if the immediate past. Multiple holocausts.

What to do?

Proposals for The World

- A World Government. A World Court. A World Bank.
- Each is elected by all citizens of the world.
- The World Government and The World Court enforce Human Rights and non-violence.
- The World Bank spreads Capital to where it is needed.
- Violence must become universally illegal. Violence within nations when citizens exercise their inalienable rights, rights to protest, to speak up and more should be planet wide illegal.
- Violence between nations: illegal. Violence on a mass scale should be illegal, period.
- First, for all nations and within nations, any armies and all war weapons should be banned. All war weapons from all countries on Earth declared illegal.

That does not mean only North Korea and Iran, nor does it mean only nuclear weapons. All of us. All weapons of war.

• The enforcement of the total disarmament of all nations is then enforced by universal unrestricted access by weapons inspectors worldwide. And then too, any attempt either to manufacture weapons or hide them or use them shall be a crime punishable through The World Court system.

• Any refusal by any government or, say, a rebel force, to allow inspectors to go anywhere and immediately confiscate any and all weaponry of any kind will bring the wrath of a well equipped million man military under the jurisdiction of The World Government and The World Court.

• Any attempt to begin a war between nations or begin a civil war within a nation or suppress human rights by whatever means, the monopoly force of The World Government and The World Court will immediately be deployed to stop the conflict and violence.

• The military force of The World Government need be about million men and women with a machinery of absolute overwhelming force that shall come proportionately by population from every nation around the world and be under the command not of their country of origin but of commanders of The World Government who in turn are chosen by that government.

• Only The World Government is charged with overseeing the use of the military and then only to stop violence. The World Government is an enterprise whose only interest is enforcing non-violence and Human Rights, not abridging them.

• Included in the mandate of The World Government would be as well as to find and punish world terrorists. It should not take a million man army as long it took the U.S. to find and punish all of Al Qaeda.

- The World Court judges any disputes between nations or within nations that could lead to wars and civil wars.
- First and foremost, every justice who sits upon the World Court must give a solemn pledge and oath to non-violence. You cannot sit upon this Court if you approve violence in any way other than to prevent violence. Moreover, every justice must swear an oath to world wide Human Rights.
- Civil and Human Rights are for everyone, everywhere. The World Court and The World Government should be enforcing Civil and Human Rights for everyone. Governments or any other social entity that tries to squelch Civil and Human Rights should be deposed and new and democratic elections held to pick a new government.

Human Rights are universal, as far as I am concerned, and should be enforced worldwide.

The response of governments like the Assad regime in Syria or the former Qaddafi in Libya or the Communist Chinese at Tianmen Square or in Tibet or the Russians in Chechnya or Kent State in the United States is disproportionate murder aimed at maintaining what is subsequently, to my mind, automatically illegitimate power. It is an immoral monopoly on violence. It should be illegal and those who perpetuate these crimes should be punished.

Super-national Human Rights does not necessarily mean that they are required to be supernatural, that is, bestowed on us from one God or another. Nor does it require Kant's Categorical Imperative, nor Thomas Aquinas' Natural Law, nor John Locke's Rights of Man, nor Jean Jacques Rousseau's Noble Savage right feelings and emotions, nor the Ninth Amendment to The Constitution. Whatever and whichever way we get to it, it would be better for all of us if we assumed it one way or another, period.

Local and personal violence is illegal and should be handled by local governments. In the U.S.A. violence and crime should be dealt with by local, state and federal law enforcement, and in other nations by appropriate authorities. However, there being no official world government yet signed onto by all nations with a military force that could enforce world peace, I think it time to think of transforming a haphazard and fairly ineffective United Nations into a World Government and a World Court and make it The preemptive force on the planet.

World Peace, enforced, period! World Law of Non-Violence.

Control will not come from a Security Council that is limited to a few of the most powerful nations, but from the highest government in the world, The World Government. Leaving disputes and the just suppression of violence to United Nation's politics as we do now is clearly not working well. One has only to see the difference between the response to the murderous Qaddafis in Libya and the Assads in Syria, almost none supporting Qaddafi but some supporting Assad and, therefore, no effective action could be taken to stop the latter until Syrians themselves took up weapons.

A universally authorized World Court should have decided long ago the dispute between Israel and the Palestinians and the disputes between the political parties in Zimbabwe or Congo or Northern Ireland or Bahrain. If there is a force to prevent violence, there must be a moral and legal force to establish justice between aggrieved parties so that they not only cannot but will not desire to do violence. Injustice is its own kind of violence.

Yet, where can we find justices fair enough and peace minded enough to decide the most difficult of mass disputes? Who shall appoint them? Certainly not government politicians with their personal or limited national agendas.

How to choose the wisest in the world to dispense the most important justice and resolve the conflicts between or within nations or communities?

There are may possible democratic ways. Simply, I would propose:

- Worldwide mass elections for a world parliament of The World Government.
- Worldwide mass elections to The World Government.

Still, whether democratic or not, unbalanced judicial favoritism can always be an issue. It is an issue now with about half the justices on the U.S. Supreme Court generally favoring a conservative agenda and the other half a liberal agenda. It is inevitable. Term limits for justices might help, but that is no guarantee either. The size of the electorate might vitiate extreme views and prejudices. You just cannot easily favor a small group or point of view of a minority if you are being elected across a continent of several billion. Not impossible for problems to arise, but less likely.

Even so, given the current mayhem and the genocides of the last centuries and many centuries before, outlawing weaponry and attempting to have The World Court manage disputes and The World Government to effectively eliminate weapons is better than what we have now, which is ad hoc piecemeal, unfair and ineffective. What would have happened if the world had been disarmed before World War II and Hitler had not been allowed to rearm Germany; or Japan would have had to give up its military? Or Italy? Or anyone? The correct answer is: No World War II. Not permitted!

As for those who fear that a world military could lead to a World Government controlled by forces that would take away your freedom, I have much sympathy for your position.

However, the danger from what we have now trumps any speculative future. We may believe that staying strong militarily will protect us and our freedoms, the United States spending more on its military than all other nations combined, but we are hardly invincible and certainly not invulnerable as 9/11 taught us.

Still, think about this: what if Iran and North Korea or Pakistan, all having or about to have nuclear weapons either sneak them into the United States or develop the capacity to send them to our coastal cities on a missile? Do you really want to chance that? Where will your precious freedom be then? Better to get rid of all that weaponry now, forthwith. Better to get rid of the possibility of that now. Better to live free and not die.

We believe that somehow a balance of military power that favors us will discourage those who wish us ill from attacking us. It is not a dissimilar doctrine to the grand balance of power that the Europeans designed before WWI that collapsed and led to WWI and then, in continuation, WWII. Thinking that we have it balanced out better than that because the balance is in our favor is fine if you like living on a knife edge ridge over a genocidal abyss on both sides of you. 9/11, in this sense, was just a warning. Mr. Cheney is right in fearing a nuclear armed terrorist group downing St.Louis and its suburbs. Frankly, it is no way to live.

The United States has neither the resources nor the will to enforce a worldwide Pax Americana and function as the current World Government presiding in D.C. And think, government budget conscious conservatives, how much does this cost us? What if the bill for The World Government, The World Court and the million man military was billed to every citizen of the planet instead of coming out of our pockets? No military defense budget for the U.S. at all equals big federal savings.

Of all my proposals this will all seem the most impossible, an impossible peaceful dream. The fear engendered by the military of others who are fearful of your military has made it appear that it would be beyond reason to expect reason. Of course, the Nazis in Germany, Fascists in Italy and the military nuts of Japan really did hold weapons and were using them in ways that would make anyone either hide out on the Moon or grab an aircraft carrier and a tank, certainly a machine gun. And we should be scared of a world with nations armed to the proverbial teeth. It is a pile of dry cord wood right next to a dry wooden house in a dry season ready for a spark to set the whole wide world on war fire and then up in smoke. It happened before: World War I and then II.

Still, instead of adding to the present defensive state and promoting fear and paranoia amongst the North Koreans, Iranians or Pakistanis, who quite rightly might be fearful of a nuclear armed United States or a nuclear armed South Korea or Israel or India, how about if we decommission all the weaponry and turn tanks into tractors and nuclear weapons into has-beens? We may all be too scared to do such a thing, but the alternative, to fear, to continually fear and in fearing and being feared, to promote a never ending evil circular loop on the whirlpool down to the abyss of nuclear Armageddon, it is not, as we say over and over again, "sustainable." We should change that forever.

Better to disarm everyone completely and have The World Court of the wisest people on the planet to help us along. A perfect alternative? Maybe not. But certainly less imperfect, far less imperfect than what we have now. Impossible, given the state of the world and our consciousness? I certainly hope not.

I believe that as the larger and more general a government becomes, right up to a world government, that as one ascends up this ladder, at each level, government should be concerned with and enforce justice and fairness that smaller government units might neglect or suppress. It is not that long ago that southern state governments in the United States complained that the federal government was encroaching on their "states' rights" in forcing those states to desegregate. The majority of citizens of these states — and they made sure that they controlled the government by not permitting or limiting some of their citizens, their black citizens, the right to vote — through their government, limited the Human Rights of a minority of their citizens, their black citizens.

States do not have rights; people have rights. States should be designed to secure and enforce those rights. These are principles of the Enlightenment, John Locke and the American Founding Fathers; and, it is worth keeping and worth keeping worldwide. Rights are universal. Read the 14th Amendment to the U.S. constitution, as well as the others from The Bill of Rights. Read The Declaration of Human Rights of The United Nations.

The larger the government entity, the less it should be providing services and doing the day to day business of business and the more it should spend its time securing and enforcing human rights. The largest of those entities, The World Government and The World Court should be doing almost nothing but that.

What should we include as Human Rights? Why should we consider them universal, that is, for everyone? In one sense, this is personal preference. Yet there is more behind this personal preference than simply, oh, I like that and isn't that just so nice.

Who are you? How do you identify yourself? Personally, I believe that my first and most important identification is with my species. I am a human being. Now, don't get me wrong, I love my dog, Besame Mucho — Bessie for short — quite a bit. I love my cat, Simon, the birds that come to the feeder, the deer who graze out in the back yard under the electric lines, even the frogs wallowing and croaking at night in the little drainage stream back of the house. And I love many, many species of mammals, fish and fowl. Who does not love a duck? But I identify with my species. I am a human being. You are a human being.

It is not that I am comprised of other identifications. I am in another sense, an American, Easterner, Western culturist, male, elderly, Jewish heritage, graduate of this and that school, husband, grandfather of three wonderful granddaughters and so on. There are numerous ways to classify me and put me into some identification or another. I might even identify with one or another of those categorizations, one more than another.

Still, first and foremost, for me, I am a human being. And I identify with all other human beings, other human beings who have their very own collection of lesser identifications.

This is not a trivial matter for me and one not simply of definition. I am a human being and the equal in what I rightly deserve in fundamental rights and respect as any other human being. I believe that every human being, like me, deserves fundamental rights and respect as a human being even before we leave the house in the morning and go out in public and after we go out the door, too, to Starbucks for our A.M. latte and off to the computer factory. In this way we are all equals. Different abilities, different proclivities, different this and that, but we are not all that different.

We do not deserve equal pay for unequal work. We do not deserve a silver spoon in our mouths. We do not deserve to be catered to and applauded throughout of lives unless we do what is worth it and praiseworthy. But we do, as human beings, as citizens of this planet, as world citizens, each and every one of us human beings have at very least the following rights: to speech, to our belief system (whether it is religious or not), to write down what we think and distribute it which is another form of freedom of speech called freedom of press and communications, the freedom to associate with whomever we choose, the right to be able to make a living, the right to migrate to any place on the planet and the right to do what we want as long as we do not cause unjustified harm to another, and, of course, the right not to be coerced unjustly, the right not to be discriminated against.

We also have the Human Right to choose who makes the rules under which we and our neighbors live. I believe that included in human rights, the right to choose you government and the head of the company you are working in is essential. That is, democracy is a human right. Regimes as in North Korea or China or Syria and many others, by the nature of their regimes, by the nature of not only suppressing dissent, but in their very being as authoritarian and undemocratic violate fundamental liberty. I believe in planet wide democracy.

"Life, liberty and happiness." The words send a delightful electric chill through my whole body. Democracy. Sends an electric chill. Tolerance. Identification with each person. Chills.

Human Rights. Amen!

This goes beyond thought or belief and to fundamental and instinctive relationship with other human beings. This is not easy to explain; although, I have heard others, friends, neighbors, colleagues, those near and far and the Dalai Lama, too, express a similar sentiment. Can you feel it? J.J. Rousseau felt it.

Not only as an individual do I identify as a human being, but I feel instinctively that we are a sociable species. Yes, we are separate and individual, but make no mistake about this, we are also wholly sociable and mostly dependent on one another. This does not mean that, at times, we might not justifiably believe that we are better than some other human being at a particular task, like making money or doing a medical diagnosis or playing ping pong or Dungeons and Dragons; or that we are, in one task or another, inferior to another, at Scrabble or racing a Nascar or medical diagnosis. That is inevitable. We cannot be the best or the worst at everything. Sometimes we are though, the best or the worst, or, at least, the better or not as good.

Be that as it may, in face to face or even beside one another or even at a distance, I feel deep in my insides, at my core, that we, as conscious human beings, are equals and deserving of better treatment than we have meted out to each other over the course of thousand of years of history, and that we deserve of each other fundamental respect and love and social fairness, that is, justice.

Where does such a strong core belief come from?

At about the same time period of The American Revolution, Adam Smith of Edinburgh, Scotland, in his The Wealth of Nations, the Bible of Capitalism — Ayn Rand and Gordon

Gecko minus the steroids — opined, and I paraphrase, 'that if we just all worked in our own self interest, it would all work out fine and we would be better off and all wealthier to boot.' What Ayn and her followers and predecessors have made of this, what many of us have made of this, is that our fundamental motivation not only should be self-interest above all else, but that underneath what appears to be altruism or caring is itself self-interest. We appear to care, but really when you get down to it, it is not true, we do not care, we are just giving the appearance of caring because we will be better off if we appear to care. Motivation is self-interest, period. So some of us believe.

And, of course, if everyone is following their own self interest and some are willing and able to work harder or are more clever than others at it to get more, then they, in a Capitalist society, will get more, and, this is as it should be. The strong not only survive, but prosper — Adam Smith and Charles Darwin combined. The rich being the strongest and the future of the species. It is not exactly an egalitarian vision. It is The Social Darwinists' vision. The poor are poor because they are not as good; the rich are rich because they are better.

Odd, too, and ironic because in contrast and almost at the same time as Adam Smith, Jefferson, Paine and even Hamilton and Madison, the American Constitutionalists, were more egalitarian in their anti-aristocratic declarations of "life, liberty and the pursuit of happiness" for all and their Bill of Rights, declaring equal rights for all. Well not really all at all; they did exclude slaves, women and those who did not own enough property. There is a fledgling universalism coming from Jefferson and the American political elite founding fathers that implies something beyond self-interest as primary motivation. Why should everyone be given equal rights if, when following their primary motivation —self-interest — they are not equals? It certainly was not in the interest of slave owners, who saw themselves as clearly superior to their slaves as well as their own wives, to hand over equal rights to slaves and their wives. And they did not. Equal Rights emphasizes some kind of fundamental equality; self-interest alone emphasizes a fundamental inequality.

I believe in both. I believe we are fundamentally equal and unequal, the same and different. We are similar. I believe we are equal in what we have a right to and unequal in what we deserve from what we do. I believe we function, too, within our personal self-interest, but we also function as human beings without thinking of ourselves first and foremost, unselfishly, altruistically, compassionately, empathetically, sympathetically and in all ways caring.

We are both and more. Some of us emphasize more the side of ourselves that is self-interested. Some of us even to the detriment of ourselves, function so interested in others that the self is entirely sacrificed to others, even unto sacrificing our very lives for others. And then, there are the rest of us, who function somewhere in the middle, neither greedy, nor saintly, more or less balanced in our lives for better and worse.

Yet, I do not think we should ever forget that the notion that motivation is always self-interested and that altruism is just a front is wrong. It just is not true as sole motivation. It could be, although I do not believe this true either, that one could dissect each self-interested act and find an altruistic motive underlying it. Ayn Rand actually cared. Ronald Reagan, Margaret Thatcher, Newt, Paul Ryan, actually care. Perhaps they do and did more than they would acknowledge. Maybe not. Maybe what they say is what they mean.

I believe that our altruism drive as well as our self-centered competitiveness drive are both instinctive. It is embedded in our neurology and DNA. As human beings, we are a social and sociable species and, on the other hand, we are individuals and care about ourselves. I understand in myself both tendencies, but both as instinct, as well as both part of the culture and personal history in which I was brought up. Nature and nurture. It is all there in some kind of balance or imbalance.

That Assad in Syria, for example, and only one example he is, could kill citizens in his country for speaking up, and that, to the shame of the others of us on the planet who could do something about such atrocities, that something is not done immediately to stop this, seems to me a fundamental breach in the instinctive relationship we have with one another. Killing or harming, doing violence to another human being for exercising their rights as human beings is a rupture in the fabric of a greater Law. How can you kill someone else if they are like you, so much like you, a human being, doing what you give yourself the right to do? You have overemphasized your selfish self-interest and forgotten who you are in wholeness.

When the Ten Commandments say "Thou shalt not kill," I do not think this should be taken lightly or contingently. Human beings should not kill or harm each other. You break with the species when you do so.

So, what should be enforced planet-wide is the end of violence and the end of any violation of our rights as human beings. Anything less would be a partial and inadequate future. That we think it impractical, I understand. That it seems the way things are now currently is The Way, seems to me the most fundamental indictment of our times.

Meeting Saint Peter at The Pearly Gates, we shall all be asked one question — in addition to all those other personal ones — "why did you go along with it?" It was a question asked of many Germans after WWII. I am afraid it could be asked of all of us too. The future will ask. Let's show them we started to do better, and then that we finally did better.

I know, I do know that it all sounds so simple and that of all the wild and wooly proposals I am making in the end this will be the most difficult to attain. The idea that we, human beings, especially male human beings, will give up the violence that at heart is the basis for maintaining privilege of one kind or another, material, social or ideational, that we should give up violence, that will take some doing. But I am reminded that when the anti-slavery movement started in the late 1700s it seemed equally impossible that slavery could be ended. There was always slavery in the human world going back to the dawn of civilization. It appeared inevitable and eternal. And that was that. And there were strong and pervasive forces aligned for its continuance. There were precious very few who began to speak up against it.

Slavery is not totally gone from this world, but it is not a dominant social arrangement anymore. It is now only a backwater and marginal practice. Could we make violence a backwater and marginal practice? Could we make Human Rights and non-violence the dominant social form and norm?

Universal Green Prosperity

• There should be international law written by The World Government that requires GREEN — sustainability practices within and across borders.

• A World Government is charged with protecting Human Rights, worldwide.

• All us have the right to live where and how we please. National borders are not sacred. There is a fundamental Human Right to choose where to live without restriction, without borders.

• Just as people should have the ability and the right to move about the planet, so should goods. Not only should there be no taxes, there should be no tariffs at all as well.

• There should be a World Bank as part of a world banking system, capital flowing from local banks to state banks to national banks and then to an international World Bank.

And prosperity? Can we have that, too, worldwide? Peace and prosperity together?

China and India, in centuries past were off and on the wealthiest civilizations on the planet. Now after a couple hundred years of hopelessly floundering about financially and in and out of colonial bondage, they appear to be pulling themselves up out of dreadful and dire poverty by their proverbial bootstraps. Some of those bootstraps, however, appear to be of American and European origin — a kind of pay back for Western colonialism. They are pulling themselves up and gaining capital to reinvest and then gaining more capital and then again reinvesting and growing, creating more and more productivity by selling us in The West every last manufactured thing under the Sun. Lots of stuff.

It is not entirely clear to that part of my mind that is reasonable and logical why they could not pull themselves up by their very own bootstraps by selling their products to themselves, to their ill paid workers who make all those products. While they do pay their workers, they do not pay them enough to buy as much as we buy from them. Nor have they created the same credit card madness that we tear our economic hairs out about, allowing their workers to buy on credit, go into fabulous middle class hock and keep buying and buying until the bubble bursts every couple of decades or so.

Of course, then the bootstraps they would be tugging on would be their own — instead of foreign ones, that is, our boots and their straps. It would then be just a sleight of hand, instead of the current heavy hand.

Our recent Western economic lot has been bursting bubbles by outsourcing our productivity. We buy from India and China but no longer produce the goods that we buy because they are producing it cheaper than we can. If our Western economy tanks any further there will be no re-hyper-inflation of the American consumer market and no further East Asian bootstrap miracle. They, all several billions of them, need us as much as we borrow and consume from them.

In Germany, this simply has not happened. And by the way, the Germany economy is now in the business of propping up the rest of the European continent. For a variety of reasons, some of which I have mentioned before, such as workers sitting on Board of Directors of companies and a workforce that is highly educated, work stayed within the country. As it should.

There is no reason why companies cannot stay put, why our greatest economic strength, our very own productivity, should say goodbye. There is no reason why expertise capital that permits business to function, cannot flow abroad so that the domestic consumers of that country can have the benefit of all that marvelous machinery and expertise, manifesting as increased productivity; yet our machinery stays put here and employs our folks. Why cannot everyone have machines to produce? "Illogical," says old Mr. Spock of old Star Trek, "highly illogical."

If we want world hunger and poverty to end and prosperity to rule the entire planet for human beings, the gains of one should not, need not, be at the expense of another. Those areas of the world that are wealthy in machinery and expertise may give freely and generously of their wealth and machinery so that others may join them in good times and consumption, but not at the expense of their own. In fact, we could sell them the machinery and the expertise to build the machines and they would be indebt and indebted to us, instead of vice versa. They might have to pay for their bootstraps. But it would not be such a bad deal for them, as they could pull themselves up by those very same bootstraps. They could pay us off when the bootstrap phase was over and they were highly profitable. But they would be profitable selling mostly to themselves and not to us.

Of course, that is the issue all along: investment, capital investment and where does it come from and to whose advantage. The way that China and India and all the rest get the machinery is by allowing foreign capital in which means that they now have productive machines; and then they, like the now good-new-boy-on-the block capitalists they have become, keep good old profit from the productivity of that machinery, sharing some of it with their capital investor buddies from The West. It is a Chinese government-western Capitalist boondoggle.

The goods thus produced they sell back to us and then the East reinvests in more machinery and then the boot-straps have some leverage and they are off and running to marvelous growth rates. Yet to get the capital initially to do all that, China and to a lesser extent India, and others, must promise cheap labor so that conglomerate Capitalist corporations and conglomerate Capitalist banks will be willing to invest in China and those corporations and banks can keep some of the bounty of depressed wages while the Chinese government and its companies gets the other part of that bounty.

However, the Chinese do not have a good enough market at home for all those goods because they cannot pay their workers quite enough because they are skimming not just the top but pretty far down the milk glass as well along with the 1% Westerners; and, therefore, to get money for their products and therefore profit and therefore capital and therefore more growth, they use consumers in more prosperous nations to buy or buy on credit these goods. Under a world Capitalist system it is logical and reasonable. And by the way, initially for consumers in the West, the goods stay cheap, certainly cheaper than the goods that are made in their own country where workers are paid more.

Yet this type of deal is neither just nor sustainable. It is logical within the Old Capitalist context of how to get your particular nation wealthy. (Adam Smith did write his The Wealth Of Nations to advise his prince, Machiavelli style, how to achieve wealth and power) but illogical in the greater context of a sustainable and mutually beneficial future. Eventually Western consumers will not be able to just run out and buy goods because they have no money because their job from their former factory has moved to China or elsewhere.

Workers here, basically, are subsidizing the capitalization of China. Workers are doing the job of the banks. And, in a different sense, so are Chinese workers. Workers here give up their good jobs so the Chinese government can fund industrialization so they can sell goods to American workers at low prices.

On the other hand, in a more generally logical and reasonable world, instead of growing the Chinese, Indian and other economies by exploiting workers, a certain percentage of capital, machinery money, could be set aside at the level of national banks flowing then to international banks — say 25% of total investment dollars — to be then sent around the world to fund business projects owned and operated locally whose products are sold locally. A true and good World Bank coordinated with national, state and local community banks could do just that. And everyone could be happy — workers, consumers, countries. There would be no need for governments themselves to hoard money to make more investments to create more companies to build up their economies. The resources for this would be built into the world system and governments would not need to scavenge capital from wealthier areas. No need then to only export to gain capital.

But even beyond machinery export there is a most important capital export of all: human capital, capital of expertise. I do not just mean the expertise of how to produce the goods only, important as all that is, but how to be in business, how to run a company and how to market a product. Hugo The Ego Chavez of Venezuela was quite progressive and generous in handing over sums of money made from the country's nationalized oil industry to cooperative worker enterprises. Yet, he forgot to show these business how to operate, especially to market their goods. He needed entrepreneurs for his socialist utopia; he needed another kind of expertise, not just capital, but business expertise.

In China and India, in Japan and Korea, in Germany and everywhere, here in America as well, the best investment of all is in education, in bringing up the expertise of people, not just in how to knit a sweater but how to run a business. Those areas of the world that have invested in their people, their well-being as well as their education, these are the areas of the world that are doing best.

What the wealthier countries should be exporting is not goods as much as technical and business technical expertise, that is, education. Knowledge, education, is everyone's future. We should be bringing students here to learn and shipping extensions of our educational institutions abroad. This would help everyone. Apple computers could still be constructed in California and around the U.S.A. The Chinese could also have an Apple factory in China, but selling those computers to the very workers who work in those factories.

Factories that manufacture socks can be bought in China as well as in Boston. Locks? No different. More iPads, socks and locks for everyone, China, Chile, The Sudan, Nashville!

It is the Apple and sock and locks company expertise that is critical. We should feel free to give away our knowledge and trade secrets as long as it does not come back to haunt via dead factories in Ohio and Silicon Valley. By the way, they are stealing them anyway!

In this way, as with Human Rights, we commit ourselves neither to our personal individual self aggrandizement alone, nor only the neighbors in our town, nor only our relatives, nor just to those in our state, nor only to our countrymen and countrywomen and country children, but to every human being our the planet.

Live long and prosper, everyone, everywhere! Your life and prosperity should not diminish mine, and mine should not diminish yours.

Free markets should never be used as an excuse to perpetuate hunger and poverty across borders nor within borders. The Social Darwinist philosophy of greed and devil may care and I do not have to care about any other living soul is contrary to the values that I and most of us hold dear. We are on this Earth together and should not make competition an ideal so perverse that it transcends goodness itself.

All for one and one for all, as those Musketeers shouted. We can do much better than just three swashbucklers.

The same basic rules that I think should apply in America, I think could apply worldwide. If you work, you and your family should not go hungry and you should not be poor. Work should be guaranteed. The bottom line is a decent living, not just the bottom line of a greedy upper echelon of 1%, whether that 1% is a Chinese bureaucrat hording capital or a corporate executive hording stock options.

It will take awhile to bring the bottom up. Yet, as Jeffrey Sachs, world economist of The Earth Institute at Columbia University and advisor to The Secretary General of The United Nations, has shown, bringing up the bottom is not nearly as costly as one might think. It is the hording wealthy we cannot afford, not the poor. For Sachs, a few well placed billions of dollars in Africa and the bottom is up, a whole continent pulled up by Sachs' bootstraps, a whole continent for a few billions — far less than anyone's debt, let alone military budget.

Please read, after this book, Sach's Commonwealth. A true and moral world economist, he has a fine tuned analysis of what is happening in the world economy and an equally fine tuned set of solutions for our world economic poverty woes. He goes into far more detail than I have of the inter-related world problems of climate change, desertification, species loss, overpopulation, lack of health care, shortage of infrastructure and much more. And importantly, Sachs has reasonable and sensible means of helping. He is an economic physician of first rank.

Yet, in the transition, given the levels of degradation and poverty, and given the effects of climate change on the poorest areas of the world especially, there will be times of straight out subsidizing other human beings with food and medicine and aid.

Boosting up economies to decent standards takes time and in famine or epidemic there is not enough time. A world fund, created even before disasters, needs to be up and running, instead of go begging at the last dire moment on CNN TV with Larry King pleading for money and food and medicine for post earthquake Haiti. It should have been there before and then forthwith dispensed when and where needed.

One of the ways that poor countries have either tried to lift themselves up by creating capital from profits or simply supported an elite that has done no such lifting up is growing agricultural products for wealthier western countries. I think we gave a name to this tendency: "Banana Republics." Land is used for cultivation of bananas or coffee or pineapples or cotton or some other commercially viable fruit of the Earth and the owner of the plantation gets rich and invests in himself and gambles it away in Monaco or, if imbued with the capitalist spirit invests in a factory in town.

It is possible that in some areas of the planet only cotton, coffee and kumquats will grow from the Earth. OK. Then these areas can only export this set of foods in order to feed themselves on imports of other foods. OK.

Yet, please, no country should be exporting food when their people are going hungry if the land can be used to feed them. Food should be grown for local consumption. Only when everyone is well fed and healthy from a good diet of local food should land be designated for any export crops.

World Green

While areas of the world like China are gaining capital and wealth by rather conventional and traditional capitalist means, they are not unlike 19th century England in despoiling and polluting their country. Not only are they doing what the English did in mistreating their workers, but they are imitating the worst features of 19th century Capitalism across the board. Capitalism in the West has in many ways transformed itself. It is still pretty bad in exploiting people and planet, but China is a very good imitator of an unrepentant and unreformed Capitalism of an earlier period, not only of product, but of exploitation and pollution.

In my practice as an acupuncturist, I had a second-generation Chinese patient with asthma, induced when he visited relatives in an industrial heartland city of modern day China. He did not have asthma before he visited; and, after several acupuncture sessions he did not have it again. It was simply the air, the severely polluted air in this city in China, worse even than any polluted city in the United States that created his temporary asthma.

The future of the world must be green. What is the point of it all, of all this productivity, of all this wealth, if we all live in misery, in planet wide ecological misery. It makes no common sense, reasonable sense, human sense, any sense at all. Need I tell you that when and if 1.5 billion Chinese start riding around in gasoline cars or in electric cars that get their electricity from coal fired plants what the entire planet will look like, what our climate will be doing?

We will be toast and not just figuratively speaking.

Yet, what is the world system that can regulate in such a way that we green up the planet and avoid ecological Armageddon and all prosper together by spreading machinery and expertise? How can we organize or use existing organizations or reorganize so that the whole species, human beings, will benefit?

There are any number of international organizations: The United Nations and its many parts, The World Court, The World Trade Organization, The World Bank and others, some private, some governmental, some non-governmental but not for profit (NGOs). I would put them under one roof, including what I have proposed before, a million man military under The World Court and The World Government. Regional unions of nations, like The United States or The EU, seem perfectly alright to me, but I think we also need a unified World Government as well to coordinate non-violence, Human Rights and universal green prosperity.

I would not only not call it "The United Nations," instead I would call it something like "The World Government." The reason I would not call it "The United Nations" is because I think nations should not necessarily be the fundamental unit of legitimacy. I am not calling for the elimination of nations. No, not at all. But when we call the world body "The United Nations" it implies that the world body is derivative of nations and nations are primary and the world body secondary.

I do not see nations as primary or sacred. They are a combination of historical events, forces and accident. How nations happened the way they happened is the topic of thousands, tens of thousands of history books filling libraries and e-libraries. I believe as social entities that help us regulate, plan and coordinate the activities and proclivities of us human beings, nations can be quite helpful. Although, too, and negatively, they have been the source of a good deal, a great deal, an incredibly enormous deal, of mischief as well.

Still, there should be a social entity for us all, all us human beings, on the planet. The effort to bring up from dire straits and poverty and disease the billions of us mired in material unhappiness of the grossest sort, requires extraordinary coordination of effort. To continue universal prosperity requires extraordinary coordination of effect and appropriate universal regulation and enforcement of peace and human rights — AND GREEN-NESS!

I believe that living on a decent and natural planet is a fundamental Human Right, too, and that we need a World Government to enforce it.

Refugee Rights

I believe that we all have a fundamental Human Right to choose which part of the planet we want to live in as well. That is, the Basques of Spain, the Kurds in Turkey and Iraq, the Tibetans in Tibet in China and so on have a Human Right to a vote to choose whether they want to be part of Spain and Turkey or China. That does not mean that once they have their country, that they can throw out wily-nily non-Basques from the Basque area, or non-Kurds from a

Kurdish country or that all Chinese are constrained to go back to Peking and the Yangtze River Valley. Not only does everyone have a right to go where they will on the planet, they also have a right to stay right where they are, if they choose.

To my mind, United States citizens do not own the land of the United States. Nobody owns the land. I believe, that those who now live in the Yucatan have a perfect right to migrate to Minnesota as Minnesotans have the right to migrate to the Yucatan or France or wherever else they want to go. The same applies to the French and the Sudanese and the Chinese. Coordinating that right so that everyone is happy with the result of that particular universal right is another matter that needs to be taken up by local, state, national and international regulatory social entities.

You may have a right to move from the Yucatan to Potsdam or from York to New York or from Croton-on-Hudson to Mogadishu, but what if a big bunch of people wants to go and what about jobs and farm land and all that.

That is the job of coordination for coordinating bodies known as governments and banks. I can assure you, each and every one of us nervous ones, that there will be a whole lot less migration if the social problems of problem areas, of poverty, of lack of education, of lack of opportunity, of lack of health care, of deteriorated environments is being taken care of. Who wants to live in tundra of northern Ontario when they can live in the Yucatan and make a living? There are no vast migrations from areas where it is all working.

Still, it should be as easy to cross the border from Tijuana to San Diego as the border from Vermont to New Hampshire. The border between Spain and France is quite easy now that there is an EU when in the past you needed a passport. Are the Spanish all picking up and moving to Marseille? Or the French emigrating by the tens of thousands to Berlin or Edinburg? The Spanish and The Scots are not living in great numbers in the suburbs of Paris.

No Taxes, No Tariffs,
Green Infrastructure

If goods as well as people can flow without encumbrance, that is without tariffs, some companies and people will prosper in that totally free and fair world market, and some will go under. Fair is fair.

Still, it is only fair on a level playing field, as we say. And, unfair practices, unfair labor practices, unfair environmental practices, unfair dumping of goods to eliminate competition, all these need regulating and policing on a world wide level. Again, Capitalist freedom and free markets require responsible governance of The System. Fair trade means fair labor and environmental practices.

A World Bank would actually and factually have the capital to help poor countries get out of the cycle of poverty and misery they are now in.

Not only could they help fund infrastructure like roads, schools, hospitals, education in general, utilities of all kinds — universal electrification and internet service planet wide — but businesses of all kinds. It is surely change that could happen and work! It sounds so simple, but it is not. The overall structure is easy to devise. How that structure functions in the practical day-to-day world, that should be difficult and interesting.

Chapter 10
**Education:
Consciousness is Everything**

Nothing I have proposed, the democratization of economics, the re-greening of the planet, respect for the rights of everyone, will work for very long or even happen without a different way of educating our children. Plato knew this all too well. Ancient Athens, an admirable relatively participatory democracy, democracy and all, fell apart. More recently, Germans elected Adolph Hitler in a fair and democratic election; and contemporary America, democratic America, is awash in political ignorance of a demoralizing kind. Democracy is not a guarantee — never was.

Frankly without an educated population, democracy will deteriorate to tyranny or anarchy and is perfectly capable of ignorance, arrogance and even evil. Dictators and authoritarians of all stripes are worse, but democracies have been, at times, just as bad. Democracy, as much as I love it, is no panacea.

Plato thought the wise philosopher should rule and rule not from the perspective of personal self interest, but serve and rule in the interest of all. I think so, too. The question then becomes, how to know who to pick, how to know which wise guy politician is a fraudulent pretender — whether sincere or not — and who really and truly knows how to DO THE RIGHT THING. Certainly, with the possible exception of Barack Obama, I see virtually no known politician on the American scene who comes close and I think Obama is drowned out in a great lake of mediocrity and foolishness. Many Republicans, to my mind, have gone off the lunatic fringe end of not just a fiscal cliff, but an intelligence cliff.

How can we pull ourselves up by the philosophical bootstraps? That is why I must write on education. Otherwise, all is for naught.

Debate on Education, For What it is Worth

Somewhere at some forum out in the intelligentsia ethers, where educational issues are supposedly thrashed about and decided, on opposite sides of an imaginary four sided table sits, on the left, Diane Ravitch writing articles for The New York Review of Books and on the opposite end and the right hand side, The Council on Foreign Relations Task Force on US Education Reform and National Security, flanked by, to Diane's further left, those arch villains of The Right, the teachers unions and school system bureacrats, and then, to the far right, corporate executives seeking to hire the best and the brightest who will make them lots more money if only we trained them properly, and then too, corporate executives of companies who want to run the school system and make money from that. The four squares of this very square table being thus fully occupied; the only ones not really seated at this table are parents, and the children and teenagers, that is, the students.

Who is engaged about this? I am all for public debate about education. However, the current discussion is elitist at best and authoritarian at worst. Education should be a prime topic of general public concern and control; and it is now far from that. If parents and students are not at that table neither is the public, in any real sense.

As I have proposed, electable state boards of education should represent, not just the interests of corporate or national security self-proclaimed elites, but the wider interests of the general public. This does not mean that CEOs trying to find well educated workers who can work in their companies or national security wonks looking for skilled CIA operatives should not have their worries and their ideas heard by boards of education or the public that hires those boards. Still, they should merely be two voices and not the dominating ones, just another citizens' concerns and desires.

The current debate itself centers around universal academic skills tests administered here and in Finland, Korea and everywhere else children are tested and whether public or private schools are better able at educating our children to score well on those tests and which should we fund and so it goes, through all those reams of newsprint and congressional hearings. What we actually teach and why in whatever kinds of schools we want, that does not seem to be on the public agenda — except when some numbskull education board in the boonies of New Jersey decides to nix Darwin and teach Creationism. The numbers on those test scores, somehow and for someone should mean something about the deterioration of the American intelligence and innovativeness and oh, the future will be so awful if those numbers do not change, our livelihoods and prosperity, our security, our very warm cozy feeling that we are in all ways best in the world at everything, a super power with super students to match. Dear, dear; my, my; they huff and puff, fume and fuss.

Not only am I not sure that the meaning of those numbers is cause for wringing of hands and gnashing of teeth but I am not all that sure either that I care all that much even if it were true — which, I and Ms. Ravitch believe, it is not.

I would like to suggest to those future state democratic boards of education a very different education system than the present one, one worthy of a fully democratized and prosperous society, a society that is both free and responsible, educating its future citizens to know how to be both free and responsible to and for themselves, their families and their communities and the world.

The education I am proposing has one purpose in four parts. Its one purpose is what education, at least to my mind, should be designed to do: prepare fledgling youth to function as full-fledged adults in the world in which they are going to live. Of course, any child and teenage now or in the future, may decide to ignore the advice of parents and teachers, ignoring what we adults want to teach and simply, in one way or another, for better or worse, set out for another territory ahead or become, much to our chagrin, delinquents, criminals or pirate captains; Free Will being what it is. But, at least we can do the best we can to help them along if they want to live cooperatively and socially.

Education, at the present moment, seems more and more to be oriented to job preparation. This is functional, but narrow. It is correct to prepare children to enter adult lives in this society possessed of the requisite skills for jobs, the more skilled the better for them. They will get paid more and can buy bigger TVs and smaller hybrid cars. That is fine as far as it goes; although if you listen to all those reports of prestigious committees and councils and those who keep test scores, we are not doing so well at that.

Whatever the case is with all that, we still have a very narrow philosophy of preparatory education. If Jesus said that "man does not live by bread alone," I would add that earning one's living to buy stone ground chapatti bread at the local Whole Foods is not all of life either. Work ain't everything; although, you would not know it by us North Americans, who work more and more, longer and longer — even more that the ever workaholic company men Japanese — and then never seem to get ahead, but work more and more to cover more and more debt, nationally and personally. Is this really it, folks? But that is what school prepares you for: for work and debt and buying rather than for life and certainly not for life as a full citizen of a free republic, certainly, not to be particularly happy either.

So now the four parts:
1. Education for Civic Citizenship
2. Basic Literacy Skills: language (reading, writing, foreign) and mathematics
3. Household (including health and fitness), Technological Living Skills and Ecological Education
4. Interests and Job Education

All four parts of the educational system I propose will teach those skills that would help a youngster graduate to adulthood having been given a foundation in how to function in this world, this society, this community, in their family and to live with themselves as well as with everyone else. It is pragmatic functional education for real life in the world as it is, however virtual it is all becoming.

1. Education to Civic Citizenship.

All one must do is turn on the boob tube and listen to the level of public political discourse to realize that the boobs on the tube would be better handicapping a Super Bowl than interminably calculating who is up and who is down by what last gaffe or which scandal that effects what poll numbers in what crucial state. Whether and why Marc Rubio stopped and sipped a glass of water just is not news to me.

Are they talking to a citizenry that actually takes moronic and gossipy politics seriously? Either we have an uninformed citizenry who actually cares about such distracting rubbish or a low consciousness journalistic class who just do not know any better themselves. One way or the other, in listening carefully to our ruling class of dunderheaded Republicans and Democrats, you realize very quickly that we are in trouble, big trouble.

So, let me place blame where blame should lie. We really and truly do not educate our citizens to be citizens. We educate our citizens to be workers and consumers. Workers are told what to do by their bosses; consumers are manipulated by the marketing departments of their bosses to buy and consume more and more. We can blame poor journalism and the likes of Rush Windbag on poor education as well.

In contrast, citizens — CITIZENS! — are in control of their society and their lives. Citizens know what is up and demand of those working to inform them of what is up, that they are properly informed. We currently do no such educating or demanding and the current political discourse is a result. A truly democratic society itself requires fully educated and informed citizens who require proper information and discussion.

Now, as my friends have asked me when I diatribe all this. "Well, dear sir, who is going to teach THAT?" Who is going to educate the educators to educate the newbies? I am not sure I have an adequate answer because it is, as we say, a bootstrap operation, picking our selves up by the proverbial bootstraps when we have neither boots nor much ground. Hmmm.

Yet do it we should. In fact, do it we must or the very foundations of a democracy will give way to one or another kind of tyranny. We still have the freedom to speak up, to demonstrate, to vote. Human Rights in America are not complete, but they are nevertheless substantive. Still and all, they are all looking more and more like an outer shell with the center corroding under the weight of moneyed elections, inflammatory demagogic rhetoric and the diminishment and disparagement of the public arena.

How to educate us out of such a mess? Raising CITIZENS is no easy task. Yet I think if we put our mind to raising our consciousnesses and raising our children to citizenship consciousness, just the knowledge that we are not doing this well and that we should make an effort to change is a beginning. That this should be discussed when we live in a poisoned public polity is difficult, but if we do not begin we can never get anywhere and frankly, we have far to go. Ask the Athenian Socrates and his hemlock poisoned ghost. Far more recently, ask Neil Postman of Teaching As A Subversive Activity. Or Noam Chomsky.

Still, CITIZENSHIP education from the beginning of school to whatever end of schooling we have in mind should always be educating for democratic citizenship. I would like it if we all began to think about, write about, discuss and debate it and then start to change it all.

Citizens should be able to listen to an argument being made by those competing to represent them in government, on school boards, bank boards, and medical boards and discern a good position from a worse, a better case from a bad one and stay informed about the context in which the argument is being made. That is, a citizen should know what is going on in their society and community and when someone is bullshitting them and handing them a line, or is genuinely interested in promoting their and the general welfare. This is no small skill. Bullshit detectors are in short supply and, therefore, according to market forces, expensive.

An informed and discerning citizenry will want a host of

points of view, not as now, what passes for different points of view, but is really only the Right-Left bleating of, as Jeffrey Sachs calls it, "The Corporatocracy." When was the last time that you heard Noam Chomsky or, for that matter, on the Right, Grover Norquist — for very long or with respect — on CNN? Or Jeffrey Sachs? Or William Greider? A true citizenry would not put up with that. Well, maybe CNN put on Jeffrey Sachs for 2 minutes and Grover for 15.

2. Basic Literacy Skills.

Not all children are going to learn to read and write and do mathematics. And of course, some will be more literate and able to do quadratic equations sooner and more quickly than others. If we expect all students to learn citizenship and learn to participate in making decisions in the society, literacy would help — you can read political discourse, not just hear it — still it is not a necessity. You can be illiterate and still be able to hear an argument and know what is what and who is on first and who is cheating off the base. And those who cannot cut any mustard scholastically, are no less citizens for the lack of their ability or inability to read Chaucer and do long division or split an atom or tweak a quark.

Still, we should make the effort as a society to try as hard as we can to educate everyone in basic literacy skills. I include mathematics as a literacy skill as I think of math as a more abstract form of language, but still language. If all those quantitative test scores are any indication about how we are doing teaching basic reading and writing skills, perhaps we need to renew our efforts.

However, I do not believe our inability to make all children and teenagers super literate is a uniform failure. The problem seems not to be with wealthy private prep schools, nor with public education in middle class neighborhoods, but with schools in poor and very poor neighborhoods where the value of our current style of education is often undermined by the ravages of poverty itself. Parents do not have enough time to help their children with school, and very likely are not very well educated themselves. If we want good universal literacy we will as a society need to ameliorate problems antecedent to school itself: poor diet, family education levels and family interest in education.

If we invest in parents as well as children, our society will be paid back many fold. To continue as we are going or blaming teachers or poor performing schools misses the point, although certainly we want the best schools and the best teachers in the most difficult educational institutions. Yet, there is a good deal of rearranging of the lives of children before and after school that will make the most difference in the long and short term. And if you are going to pay for students from poor families who are doing poorly in public school to migrate to a rich person's prep school, as George Bush thought, they will need some of the family and social support that going to that school requires as well.

"No Child Left Behind," may also require of society that no parent and no person be left behind either. As a society we need to take our social work far more seriously and be sure that everyone succeeds, and that that success, however modest, is passed on to the next generation instead of some of the failure we now see in the South Bronx, on the Southside of Chicago and, in general, in rural Mississippi schools.

Return parents to school. (Remember that all education is now paid for.) Return parents to school with classes for child rearing and child education, as well as nutrition, among others.

Parental income should be better if and when a living wage is the minimum wage and only one job is necessary to attain a decent living and a decent upbringing for children. So that would help, too.

And if all that does not work, remedial studies should be standard for those students and even those families who are not doing well. Standard.

Now, still, there will be some who for one reason or another are not readers or writers or are unable to learn math. Some of us really and truly are learning disabled. It should not disable us to either live or work. There should always be employment for those who are willing to work but are not literate. Not all jobs — especially relatively low tech jobs — require good literacy skills. A society that guarantees some kind of work will leave nobody behind, and everyone will be contributing what skills they have for the collective good.

3. Basic Life Skills.

If you are going to live in this world and pursue happiness, it is a very good idea to know what is around and how to get around. It may have been a waste of time to teach my son, more interested in theatre and art and politics, how to do calculus. Yet it would not have been a waste of time to teach him how to cook, as when he was away at college and thereafter, his cooking skills were not non-existent, but not all that good either. Given all his interests and then all those unnecessary school requirements, perhaps he would have been better able to fend for himself if I had been more insistent on him learning cooking. I take some blame there.

I think it would behoove us as a society if we brought the skills of living day-to-day here and now to our schools instead of insisting on such esoteric skills as chemistry. Nothing wrong with chemistry. Happened to be my best subject in high school, and I like it quite a bit. But as a requirement for everyone, not as important as learning about personal fitness, personal hygiene, diet and cooking. Moreover, in this society, how to buy — how to be an astute consumer — and how to sell — we all wind up selling something here and there, some of us do it for a living even — are essential skills. We need to know how to buy a house. How to buy insurance. How to keep a checking account. How to apply for credit. How to be credit worthy.

Essential life skills in this kind of society and should be taught across the board. How to keep house. Basic sanitation. How to raise children. The list goes on and on. Basic psychology. How to deal with and live with our thoughts and moods. How to interact with other people, with those younger, with peers, with those older, with parents, with mating, with adulthood, with society, with the world. Given the percentage of the population requiring drugs to medicate their moods, we need far more education in psychological health as well.

Basic current technology and machines. Currently, every child should know about computers. Every child should have some basic knowledge about machinery from cars to appliances and on to more complex systems. Know how to live with all of this and well.

Exercise and personal hygiene. Basic medicines and how to use the medical system.

Ecology and Nature. Either we educate everyone about ecology and how to live on this planet or we will not have a suitable planet to live on. As with transforming to a green economy, I cannot emphasize enough how much we need a green education.

Spirituality and religion and philosophy. The bias in our present education is facts and science. Scientism has become the religion of the intellectual class for the most part. I believe we need to reinvigorate discussion and debate about belief itself. I am not urging that we adopt one religion or another, one philosophy or another, not at all. But part of education must be to talk about foundations of belief and ethics.

I am not giving details on much of the above. That is not only a whole other book, it is many books. Curricula must be developed in all these areas and included in the basic education of our children. We could fill textbooks on how to do all this. They should be written, if they are not already.

As a society, we must educate our youngsters about how to live in this world rather than leaving the learning of these skills to chance and to the all too busy and stressed families that have neither the time nor patience, nor all too frequently, the knowledge.

4. Interests and Job Training.

At the end, when all is said by teachers and done by students, when the graduation certificates are all handed out or not, as caps or hats are thrown up in the air as graduates or non-graduates, students go out into what they now call "real life," educational institutions being not where you would choose to spend your reality, but a preparatory step into the real of life. Unless, of course, one becomes a teacher and saunters back to a real life in school with students who are preparing for real life even if they become teachers.

Still and all, we hope, that those who are getting out of school go out into real life and do what they really want to do in real life. That is, they work at what they really would like working at and live well and prosper in their work life, whether it is dentistry, masonry, child raising, rocket science, assembly line work at the clothes pin factory or something so eccentric and creative that none of us have thought of doing something like that before or farming or picture framing.

Yet, from what I remember at school, the standardized curriculum of a pretty fair high school in Brooklyn, New York in the 1960s, finding one's interests and learning to pursue them is not on the curriculum. Until senior year, all the choices, for the most part, are made for you. Decades later when my son, in the 1990s, went to a pretty fair high school in Moretown, Vermont, the standardized curriculum that I trudged through successfully in Brooklyn, was ever so similar, if not a downright duplicate of the curriculum I was taught.

Still and all, even though my son was valedictorian of his class — and I, an honor student — as my son pointed out from time to time (especially when he was especially bored with math classes all the way through calculus that he was getting all As in) "it is just such a boring waste of time, dad, and when will I ever use this is my life?" Theatre and art were his forte. Mine, I did not know.

Why they put him and me through all that nonsense is beyond my understanding. Although in an entirely different way, I do understand. You are being groomed to be an agreeable and flexible and obedient robot. They tell you what to do; you do it. Life in America. You will fit on the factory floor. You will fit in front of the computer screen. You will fit. And, perchance, if you are very, very perceptive and smart, like Steve Jobs or Bill Gates, you will realize it would be better if you dropped out of all of that, go out on your own, invent something really cool and have all the 'bots work for you. Of course, there are those who, being also very perceptive and smart who go through the system and instead of becoming robots do not get quite as rich as Misters Jobs and Gates and the face behind the Facebook, but who do quite well and even what they want to do and contribute mightily to themselves and humanity to boot.

Yet, I think it better if the exceptions become the rule, and we retool education to allow children to follow their personal blissful path; not only allow but actively encourage not only independent thinking citizens but creative and independent thinking and acting human beings.

Will corporate leaders and corporations get the skilled labor force they need for the future? Perhaps, perhaps not. The question for me is, which future? The future that corporate elites choose — and that, of course, benefits them above all others and the money and effects trickle and dribble down to the rest of us — or do we all choose what future we all want? A preordained future with a preordained set of workers fits a preordained agenda of corporate elites, elites whose decisions are only now showing up as decimating the planet. In that future do we want our children living and working? What I am proposing does not fit that future.

I am envisioning an unknown future decided upon by, not me, not Witless Mitt and his Multi-Millionaire Minions, but by well educated citizens, who know who they are, what they want to do, what will get them there and what effect they will have on others, that future can be prepared for with a different kind of non-standardized curriculum.

I would like to recommend to you a college course put out by The Teaching Company (you can purchase it on their website if you would like) called "The Joy of Science." I think it would be easy to adapt this college level survey course to high school or even elementary school. The course consists of a couple of lectures on each of the many branches of science. In one way, it creates scientific literacy for adults. You will have some idea coming out of this course of what all kinds of science scientists are doing as scientists. In another way, this course is a turn on. I personally found each of the many kinds of science as presented absolutely fascinating, and I am quite sure that many if not most of the scientists in each of these fields find their field fascinating as well. Even a science that I thought might be a huge bore, like "Materials Science," was surprisingly and astoundingly interesting.

Now, not everyone, I am almost certain, would find tectonic plates or DNA molecules or cosmological constants as interesting as I. Still, I find it difficult to believe that there would be no branch of science that each and everyone of us might not find interesting in some way. Moreover, I think presented to young and older children, a good introduction to the many branches of science would generate enormous interest. In fact, it would not be difficult once such an introduction was conducted to find out which of these subjects individual students would find interesting. Maybe one. Maybe, like me, all.

And guess what? In an educational system geared to the individual student, finding these interests, generating these interests can create the greatest of educational moments, the greatest of teaching moments and the beginning of life long careers or, at least life long hobbies. Show them what is out there and they shall come. Even bring them out to where actual scientists are at work, give them a tour of a lab or an observatory, a computer factory or … an automobile assembly line …. or … the possibilities and interests are fairly endless. And then, we should help each and every student pursue their new interests as long and as far as these take them. If they lose interest and go onto something else, at least they have developed the discipline to pursue an interest further and when they pursue a later interest, they will know better how to go about doing so.

In our current system, we are not geared for this kind of individualized education. We do factory education, standardized education. We will need more teachers, more para-professionals, and I hope, more grandparents to staff our schools to help nurture students on their very own personal path. Remember that one year of required service after age 50? Great use of that kind of service.

Moreover, interest survey courses should not just stop with science. Students may survey the arts as well. Give children a good idea of what are the things that people have done in the past that they might like to do in the future. Visual arts. Theatre arts. Construction arts. And on and on.

Somewhere in the subjects of science and in arts a child may become engaged in pursuing with interest their future profession. And at some point earlier or later, if none of these interests interest them, they might have to invent their very own interests and careers, unique and inventive careers.

But if it is a system designed to interest students and then teach from their new enthusiasm for learning, I would suggest that teaching independent learning skills, that is, how to pursue your interests, how to learn, how to follow what you want to learn, how you will learn what you want to do and then find out how to do it, that teaching, of the skill of how to learn will be as important as what students are learning in content.

I took an independent study Master's degree in Psychology at Vermont College several decades ago. There are a few programs like this scattered across the country, Vermont College, Godard College — down the road in rural Vermont — The Union Institute in Ohio, Prescott College in Arizona and, perhaps others that I am not familiar with. A professor representing the school reads your papers and approves your study. You choose your mentor, someone with a Ph.D. in your field who you want to work with more regularly. For the first several months, with the help of your mentor, you design your curriculum. For the rest of your time, you do what you said you were going to do — read pertinent books, write papers — in pursuit of intellectual happiness and in answer to the questions you formulated from the beginning.

Considering that our educational system is not at all designed to foster independent study and learning skills, these programs are not easy. I know not a few graduate students who started but could not finish these programs. However, for those who persevere or are naturally good independent learners, the rewards both in the specifics of what is learned, but far more importantly, how to go about learning, making reasonable questions in a field, establishing what field you want to question, how to gather information and materials and then how to digest and process information and materials, how to express what you have learned and done, these skills are even more important and have influenced me for the rest of my days. I could not write this book in my spare time if not for what I learned about learning and persevering, if not for what I taught myself at Vermont College, if not for the wise counsel of my mentors and my professor, Eleanor Ott, Walter Zeichner and Verbena Pasteur.

But why not slowly but surely from the very beginnings of schooling teach independent learning and learning from what would interest the one learning — little by little from the beginning. At first, more teaching personnel is required. By the time students get to what is now high school, teaching personnel would be fewer in number, perhaps, and with an entirely different set of duties, less active lecturing, more supervising students independently pursuing their interests in independent or group independent learning.

Will students from non-standardized education do well on standardized tests? My guess is that they will but, I am not sure I really care. If we have a country of low scoring students and all that anyone wants to do is make a minimum living wage in a totally routine job, well, then, if that what is desired by the population of America, I think we would be a country of simple factories manufacturing simple products, making enough to get by. Perfectly sustainable, and who knows, maybe happier than we are now, we being on any standardized happiness scale, not especially happy.

Somehow, given the character of the characters in the United States, I have a feeling this will not be our scenario. It will be the pursuit of happiness for some, to live a simple if materially modest existence at work that is of value, but not dynamic or creative. For others, the thrill of invention and great triumphs might be the way. Or, as my Organic Chemistry professor at Durham Tech Community College opined: "I just really love doing this." And as love of a subject is contagious, I loved Organic Chemistry, too; and while I have not followed that path, I could easily see doing it.

For some, life is painting a house. For some, it is painting "The Mona Lisa." For others, it is geological oceanography. For Billy Graham and Barack Obama, stirring sermons or inspirational speeches are a satisfying thrill. For my Organic Chemistry teacher, working at a lab for a pharmaceutical company and teaching us the intricacies of tinker toy like organic diagrams, ah, bliss. For me, it is sitting at a computer and talking to you.

And, for you? Do you know? Were you educated to know? Did you have to fight against the grain to know and to do? Do you know and never got to do it?

And, God bless them everyone, I know those who love to do accounting. It is beyond my understanding, but for some of us, organized numbers do it for them. Lawyers. Doctors. Lab technicians. Cooks. Waiters and waitresses. Production supervisors. Farmers and barbers. Architects. Builders. I might not want to do it, but for someone else, perhaps. I know someone in each of these fields who loves it. More power to us all! And, I believe, if students figure it out earlier and pursue their interests more fully that the lawyers and doctors and cooks and everyone will be sooooo… ever much better, will be, as we say, world class!

How long should formal schooling go on then in this system? I am quite sure that in this type of system, timing will change and the old distinctions of elementary, junior and then senior high schools and college, undergraduate and graduate will entirely breakdown.

As the system is free education cradle to grave, anyone can go in and out of the system as they so choose. Yet, at all levels, beginner to the most advanced, the schooling system is available to anyone at anytime. Don't feel like pursuing much of anything at 18 years old, but playing football in the park? Your choice. Want back in at 28. You're back in at whatever level. Checking out what is there and then finding your interests and then pursuing your interests will always be there.

Want to just work in a simple place serving food at the lunch counter until your are 50? Okay. And then, you are struck with inspiration to pursue particle physics or the history of religious evangelism from 1200 to 1992 A.D., go for it. Tired of simple work at a minimal wage. Want to pursue entrepreneurialism? Need to figure that out. Go back to school. It is there for you.

What we should require of children in our society is that they stay in school long enough to know how to be citizens, that they are reasonably literate and that they know reasonably how to function in this society with other people, within the law and social structure of the country and with the existing technology. Required.

Otherwise? All along, schools should also be trying to entice students to learn by showing them what is available to learn more about and teach them how to pursue their interests. But no body should ever be required to go through a standardized curriculum that is irrelevant to their interests and lives and which can only alienate them from further learning.

From this type of education, I think we should be able to generate a conscious citizenry able and willing to put into power, whether political or economic, those exceptionally wise individuals who will best serve everyone's interest.

We need it!

Conclusion:
Of All Proposals Great & Small

How? How in this world does any of this, whole or in part, get done? Ah. Here is where it gets difficult, but not really. So what I would like to propose about the how and now — the day after tomorrow now — is to start by forming a new political party in the U.S.A. The name of this party could be perhaps The Party of Human Beings. One constructs a political party to give mutual aide in getting elected to office and following what is called "a platform," that is, the sum of the ideas of The Party, so that, in free and fair elections and then with wide majorities, the ideas of The Party of Human Beings become the laws of the land. Would be nice, eh?

Of course, I believe my ideas from this book will be a starting point; and, I trust that many of them will become part of the platform of The Party of Human Beings; although, I am certain that not all and/or that some others will be tweaked this way or that, but still retain their basic shape. And, then, too, there will be other proposals from other thinkers added to the platform as well.

I hope then that these ideas spread, too, to other parts of the world, and that in elections The Party of Human Beings gets elected, forms majorities and enacts these ideas into law around the world. I think, perhaps, that once the democratic countries adopt these ideas, there will be movements to spread these ideas to non-democratic countries and transform them into democratic countries.

Then, naturally, once it is everywhere, and The Party of Human Beings has created a democratic polity that follows Human Rights and non-violence everywhere, then perhaps The World Government and universal peace and harmony and prosperity will be the norm.

Simple really. Take some time actually. A walking journey of a thousand miles may start with one step and a political social economic rights movement may start with one vote or even before that, the right to vote. Best of luck everyone; let's get on with it.

A Tentative Platform,
All Proposals Big and Bigger

• Taxes: none whatsoever.

• Government:
- is not a social service agency.
- is confined to making rules and regulations and enforcing them. Law. Prisons. The military.
- is not allowed to go into debt.
- All businesses whatsoever are regulated by a regulatory board that is appointed from one central board that is created by the government. One regulatory board per industry covers all regulation for that business. All regulatory boards are paid for by the businesses in that business.
- Each citizen is billed equally for the cost of government making and enforcing laws each year.

• Social Services:
- Medicine: Statewide Medical Board bills all citizens equally for all medical expenses of all citizens in the state; Board is elected by the all citizens of the state; Board controls the medical system;
- All citizens have a right to have all their medical expenses covered.
- Education: Statewide Education Board bills all citizens equally for all educational expenses for all citizens in the state; Board is elected by all the citizens of the state; Board controls the educational system
- All citizens have a right to cradle to grave education paid for by the state board.
- All other services: decided by the citizens of each locality whether each service is public or private or otherwise.

• Banking: Community Banks/State Banks/National Bank/International Bank

- The Board of Directors of each and every Community Bank is elected by the citizens of the locale of the bank.

- Community banks elect the Board of Directors of The Statewide Bank that in turn elects the Board of Directors of The National Bank that in turn elects the Board of Directors of The International Bank.

- These banks are the one and only source of investment capital. There is no private investment permitted. No stock markets. No money markets. No private investment firms. None of that.

- Community banks choose 50% of the Board of Directors of all companies in the community that they have invested in. The community banks receive back 50% of the profits of all businesses they have invested in. The same pattern applies to banks at all levels.

- Community banks send one-third of their revenues, after bank operating expenses, from profits to state banks and state banks send one-third to national and then one-third goes to the international bank. One-third of revenue of community banks goes to unemployment and disability insurance, etc. and one-third is invested in new or existing local businesses or infrastructure projects.

- At all levels banks invest in businesses, insurances, and infrastructure projects.

• Companies

- Founding entrepreneur can be head of Board of Directors for 1st ten years of company.

- 50% of Board of Directors comes from the Community Bank (or state or national or international bank depending on which is investing); 50% elected by all employees of company.

- 50% of profit divided equally to all employees; 50% to appropriate bank.

- All wages must be living wages, suitable to sustain a family of four.

- Wages need not be equal, the differential decided by Board of Directors.
- Maximum salary for anyone in any company can be determined by government law and regulation; salary differential, too, from top to bottom can be determined by government law and regulation

• Jobs
- Everyone is guaranteed a job.
- If laid off, each worker is paid from unemployment insurance at past salary for one year.
- You may quit job and receive unemployment insurance. Limit in lifetime to number of times one can do this.
- If no job then after unemployment insurance runs out, an infrastructure job should be offered, salary dependent on going wage for that job.
- If disabled, receive equivalent of living wage from disability insurance.
- If unwilling to work: receive nothing.
- Provisions should be made for artists, entrepreneurs and others who cannot or are not yet ready to work in the regular economy.
- New mothers or infant/young child care giver: 2 years of full unemployment insurance; job back after 2 years.

• The Four Zones
- Within all zones, ownership of the means of production follow the same rules. Everyone who works in a company or on a farm or on a ranch "owns" that social entity and has a right to an equal share of 50% of profits, depending on hours worked. Each zone is regulated by lawful regulatory boards.
- City and suburb: grow up and not out; green up.
- Farm: only ownership of farm but not land; cannot be evicted from land in perpetuity unless grossly negligent; farmland cannot be converted to city or suburb; no distant ownership of farms or farm animals.
- Smaller and organic farms. Revitalization of farms and

farm life. More people farming. Prosperous farm life.

- Ranch: herds are allowed to roam freely and ranchers harvest from freely roaming herds. More people ranching. Prosperity on the ranches.

- Revitalization of ranches and ranch land.

- Wilderness: greatly expanded; lifestyle is living off the land; revitalization of tribal societies

• International

- Human Rights: life, liberty, speech, belief, non-discrimination, security, choice of government officials, choice of officials in all social entities.

- Democracy is a Human Right.

- No wars, between nations or within nations. War, internal or external, is illegal.

- No weaponry permitted at all; international inspection without boundary. Planning for war is illegal.

- A World Court to settle disputes of any kind between nations or within nations when not resolvable by national courts.

- A World Government million person military to enforce any edict of World Court and stop any violence.

- A World Government to coordinate and regulate economics and law according to Human Rights and sustainable economies and environment.

So, dear reader, friend, citizen are you ready? Want to make that American Revolution 2.0? Want to change the world? Want to clean up the current dystopian New World Odor? Let's go!

I have not dealt with how to transition from The Old World Odor to a world of Green Democracy. While the proposals and ideas replace that old stink, how actually to change without much pain and disruption, now that will be a good trick. But that too is another book, if not several and needs to be written not only on paper but in history. I hope we will be doing it together. It will take some time and even more thought and sensitivity than I have tried to demonstrate here.

This is only a beginning and an outline of a beginning at that. But better a beginning than the end of the good earth and the poor human beings of it.

AN AFTERWORD:
INSPIRED YET?

Even though what I have written is a beginning and an outline, there is just a bit more exhortation beyond "let's get our butts out there and think and do" to talk to you about still.

Proposals themselves are generally not seen as particularly inspiring, and, for this enterprise, considering the forces that will be aligned against such green and democratically radical solutions and even without those oppositional powers-that-be-and-do-not-want-to-change, even without all that, there is a prodigious amount of work to be done. It would seem impossible, frankly, without a kind of, what we might call, "a religious fervor."

Proposals and rational ideas may not equal the inspired rhetoric of really good speakers, even if those speechmakers say very little or say the wrong thing. A very good preacher can march us just as well to Hell, believing we are headed to "the promised land," as a very good preacher can lead us out of Hell and to "the promised land." Hitler is an example of the former, Moses, speech impediment and all, the latter.

So, a book with just a set of proposals, an outline of proposals and a little flourish of written rhetoric here and there might not be moving enough to get us moving enough. But if I might make a suggestion to you. Let these ideas, these proposals sink in a bit. Take some time with theme. Think about them; feel them out. The sum of them really, to my mind and heart, is greater than the sum of parts and the parts are not too bad either.

Yet, added together and marinated with brain juices over a period of time, I think that they are the equal of any really good speech by any politician around. But even more than that, I believe, they are and should be a good, a very good, an extremely excellent plan for the future of human beings on this planet.   Human Rights. Democracy. Ecology. If there were themes that this book has been all about, it is these. And those, citizens, are in fact the continuation and reinvigoration of revolutions that began with The American and The French, and more rebellions and revolutions that could be even named in a short book, the continuation, reinvigoration, the realization of Human Rights, Democracy, a fair, clean and equitable world. I trust that those might inspire us all. The proposals of this book are simply an expression, a filling out of the implications of HUMAN RIGHTS and DEMOCRACY and ECOLOGY.

Now, I think, we are ready for the Nike expression: "JUST DO IT!" We have some idea, now of what the "IT" is that we want to "JUST DO."

See you at the party convention. Sign up, sign in, seize the day, change the world.

About The Author

Philip Kosdan, M.A., M.Ac., L.Ac., The Wiseacre, has been a practicing and licensed acupuncture and herbalist for 30+ years. He has two masters degrees, one from New England School of Acupuncture (Chinese Medicine) and another from Vermont College (Psychology), as well as a B.A. from New York University (Sociology).

Phil grew up first in the Bronx for 5 years, then on to Chicago's Northside for 5-6 years, back to New York and Brooklyn for another 10 or so years, Vermont and New England for 20 and now to North Carolina for 18+. Phil resides in Carrboro, North Carolina with his wife of 23 years, their long black cat, Simon Linguine, their short fluffy dog, Bessie (Besame Mucho), where he is visited not infrequently by three granddaughters, Vivian, Averi, and Keeli and two grandsons, B.J. and Brendan and their parents, daughters Alexandra and Lorin and their partners, Brian and Jasin. He tragically lost a son, Gabriel, at the age of 28 to Cystic Fibrosis

He is also at work on two other books, tentatively titled: A Hub For The Wheel Of An Integrated Medicine and Medicine As A Revolutionary Activity.

Acknowledgements

I would first like to thank the coffee bean. When Larsen, the cartoonist, was asked to what did he attribute his funny and odd creativity, he opined that it was his morning coffee. After the cup, he simply sat down at his drawing board and out came those wonderful and weird drawings. Well, I am with Larsen on the benefits of coffee. Most of the ideas and proposals in this book came along after a cup of coffee or two while I was either driving to work in Vermont or on family visits to New York City from North Carolina. Not only did I solve all possible social problems forthwith while plummeting down the highway, but I assure you I did advanced work in Cosmology as well, deciding on the shape, size and longevity of the entire Universe and the meaning of everything under the stars. Coffee is marvelous.

Filtering through what is of value and what is caffeinated delusion and illusion, now that is something else again. To that, I must acknowledge not only a different part of my personal psyche but also how that psyche was formed and informed by teachers, authors of other books, friends, enemies and family. An adrenalized mind requires tempering.

I owe so much to the very many teachers who spent a portion of their lives educating me. In high school, my English teacher especially, Mr. Trachten; and in history, the ever flamboyant history teacher, Mr.deLeon; and, in music, the wonderful Mr. Iijima. I cannot thank them and several other high school teachers, Mr. Spector in Chemistry, Mr. Schraeger in Math. enough. And then at N.Y.U., sociology department professor and advisor, Dr. Corwin, without whom I would have never graduated, given the chaos of the late 1960's. My history teacher and leftist radical professor, Dr. Robert Wolfe, who showed me that history was not exactly as I had learned it and that it was possible to think creatively about social arrangements. Then Neil Postman, another N.Y.U. professor whose classes I never attended but whose presence and books have always been a seminal inspiration. Ted Kaptchuk at New England School of Acupuncture. Sandra Ingerman at The Foundation for Shamanic Studies. Eleanor Ott, Walter Zeichner, Verbena Pasteur at Vermont College. All helped form an enthusiastic if sometimes ill-tempered mind.

Writers and speakers? More than I could ever list, but especially my teenage intellectual hero Erich Fromm, the anti-guru iconoclastic Krishnamurti, Howard Zinn, George Lakoff, Ludwig Wittgenstein, the many professors at The Teaching Company in the Great Courses Series, and, too, Paul Unschuld, Gandhi, Lewis Lapham and on and on. I cannot begin to thank them all or even begin to list them all. Well, actually, I will list some more in this book's bibliography.

And then, most importantly, I wish to thank friends and family, many of who have had to endure numerous writings of the material that has eventually become this book. My loving wife and part time editor of my rants and raves, Pat. I simply could not even approach doing this without her. My best friend from N.Y.U., Eunice (Poulos) Siegaltuch who decades later, still agrees to read and edit my works. And, Bea Bookchin — whose deceased ex-husband, Murray Bookchin, was director of The School of Social Ecology at Goddard College, and a writer and activist who has many an opinion about topics and problems that we have similar, if not at all the same, solutions for — I am ever so grateful for all of our many conversations about everything but especially the state of the world and politics; and, she too has read and helped me to clarify and edit this work.

And so many other friends, Donna and Dave Gulick, Don and Merrillee Narensky, Alan Spalt, and so many others who put up with my pressure to read my book as soon as possible so I can get their comments back so I can revise, revise, revise.

And of course, the extended family with which I am in love, every last one, daughters, granddaughters, many in laws, and cousins and aunts and uncles, my deceased parents and, especially my son, Gabriel — as well as his many friends, who, too became my friends; especially Martin Nibali without whose expertise in self-publishing this book would not be in your hands. And last and most certainly not least, my esteemed copy editor, Jennifer Weaver, who made this manuscript far more readable and was especially good at removing at least 764 unnecessary commas and semi-colons that would have annoyed my readers to death.

BIBLIOGRAPHY

Alexander Hamilton, John Jay, James Madison. The Federalist Papers: Public Domain Books.

Aristotle. Politics: A Treatise on Government. Translated by William Ellis. London; New York: J M Dent & Sons, Ltd.; E P Dutton & Co., 1912,1912,1923,1928.

_____. Nicomachean Ethics. Translated by Terence Irwin. Second Edition ed. Indianapolis, Indiana: Hackett Publishing Company, Inc., 1999.

Atkins, P.W. The Second Law. New York: Scientific American Library, 1984.

Audi, Robert. Epistemology. second ed. New York, London: Routledge, 2003.

Ayer, Alfred Jules. Language Truth and Logic. New York: Dover Publications , Inc., 1952.

Bacon, Francis. Novum Organum. Translated by Peter Urbach and John Gibson, Edited by Peter Urbach and John Gibson. Chicago: Open Court, 1998.

Belenky, Clinchy, Goldberger,Tarule. Women's Ways of Knowing. New York: Basic Books, 1986.

Bellamy, Edward. Looking Backward   2000-1887. New York: New American Library, 2000.

Benedict, Ruth. Patterns of Culture. Boston: Houghton Mifflin Company, 1934.

Berger, Peter L. Invitation to Sociology. New York: Anchor Books, 1963.

Berger, Thomas Luckman; Peter L. The Social Construction of Reality. New York: Anchor Books, 1966.

Berne, Eric. Games People Play: Castle Books, 1964.

Berry, Wendell. What Matter? Economics for a Renewed Commonwealth. Berkeley: Counterpoint.

_____. The Art of the Commonplace, the Agarian Essays of Wendell Berry. Berkeley: Counterpoint, 2002.

Best, Steven. The Politics of Historical Vision. New York: The Guilford Press, 1995.

Blackmore, Susan. Consciousness, an Introduction. New York, NY: Oxford University Press, Inc., 2004.

Blakeslee, V.S. Ramachandran; Sandra. Phantoms in the Brain. New York: William Morrow Company, Inc., 1998.

Bly, Robert. Iron John. New York: Addison-Wesley Publishing Co. Inc., 1990.

Bookchin, Murray. The Ecology of Freedom. Palo Alto, CA: Cheshire Books, Inc., 1982.

_____. Social Ecology and Communalism. Oakland, CA.: AK Press, 2007.

Briskin, Alan. The Stirring of Soul in the Workplace. San Francisco: Jossey Bass, Inc., 1996.

Brown, Dee. Bury My Heart at Wounded Knee. New York: Holt, Rinehart, and Winston, 1970.

Brownlee, Shannon. Overtreated, Why Too Much Medicine Is Making Us Sicker and Poorer. New York: Bloomsbury, 2007.

Brownson, O.A. The American Republic, Its Constitution, Tendencies, and Destiny. New York: P. O'Shea, 1866.

Bruner, Jerome. Acts of Meaning. Cambridge, MA: Harvard University Press, 1990.

Bryson, Bill. A Short History of Nearly Everything: Special Illustrated Edition. New York, NY: Broadway Books, a division of Random House, Inc., 2005.

Budd, Malcolm. Wittgenstein's Philosophy of Psychology. New York & London: Routledge, 1989.

Buddha. The Diamond Sutra Andthe Sutra of Hui Neng. Translated by A.F. Price andWong Mou-Lam. Berkley, CA: Shambala Publications, 1969.

Burke, Edmund. The Works of the Right Honourable Edmund Burke, in Twelve Volumes. London: John C. Nimmo.

Calloway, Colin. One Vast Winter Count, the Native American West before Lewis and Clark History of the American West, Edited by Richard W. Etulain. Lincoln and London: University of Nebraska Press, 2003.

Campbell, Jeremy. Grammatical Man. New York: Simon and Schuster, 1988.

Camus, Albert. The Rebel. New York: Vintage International, 1991.

Capra, Fritjof. The Tao of Physics. New York: Bantam Books, 1975.

_____. The Web of Life. New York: Anchor Books/ Doubleday, 1996.

Casey, James. The History of the Family. New York: Basil Blackwell, 1989.

Casti, John L. Complex Ification. New York: HarperCollins, 1994.

Chardin, Teilhard de. The Phenomenon of Man. New York: Harper Colophon, 1975.

Ching, Frank. Ancestors, 900 Years in the Life of a Chinese Family. New York, NY: Ballantine Books, a division of Random House, Inc., 1988.

Chomsky, Noam. Knowledge of Language. New York: Praeger Publishers, 1986.

_____. Language and Problems of Knowledge. Cambridge, MA: The MIT Press, 1988.

_____. Hegemony or Survival, America's Quest for Global Dominance. First Edition ed. New York, NY: Metropolitan Books, 2003.

Churton, Tobias. The Gnostics. New York: Barnes & Noble, 1987.

Cicero, Marcus Tullius. The Orations of Marcus Tullius Cicero, Volume 4. Translated by C.D. Yonge, 1903.

Clapham, Andrew. Human Rights, a Very Short Introduction A Very Short Introduction, Edited by Oxford University Press. Oxford; New York: Oxford University Press, 2007.

Cohen, Mark Nathan. Health And The Rise of Civilization. New Haven and London: Yale University Press, 1989

Confucius. Confucian Analects. Translated by James Legge.

Croly, Herbert. The Promise of American Life. New York: Norwood Press, The Macmillan Company, 1909, 1910, 1911,1912.

Cumming, Robert Denoon. The Philosophy of Jean-Paul Sartre, Edited by Robert Denoon Cumming. New York: Vintage Books, 1965.

Cusset, Francois. French Theory, How Foucault, Derrida, Deleuze, & Co. Transformed the Intellectual Life of the United States. Translated by Jeff Fort. Minneapolis, Minnesota: University of Minnesota Press, 2008.

Darnton, Robert. Mesmerism and the End of the Enlightenment in France. Cambridge, Mass.: Harvard University Press, 1968.

Daschle, Tom. Critical, What We Can Do About the Health-Care Crisis. New York, New York: St. Martin's Press, 2008.

Deloria, Vine, Jr. God Is Red, a Native View of Religion. Golden, Colorado: Fulcrum Publishing, 1994.

Dennett, Daniel C. Consciousness Explained. Boston: Little, Brown and Company, 1991.

Derrida, Jaques. Acts of Literature, Edited by Derek Attridge. New York: Routledge, 1992.

Dewey, John. Democracy and Education.

_____. Experience and Education. New York: Collier Books, 1938.

Dubner, Steven D. Levitt & Stephen J. Freakonomics. New York: William Morrow, An Imprint of Harper Collins Publishers, 2005.

Dubos, Rene. A God Within. New York: Charles Scribner's Sons, 1972.

Duby, Philippe Aries and Georges. A History of Private Life, Edited by Paul Veyne. Cambridge, MA: The Belknap Press of Harvard University Press, 1987.

Eagleton, Terry. Literary Theory. Minneapolis, MN: University of Minnesota Press, 1983.

Editor, Ben Ray Redman. Voltaire, Edited by Ben Ray Redman. New York: Penguin Books, 1978.

Eidinow, David Edmonds & John. Wittgenstein's Poker, the Story of a Ten-Minute Argument between Two Great Philosophers. Great Britain: Harper Collins, 2001.

Emmerson, Ralph Waldo. Selections from Ralph Waldo Emerson, Edited by Stephen E. Whicher. Boston, MA: Houyghton Mifflin Co., 1960.

Engels, Karl Marx and Frederick. Selected Works. New York: International Publishers, 1969.

Fanon, Frantz. The Wretched of the Earth. Translated by Richard Philcox. New York: Grove Press, 2004 (English Translation).

Fischer, Louis. The Life of Mahatma Gandhi. New York: Harper & Row, 1950.

Fitzhugh, George. Cannibals All! Or Slaves without Masters. Richmond, VA.: A. Morris, 1857.

Foucault, Michael. The Order of Things. New York: Vintage Books, 1970. Reprint, 1973.

_____. The Arcaeology of Knowledge. New York: Pantheon Books, 1972.

_____. The Birth of the Clinic. New York: Vintage Books, 1973. Reprint, 1975.

Foucault, Michel. Foucault--an Introduction. Translated by Edward Dixon. Philadelphia: Pennbridge Books, 1992.

Fromm, Erich. The Sane Society. London & New York: Routledge Classics, 1955 Orig.; 2002.

Galbraith, John Kenneth. The Age of Uncertainty. Boston: Houghton Mifflin, 1977.

Gandhi, Mahatma. Freedom's Battle, Being a Comprehensive Collection of Writings and Speeches on the Present Situation: A Public Domain Book, 1922.

Gaskin, Stephen. Sunday Morning Services on the Farm – Summertown, TN: The Book Publishing Company, 1977.

Gladwell, Malcolm. Blink, the Power of Thinking without Thinking. New York: Little, Brown and Co., 2005.

Glasser, William. The Identity Society. Revised ed. New York: Harper and Row, 1975.

Gleick, James. Chaos. New York: Viking Press, 1987.

Goffman, Erving. Interaction Ritual. Garden City, NY: Anchor Books, 1967.

Goldman, Emma. Anarchism and Other Essays.

Goldsmith, Margaret. Franz Anton Mesmer, a History of Mesmerism. Garden City, New York: Doubleday, Doran & Company, Inc., 1934.

Goldsmith, Neil deGrasse Tyson and Donald. Origins, Fourteen Billion Years of Cosmic Evolution. First Edition ed. New York, NY: W.W. Norton & Company, Inc., 2004.

Goodman, Paul. Growing up Absurd, Problems of Youth in the Organized Society. New York: The New York Review of Books, 1956

Gornick, Vivian. The Romance of American Communism. New York: Basic Books, 1977.

Grabar, G.W. Bowersock Peter Brown Oleg. Late Antiquity. Cambridge, MA: The Belknap Press of Harvard University Press, 1999.

Greider, William. The Soul of Capitalism, Opening Paths to a Moral Economy. New York: Simon & Schuster, Inc., 2003.

Habermas, Jurgen. On Society and Politics, a Reader, Edited by Steven Seidman. Boston: Beacon Press, 1989.

Hadler, Nortin M. M.D. The Last Well Person: How to Stay Well Despite the Health-Care System. Quebec, Canada: McGill-Queen's University Press, 2004. Reprint, 2005.

Haich, Elisabeth. Initiation. Translated by John R. Robertson. Third ed.: London, 1965.

Hammurabi. The Oldest Code of Laws in the World, by Hammurabi, King of Babylon. Translated by M.A. C.H.W. Johns. Edinburgh: T. & T. Clark.

Hampden-Turner, Charles. Maps of the Mind. New York: Macmillan Publishing Co., 1981.

Harner, Michael. The Way of the Shaman. New York: Harper and Row Publisher's, Inc., 1980.

Harris, Marvin. Cows, Pigs, Wars and Witches. New York: Vintage Books, 1974.

_____. Cannibals and Kings. New York: Random House, Inc., 1977.

_____. America Now: The Anthropology of a Changing Culture. New York: Simon and Schuster, 1981.

Harrison, Joohn A. The Chinese Empire. New York, London: Harvest/HBJ Book, 1972.

Hartnack, Justus. Wittgenstein and Modern Philosophy. Translated by Maurice Cranston. Garden City, NY: Anchor Books--Doubleday & Company, Inc., 1965.

Hegel, G.W.F. Phenomonology of Spirit. Translated by A.V. Miller. Oxford: Oxford University Press, 1977.

Hegel, Georg. The Philosophy of History.

Henry, Jules. Culture against Man. New York: Vintage Books, 1963.

Herodotus. Herodotus-- the Histories. Translated by Aubrey de Selincourt. Baltimore, MD: Penguin Books, 1954.

Herrick, James W. Iroquois Medical Botany, Edited by Dean R. Snow. Syracuse, New York 13244-5160: Syracuse University Press, 1995.

Hesse, Herman. The Glass Bead Game (Magister Ludi). New York: Henry Holt and Company, Inc., 1943.

Hobbes, Thomas. Leviathan. The Green Dragon in St. Paul's Churchyard: Andrew Crooke, 1651.

Hofstadter, Douglas. I Am a Strange Loop. New York, NY: Basic Books, A Member of the Perseus Books Group, 2007.

Hume, David. A Treatise of Human Nature, Edited by David Fate Norton and Mary J. Norton. New York, NY: Oxford University Press, Inc., 2000. Reprint, 2001, 2002, 2003 (twice).

Husserl, Edmund. Ideas. Translated by W.R. Boyce Gibson. New York: Collier Books, 1962.

James, William. Pragmatism.

Johnson, George Lakoff; Mark. Metaphors We Live By. Chicago; London: The University of Chicago Press, 1980.

_____. Philosophy in the Flesh. New York: Basic Books, 1999.

Jr., Vine Deloria. Evolution, Creationism, and Other Modern Myths: A Critical Inquiry. Golden, CO: Fulcrum Publishing, 2002.

Kant, Immanuel. Critique of Pure Reason. Translated by J.M.D. Meiklejohn. Buffalo, NY: Prometheus Books, 1990.

Karen Horney, M.D. Feminine Psychology. New York   London: W.W. Norton & Company, 1967.

Kazin, Michael. A Godly Hero, the Life of William Jennings Bryan. New York, NY: Alfred A. Knopf, a division of Random House, Inc., 2006.

Keane, John. The Life and Death of Democracy. New York, London: W.W. Norton & Company, 2009.

Kellner, Steven Best and Douglas. Post-Modern Theory--Critical Interrogations. New York: The Guilford Press, 1991.

Kidder, Tracy. Mountains Beyond Mountains: The Quest of Dr. Paul Farmer, a Man Who Would Cure the World. New York/Toronto: Random House, Inc., 2004.

Konner, Melvin. Why the Reckless Survive. New York: Viking, 1990.

Korten, David C. The Post-Corporate World. San Francisco: Berrett-Koehler Publishers, Inc., 1999.

Kramnick, Isaac. Enlightenment Reader. New York: Penguin Books, 1995.

Krishnamurti, J. Education as Service. Chicago: The Rajput Press, 1912.

_____. The Awakening of Intelligence. San Francisco: Harper and Row Publishers, 1973.

_____. The Years of Awakening. New York: Avon Books, 1975.

_____. The Flame of Attention. San Francisco: Harper and Row, 1984.

Kuhn, Thomas S. The Structure of Scientific Revolutions. Chicago: The University of Chicago Press, 1970.

Kushi, Michio. The Order of the Universe. Vol. three. Boston, MA: East West Foundation, 1977.

Laing, R.D. The Politics of Experience. New York: Ballantine Books, 1967.

Lakoff, George. Women, Fire, and Dangerous Things. Chicago/London: The University of Chicago Press, 1987.

Leitch, Vincint B. Deconstructive Criticism. New York: Columbia University Press, 1983.

Lin, Jami. Contemporary Earth Design, a Feng Shui Anthology. Miami: Earth Design Inc., Literary Division, 1997.

Locke, John. Two Treatises of Government. London: Everyman, J.M. Dent, 1993.

Machiavelli, Niccolo. The Prince. Translated by W.K. Marriott.

Magee, Bryan. The Story of Thought. New York: Quality Paperback Bookclub, 1998.

Mannheim, Karl. Ideology and Utopia. New York: Harvest/HBJ Books, 1936.

Marcuse, Herbert. Eros and Civilization. New York: Vintage Books, 1955.

Marx, Karl. Capital--Volume I. Translated by Ben Fowkes. Vol. Volume I. New York: Vintage, 1977.

_____. The Communist Manifesto. New York: W.W. Norton and Co. , Inc., 1988.

McCullough, David. John Adams. First Touchstone Edition, 2002 ed. New York, NY: Touchstone, 2001.

McKeon, Richard. Introduction Ton Aristotle. New York: The Modern Library, 1992.

Mill, John Stuart. On Liberty. London and Felling-on-Tyne, New York and Melbourne: The Walter Scott Publishing Co., Ltd.

_____. Utilitarianism. London: Longmans, Green and Co., 1879.

Miller, David. Political Philosophy, a Very Short Introduction A Very Short Introduction, Edited by Oxford University Press. Oxford, New York Oxford University Press Inc., 2003.

More, Thomas. Utopia. Baltimore, MD: Penguin Books, 1965.

Munitz, Milton K. The Question of Reality. Princeton, NJ: Princeton University Press, 1990.

Nadeau, Menas Kafatos Robert. The Conscious Universe. New York: Springer-Verlag, 1990.

Nearing, Helen & Scott. The Maple Sugar Book. New York City: Galahad Books, 1950, 1970.

Nietzsche. A Nietzsche Reader. Translated by R.J. Hollingdale. New York: Penguin Books, 1977.

Norris, Christopher. Derrida. Cambridge, MA: Harvard University Press, 1987.

Pagels, Heinz R. The Cosmic Code. New York: Simon and Schuster, 1982.

Paine, Edmund Burke; Thomas. Reflections on the Revolution in France and the Rights of Man. Garden City, NY: Dolphin Books, 1961.

Paine, Thomas. Common Sense: Joust Books.

Passmore, John. A Hundred Years of Philosophy. Baltimore, MD: Penguin Books, 1968.

Paul H. Ray, Ph.D., and Sherry Ruth Anderson, Ph.D. The Cultural Creatives, How 50 Million People Are Changing the World. First Edition ed. New York, NY: Harmony Books, 2000.

Peat, David Bohm and F. David. Science, Order, and Creativity. Nerw York: Bantam Books, 1987.

Pinch, Harry Collins & Trevor. The Golem. Cambridge: Cambridge University Press, 1993.

Pinker, Steven. The Language Instinct. New York: W. Morrow and Co., 1954.

Plato. Laws. Translated by Benjamin Jowett.

_____. The Dialogue's of Plato. New York: Bantam Books, 1986.

_____. Republic. Translated by G.M.A. Grube. English ed. Indianapolis, Indiana: Hackett Publishing Company, Inc., 1992.

Plechanoff, George. Anarchism and Socialism. Translated by Eleanor Marx Aveling. Chicago: Charles H. Kerr & Company.

Polanyi, Karl. The Great Transformation, the Political and Economic Origins of Our Time. Boston, MA: Beacon Press, 1944. Reprint, 1957, 2001.

Porter, Roy. A Social History of Madness. New York: E.P. Dutton, 1989.

Prigogine, Ilya. Order out of Chaos. Toront New York London Sydney: Bantam Books, 1984.

Proudhon, P.J. Essential Proudhon.

_____. What Is Property? An Inquiry into the Principle of Right and of Government.

Rand, Ayn. The Virtue of Selfishness, a New Concept of Egotism: A Signet Book, 1961, 1964.

Randall, Willard Sterne. Jefferson--a Life. New York: Henry Holt and Company, 1993.

Rousseau, Jean-Jacques. The Social Contract and Discourse on the Origin of Inequality. New York, New York: Washington Square Press, 1967.
Rude, George. The French Revolution. New York: Grove Press, 1988.

Sachs, Jeffrey. Common Wealth, Economics for a Crowded Planet. New York: Penguin Press, 2008.

_____. The Price of Civilization, Reawakening American Virtue and Prosperity. New York: Random House, 2011.

Sachs, Jeffrey D. The End of Poverty, Economic Possibilities for Our Time. New York, NY: Penguin Press, 2005.

Sanford, T.W. Adorno; Else Frenkel-Brunswik; Daniel J. Levinson; R. Nevitt. The Authoritarian Personality, Edited by Max Horkheimer; Samuel H. Flowerman. New York: Harper and Brothers, 1950.

Sartre, Jean-Paul. Search for a Method. New York: Vintage Books, 1963.

_____. Being and Nothingness. Translated by Hazel E. Barnes. New York: Washington Square Press, 1966.

Schafer, Roy. Retelling a Life. New York: Basic Books, 1992.

Schor, Juliet B. The Overworked American. New York: Basic Books, 1991.

Schulte, Joachim. Wittgenstein an Introduction. Translated by William H. Brenner & John F. Holley. Albany, NY: State University of New York Press, 1992.

Schumacher, E.F. Small Is Beautiful. New York: Perennial Library--Harper and Row, 1973. Reprint, 1975.

Searle, John R. Mind, a Brief Introduction. New York, NY: Oxford University Press, 2004.

Service, Robert. Lenin. Cambridge. MA: Havard University Press, 2000.

Skinner, B.F. Beyond Freedom and Dignity. New York: Bantam Books, 1971.

Slater, Philip. The Pursuitnof Loneliness. Boston, MA: Beacon Press, 1970.

_____. Earthwalk. New York: Anchor Books, 1974.

Smith, Adam. The Wealth of Nations. New York: The Modern Library, 1994.

Smith, J.W. The World's Wasted Wealth 2. Cambria, CA: The Institute For Economic Democracy, 1994.

Smith, Neil. Chomsky, Ideas and Ideals. Second Edition, 2004 ed. Cambridge, United Kingdom: Cambridge University Press, 1999.

Sontag, Susan. Against Interpretation. New York; London; Toronto; Sydney; Auckland: Anchor Books/Doubleday, 1966.

Spence, Jonathan. Mao Zedong. New York: Viking, 1999.

Spencer, Herbert. Essays: Scientific, Political & Speculative. Vol. One. London & Edinburgh: Williams and Norgate, 1891.

Steele, James. Sustainable Architecture. New York: McGraw-Hill, 1997.

Stenmark, Mikael. How to Relate Science and Religion. Grand Rapids, Michigan: William B. Eerdmans Publishing Company, 2004.

Stephen. Monday Night Class. Santa Rosa, CA: Book Farm, 1971.

Sumner, William Graham. What Social Classes Owe to Each Other: Harper & Brothers, 1883.

Sun-tzu. The Art of War. Translated by John Minford. New York: Viking, 2002.
Szasz, Thomas S. The Myth of Memtal Illness. New York: Perennial Library, 1974.

Talbot, Michael. The Holographic Universe. New York: HarperCollins Publishers, 1991.

Tannen, Deborah. The Arguement Culture. New York: Random House, 1988.

_____. You Just Don't Understand. New York: Ballantione Books, 1990.

Thomson, Garrett. An Introduction to Modern Philosophy. Belmont, CA: Wadsworth Publishing Company, 1993.

Thoreau, Henry David. Walden and Civil Disobedience. first ed. New York: W.W. Norton and Company, 1966.

_____. Civil Disobedience and Other Essays. New York: Dover Publications, Inc., 1993.

Thorstein, Veblen. Theory of the Leisure Class.

Tocqueville, Alexis de. Democracy in America. Translated by Henry Reeve.

Trungpa, Chogyam. The Myth of Freedom. Boston & London: Shambhala, 1976.

_____. Shambala--the Sacred Path of the Warrior. New York: Bantam Books, 1984.

_____. Journey without Goal. Boston & London: Shambhala, 1985.

Volk, Tyler. Metapatterns. New York: Columbia University Press, 1995.

Voltaire. The Portable Voltaire, Edited by Ben Ray Redman. New York: Penguin Books, 1977.

Wacks, Raymond. Philosophy of Law, a Very Short Introduction A Very Short Introduction, Edited by Oxford University Press. Oxford, New York: Oxford University Press, 2006.

Ward, Colin. Anarchism, a Very Short Introduction A Very Short Introduction, Edited by Oxford University Press: Oxford University Press, 2004.

Warner, Donald Batchelder and Elizabeth G. Beyond Experience: The Experiential Approach to Cross Cultural Education. Brattleboro, VT.: The Experiment Press, 1977.

Watson, John B. Behaviorism. New York London: W.W. Norton & Company, 1930.

Weber, Max. The Protestant Ethic and the Spirit of Capitalism. Blacksburg, VA.: Wilder Publications, 2010.

Wells, H.G. A Modern Utopia: A Public Domain Book.

_____. A Modern Utopia. Lincoln, NB: University of Nebraska Press, 1905.

Wheen, Francis. Karl Marx--a Life. New York: W.W. Nortoon and Company, 1999.

Wilentz, Sean. The Rise of American Democracy, Jefferson to Lincoln. First Edition ed. New York, NY: W.W. Norton & Company, Inc, 2005.

Wilson, Rudolf J. Freund/ William J. Statistical Methods. San Diego: Academic Press, 1997.

Wittgenstein, Ludwig. The Blue and Brown Books. New York: Harper Torchbooks, 1958.

_____. Philosophical Investigations. Translated by G.E.M. Anscomb. Third ed. New York, 1958.

_____. Tractatus Logico-Philosophicus. Translated by C.K. Ogden. New York: Routledge, 1990.
Wolff, Richard. Democracy at Work: A Cure for Capitalism. Chicago: Haymarket Books, 2012.

Yack, Bernard. The Longing of Total Revolution. Oxford, England: University of California Press, 1992.

Zakaria, Fareed. The Future of Freedom. New York; London: W.W. Norton and Company, 2003.

Zinn, Howard. A Poeple's History of the United States. New York: HarperCollins Publishers, 1999.

The following university level courses from The Teaching Company have been of enormous value in writing this book and for my continuing education:

- Economics, Professor Timothy Taylor
- Contemporary Economic Issues, Professor Timothy Taylor
- Foundations of Economic Prosperity,
Professor Daniel Drezner
- The History of the United States,
Professors Darren Staloff, Louis Masur
- The American Identity, Professor Patrick Allitt
- The Skeptic's Guide To American History,
Professor Mark Stoler
- Turning Points in American History,
Professor Edward O'Donnell
- Cycles of American Political Thought,
Professor Joseph Kobylka
- Thinking About Capitalism, Professor Jerry Muller
- Foundations of Western Civilization, I & II, Thomas Noble,
Robert Bucholz
- History of The Middle Ages, Professor Phillip Daileader
- The Terror of History, Professor Teofilo Ruiz
- Transformational Leadership, Professor Roberto
- The Great Ideas of Philosophy, Professor Daniel Robinson
- Freedom: The Philosophy of Liberation,
Professor Dennis Dalton
- Power Over People: Classical and Modern Political Theory,
Professor Dennis Dalton
- Practical Philosophy, The Greco-Roman Moralists,
Professor Luke Timothy Johnson
- The Modern Intellectual Tradition,
Professor Lawrence Cahoone
- Natural Law and Human Nature,
Professor Father Joseph Koterski
- The Rights of Man, Great Thinkers and Great Movements,
Professor Paul Gordon Lauren